ROCKY

MOUNTAIN

EMPIRE

BOOKS BY SAMUEL W. TAYLOR

Fighters Up (with Eric Friedheim)
The Man with My Face
Family Kingdom
I Have Six Wives
The Grinning Gismo
Heaven Knows Why
Uranium Fever; or, No Talk Under $1-Million
   (with Raymond W. Taylor)
Nightfall at Nauvoo
The Kingdom or Nothing

SCHEDULED FOR PUBLICATION:

The John Taylor Papers
   Vol I. The Apostle
   Vol II. The President

Samuel W. Taylor

ROCKY MOUNTAIN EMPIRE

THE LATTER-DAY SAINTS TODAY

Macmillan Publishing Co., Inc.

NEW YORK

Macmillan Publishing Co., Inc.
866 Third Avenue, New York, N.Y. 10022
Collier Macmillan Canada, Ltd.

Library of Congress Cataloging in Publication Data

Taylor, Samuel Woolley, 1907–
  Rocky Mountain Empire: the Latter-day Saints today.

  Bibliography: p.
  Includes index.
  1. Church of Jesus Christ of Latter-day Saints—
History. 2. Mormons and Mormonism in Utah—History.
3. Utah—Church history. I. Title.
BX8611.T37   289.3'3   78-9655
ISBN 0-02-616610-0

First Printing 1978

Designed by Jack Meserole

Printed in the United States of America

To Lillian, one of the chosen few.

Contents

Introduction

AN ESTIMATED 96 percent of the area of Utah is primarily scenery. The Wasatch Range of the Rockies runs down the center of the state, north to south. To the east is the broken wilderness of barren slickrock draining into the gorge of the Colorado River. To the west is Great Salt Lake, the Bonneville Salt Flats, and the sweep of the alkali desert. Most of the tillable land lies in the strip of central valleys nestled against the western foothills of the mountains. This is the Wasatch Front, stronghold of Mormonism.

Utah is more than a state. It is a state of mind. The mental wall surrounding it has been called the Zion Curtain. Few outsiders have penetrated it, except for the guided tour. Gentiles know little about the Peculiar People, beyond that their Word of Wisdom prohibits coffee, tobacco, and liquor; that they send out hordes of young missionaries; and that, of recent years, they hold family home evening once a week. Superficial as this concept may be, it does indicate a profound change in the modern culture as contrasted to pioneer Mormonism.

It has been pointed out that the founder of the faith, Joseph Smith, would at present be denied entrance to the temples because of his casual attitude toward the Word of Wisdom, while Brigham Young would be unable to enter Brigham Young University (BYU) because his beard and haircut wouldn't conform to modern grooming standards.

It is a question whether Joseph Smith would be amazed or amused by the modern emphasis on the Word of Wisdom, which originally was intended merely as wise advice, "not by commandment or constraint." He was tolerant on the subject.

Chances are that Brigham Young would give hearty approval of modern grooming and dress standards at BYU, for he continually hectored the women regarding the immodest and extravagant fashions of the wicked outside world. He even counseled the men to have the fly of their trousers on the side rather than in front. He had founded the Y as the intellectual and cultural center of Mormonism, and he would find it so today.

The reaction of John Taylor to the modern scene, however, might be of a different nature. The man who led the church during the violent and desperate decade following Brigham Young's death had adamantly refused to obey the laws of the United States which conflicted with the pioneer concept of the law of God. He counseled the people to resist and even went underground himself during the final two and a half years of his life rather than compromise his faith. He warned of the consequences of appeasement and predicted with amazing accuracy the future course of the church if it capitulated. John Taylor was, quite literally, the last pioneer; he was the final man in authority to hold to original principles and values. After his death came the Manifesto of 1890, which officially abandoned plural marriage and ushered in other changes of the modern culture.

In tracing the metamorphosis, "The decisive period was that between the Woodruff Manifesto of 1890," Bernard DeVoto stated, "and the adoption by the United States Senate in 1907 of the minority report of its Committee on Privileges and Elections which confirmed [the seating of] Reed Smoot."[1] The right of this Mormon apostle to hold his Senate seat had been challenged four years previously by the Salt Lake Ministers' Association

for the reason that he is one of a self-perpetuating body of fifteen men who, constituting the ruling authorities of the Church, . . . shape the belief and control the conduct of those under them in all matters whatsoever, civil and religious, temporal and spiritual, . . . uniting in themselves authority in church and state. . . .[2]

During the years of the Smoot hearings in the U.S. Senate, the church literally was fighting for its life. "During that time the Church learned not only that it must outwardly conform to the requirements of the American system," DeVoto said, "but also that it would lose nothing by doing so." Out of the trauma, the modern culture emerged.

This is the story of that adaption to unrelenting pressure, and

1. "The Centennial of Mormonism: A Study in Utopia and Dictatorship." *American Mercury*, January 1930.
2. See *Proceedings* of the Smoot investigation.

particularly of the impact it had upon individuals involved. I have not been primarily concerned with details of the faith, but rather, in what that faith did to the people.

Temple Square is sometimes called the heart of Mormonism. So it is; but, more correctly, it is a showcase of the faith, for the heart was beating before Temple Square existed. The imposing Church Office Building is the nerve center of the modern church body. The ruling hierarchy is the administrative brain directing all actions.

The heartbeat is found in the basic unit of the local ward congregations. More than anything else, this is the story of ward members. Here is the faith and the culture of the Wasatch Front, the way of life of the Peculiar People.

I would like to thank the apparatus of the Taylor Spy Network for keeping me informed on Secret Matters behind the Zion Curtain. The underground material of the Salt Lake *samizdat* is not only enlightening but lively reading.

I appreciate the friendly cooperation of university librarians: Everett L. Cooley at University of Utah; Chad Flake at Brigham Young University; and John J. Stewart at Utah State University, together with their staffs. The Utah State Historical Society also supplied valuable material.

Perhaps most important of all was the contribution of the late Raymond Taylor. His correspondence over a period of years constitutes a most penetrating assessment of the Mormon culture.

SAMUEL W. TAYLOR

Redwood City, California

BOOK ONE

Latter-day
Laocoön

*You Gentiles make a mistake in thinking always
of us Mormons in terms of polygamy. You have
the same institution, but you call it stenography.*

—PRESIDENT HEBER J. GRANT,
San Francisco, 1935[1]

1

Meanest Man in Deseret

AS HE WAITED behind the tree, the windows of the white frame house across the road went black, room by room, until there was only the yellow slit from a lamp beyond the drapes of an upstairs bedroom. Presently the lamp snuffed out and the house was dark. Charles Mostyn Owen checked his gold pocket watch by the light of the moon. Quarter past eleven. It was a bitter February night, and after a vigil of more than three hours at the tree he was shivering, teeth chattering, chilled to the bone despite wool underwear, sweater, overcoat, muffler, mittens, earmuffs, and heavy socks.

Everybody in bed. Probably nothing would happen tonight. Yet, perhaps. . . . Why not wait awhile longer? Discomfort meant little to Owen; he was a dedicated man. He swung his arms vigorously and stomped his boots in the thin snow to restore circulation.

More than an hour later his patience was rewarded. The yellow slit appeared at the upstairs window again. Presently the rear screen door slammed. From behind the tree Owen saw the burly figure of the ward bishop hurrying toward the barn. A short time later the bishop drove out the lane in his white-top and headed the team north along the road at a brisk trot.

Owen smiled, conscious of the peaceful beauty of the scene, the farmhouses and winter fields of the Salt Lake valley. The Wasatch Range rose abruptly to the east, glittering white against the night sky. At the south end of the valley he could see the silhouette of the Point of the Mountain at Jordan Narrows, and to the

1. Herb Caen's column, San Francisco *Chronicle,* September 16, 1976.

north Ensign Peak, at whose base stood Temple Square, the heart of Mormon country.

When the white-top returned, a woman's bundled figure was beside the bishop. That, Owen knew, would be the midwife. Presently lights began coming on in the lower windows, and at three minutes past 1 A.M. the man behind the tree heard the wail of a newborn infant.

Next morning Charles Mostyn Owen appeared before Salt Lake County Attorney Putnam and swore out an information that a woman who was "by common habit and repute in the community the plural wife" of the bishop had been delivered of a child, making its father guilty of unlawful cohabitation contrary to the provisions of Sections 4209 and 4910 of the Compiled Laws of the State of Utah.

The county attorney was frank. Though a Gentile himself, he couldn't take action of the complaint against a ward bishop without inviting defeat at the polls at the next election, what with the overwhelming majority of Mormons in the county. Sorry.

Owen thanked him politely, and took his complaint to the opposition paper, the Salt Lake *Tribune,* which was most happy to publish it. After this circumstance, there was nothing left for County Attorney Putnam to do but take action.

The complaint against the bishop was another of more than a hundred such cases Charles Mostyn Owen had brought to public attention in the past two years alone, at a time when plural marriage officially had been abandoned more than a decade previously. This was a source of extreme embarrassment to the Mormon Church and the people of Utah. In fact, the activities of this professional snoop had given him the status of the most despised villain of the entire history of the Saints.

Others had been more hated, it is true, notably Governor Lilburn W. Boggs of Missouri, who in 1838 had issued the notorious order that all Mormons in that state must be expelled or exterminated.[2] Apostates who had turned against the faith, such as Phi-

2. The *Deseret News* of June 26, 1976 noted that after 137 years, Governor Boggs' extermination order "was rescinded by Gov. Christopher S. Bond, who called the incident a dark chapter in Missouri history." This action evidently means that from 1838 to June of 1976 the order was still in force, making it dangerous to life and limb for a Mormon to set foot in Missouri. Otherwise, why was it necessary to rescind it?

lastus Hurlbut, John C. Bennett, Thomas B. Marsh, and Bill Hickman, were simply consigned to the buffetings of Satan, their lurid exposés rejected as tissues of lies.[3] But for scorn and contempt, no name was held in such disdain as that of Charles Mostyn Owen, meanest man in Deseret.[4]

Two weeks after Owen's latest complaint, Abel John Evans presented the plan to spike the guns of the professional snoop. Abel John Evans was president of the Utah Senate and was also a prominent businessman, a self-taught lawyer, and of good church position as counselor in the presidency of Alpine Stake of Zion.[5]

The official posture assumed by Abel John Evans and other faithful Saints was that polygamy had been abolished by the Manifesto of 1890, eleven years previously, that no further plural marriages had been contracted since that time, that those who had entered "the Principle" prior to that date were becoming fewer and fewer as time took its toll, and that when the last of these were gone the entire issue would be a thing of the past. So why rake up old scores? Why persecute old men for maintaining family obligations contracted many years previously?

But Charles Mostyn Owen was busily demolishing this pretty picture. Except for Owen, the insinuations of the Ministers' Association of Salt Lake City and of the *Tribune,* that polygamy was still secretly flourishing, might have been ignored. Owen was filing

3. Hurlbut gathered the unfriendly affidavits used by Eber D. Howe in compiling his *Mormonism Unvailed* (Painesville, Ohio, 1834). Although John C. Bennett had been assistant president of the church before defecting, and thus knew whereof he spoke—regardless of how venomously he presented it—Mormon apologists have studiously avoided recognizing his *History of the Saints* (Boston, 1842). Thomas B. Marsh, who had been the first president of the Twelve Apostles (a position which fell to Brigham Young when Marsh defected), made affidavit in October 1838, regarding Danite activities in Missouri. Subsequently, prematurely old and a broken man, he repented, and Mormon historians have time and again quoted the affidavit as the cause of Marsh's subsequent fate, an example of the fruits of apostasy. However, even though the affidavit is presented as completely false, its most damaging portions are still suppressed. As for Bill Hickman and his *Brigham's Destroying Angel* (New York, 1872), both he and it have been totally ignored.

4. Curiously, the name of the man who precipitated the last great crisis in Mormon history isn't mentioned in B. H. Roberts' official *Comprehensive History of the Church,* 6 vols. (Salt Lake City, 1930) (hereafter "CHC").

5. At this time, March 1901, there were forty-five stakes. Alpine Stake included wards at American Fork, Lehi, Pleasant Grove, Linden, Alpine, and Cedar Valley. The stakes were situated primarily in the Great Basin, except for one in Mexico and one in Canada. (See Andrew Jenson, *Church Chronology.*)

complaints of babies born to plural wives who had been mere children eleven years ago. He bombarded the New York *Journal* with stories of plural marriages in Mexico, on the high seas, and in private homes; he presented evidence that it was no longer necessary for such marriages to be solemnized in the temples. He was corroborating the charges of the *Tribune* and the Ministers' Association that polygamy had not stopped but had merely gone underground, being practiced as in an earlier day at Nauvoo—officially denounced by the church, but secretly fostered as essential to celestial glory.

Owen was self-righteous about his snooping. "It was the duty of any person calling himself a good citizen to institute proceedings in a legal manner for the conviction of such persons," he declared. He didn't bother with small fry, but went after big game—church officials, holders of public office, men of affairs. He had initiated the prosecution of Apostle Heber J. Grant,[6] and of Angus M. Cannon, president of the Salt Lake Stake. When he filed a complaint against Church President Lorenzo Snow, a man in his eighty-sixth year, even the Gentiles were shocked. Judge George C. Bartch, justice of the Supreme Court of Utah, personally remonstrated.

At the time the complaint was pending, "He approached me one night on West Temple Street, near the *Tribune* office," Owen said. "He told me that he thought the information was ill advised, that Mr. Snow was an exceedingly old man and the head of the church, and it would cause a good deal of resentment by the Mormon people.

"I asked him if it was not a fact, whether he knew it or not, that Mr. Snow had a very young infant in the family by the ninth wife," Owen told Judge Bartch. This was, Bartch said, news to him. "Mr. Bartch, for your information I will state that he has," Owen said.[7] "And the reason of my prosecution of Mr. Snow is

---

6. Grant subsequently became president of the church.

7. Remarkable, but true. However, it should be understood that men who had entered the Principle prior to 1890 had absolutely no intention of putting aside plural families. For this attitude, see *Proceedings before the Committee on Privileges and Elections of the United States Senate in the Matter of the Protests against the Right of Hon. Reed Smoot, a Senator from the State of Utah, to Hold His Seat.* 4 vols. (U.S. Government Printing Office; Washington, 1904, 1905, and 1906) (hereafter "SI"). The quotations of Owen's dialogue are taken from his testimony at the Senate investigation.

6

this, that I have never desired to prosecute any of the rabble, so to speak, of the Mormons—the poor class, those who are financially unable to help themselves." Owen further said, "It was the leaders of the church and those most offensive that I was after." As president of the church, Snow "had unlimited funds from the tithing fund to protect himself."

Though the county attorney refused to prosecute the church president on the ground that there was insufficient evidence to convict, just one week after making complaint against Snow, Owen swore out another, charging Congressman-elect B. H. Roberts, the eminent LDS historian and member of the First Council of Seventy, with adultery.

By this time Owen's activities had reached the point that he abandoned his profession as engineer to devote full time to snooping. The New York *Journal* had hired him as its Utah correspondent in the paper's campaign to unseat Roberts, an admitted polygamist, in Congress. Owen then was retained by the Woman's Interdenominational Council to continue his valiant work, his salary and expenses being paid by Dr. William M. Paden, pastor of the First Presbyterian Church of Salt Lake City and leader of the Ministers' Association of that city.

As an engineer, Owen's work had taken him into virtually all parts of Mormon country except for a small section of southern Utah. With that exception, "I think I can say that I have been over the whole of Utah, almost settlement by settlement," he said; also "over a large portion of southeastern Idaho, and western Wyoming completely."

He found little difficulty gathering information against polygamists in Deseret. "There is hardly a settlement," he said, "where there is not either an apostate, or a member of the church in good standing who is opposed quietly to the practice," and willing to be an informant. "They do not dare to express themselves openly, but under the seal of confidence and protection as to their identity I have undoubtedly the closest information possible."

Though professing the highest motives in his valiant work of stamping out the abomination of polygamy, Owen's petty meanness was revealed when he posed for pictures depicting the clothing worn in the temples and the various rites of the endowment ceremonies. This outraged the Saints and shocked the Gentiles.

7

Such was the man whom Abel John Evans, in cooperation with church authorities and the Utah legislature, was determined to stop through passage of legislation against his activities. But just what would be the provisions of such a law? Utah had gained statehood five years previously only by endorsing a constitution that prohibited polygamy forever. Any attempt to alter this provision, at the very time of the nationwide furor over the seating of the polygamous Roberts in Congress, was unthinkable.

After prayerful consideration, and counsel from church authorities, Abel John Evans came up with what seemed a brilliant idea. He drafted a bill amending existing law to read that no prosecution could be instituted for adultery except on complaint of a close relative, and that "no prosecution for unlawful cohabitation shall be commenced except on complaint of the wife or alleged plural wife of the accused." This neatly would throw Charles Mostyn Owen out of a job.

In introducing the bill, Evans reminded the legislature that the Manifesto did not "annul the compacts and contracts already entered into, the holiest of all contracts, contracts that men with a spark of honor could not break." And, he declared, the bill would "cut off the heads of cravens who creep around for petty revenge, discovering evils where they do not exist and trying to get honest people into shame and disgrace.

"They say the passage of this act will create a furor," Evans admitted prophetically. "Well, let it come. I call upon you to vindicate Utah."[8]

"The whole nasty business is a monumental dishonor," the *Tribune* declared next morning, "and it renews the suspicion that the whole [church] institution is but a vast commercial, political machine, with polygamy as the cement of the nefarious system."

"The bill will work far-reaching injury to the state and its people," the *Herald* warned the following day. Its adoption "will be accepted by the outside world as a direct defiance of the national sentiment, a repudiation of pledges made to secure statehood."

The legislature promptly passed the measure, indicating church sponsorship. As it awaited the governor's signature, the *Herald* on March 13 recalled the struggle of forty-five years for statehood, the tyranny of carpetbag government under territorial status, warning

8. *Deseret News*, March 7, 1901.

that the "final enactment into law would at once be the signal of an outburst of wrath and a retaliation beside which previous experiences would be mild."

Next morning's *Tribune* contained a petition by the Ministers' Association for the governor to veto the measure, whose passage, the newspaper charged, was "to make it easy and secure for Mormons to insidiously re-introduce polygamy into Utah," it being "a clear case that statehood was obtained by fraud."

As the national press took up the cry, it became obvious that the bill was a mistake. Governor Heber M. Wells, though admitting that he was "a product of that [plural] marriage system, taught from infancy to regard my lineage as approved of the Almighty, and proud today, as I have ever been, of my heritage," vetoed the measure, because it would be "employed as a most effective weapon against the very classes whose condition it is intended to ameliorate. Furthermore," he said, coming to the crux of the matter, "I have every reason to believe its enactment would be the signal for a general demand upon the National Congress for a constitutional amendment" outlawing polygamy.[9]

What Utah feared was a resurgence of anti-polygamy frenzy, which had led to such extremes in the 1880s, with church property confiscated by the government, and prominent officials imprisoned or fugitives. "The nation has once more been inflamed," the *Deseret News* admitted, two days after veto of the bill, blaming the "conscienceless disseminators of falsehood who struck the match and applied the torch." Though the *News* was confident that "The country will come to its senses when the facts gradually appear," a Mormon historian concluded that passage of the bill by the legislature "caused a nationwide war on the Mormons."[10] Within a week the fire had swept the country, the national press accusing the LDS Church with attempting to cover up the revival of polygamy. The *Literary Digest* claimed that the bill's objective was to "gradually restore and continue" plural marriage. "The widespread publicity given to this action," the Washington *Post* said, "awakened everywhere a sentiment of antagonism not unmixed with disgust." *The Outlook* pointed out that while the State Constitution made it impossible to legalize polygamy in Utah, the legislature had passed

9. "Executive Communication," March 14, 1901.
10. Wayne Stout, *History of Utah*, 2:122 (Salt Lake City, 1968) (hereafter, "Stout").

a law "which will practically prevent all prosecution for polygamy."

Certainly the aims of Charles Mostyn Owen, as stated to Judge Bartch, had been fulfilled beyond his wildest dreams.

The Evans Act "aroused a protest throughout the country," the Ministers' Association declared, in making formal protest to the U.S. president and Senate that the leaders of the LDS Church constituted "a self-perpetuating body of fifteen men," who claimed "supreme authority, divinely sanctioned, to shape the beliefs and control the conduct of those under them in all matters whatsoever, civil and religious, temporal and spiritual," and who, "uniting in themselves authority in church and state," used their power to foster the practice of polygamy "regardless of the pledges made for the purpose of attaining statehood."

Getting down to the nitty-gritty, the protest claimed that "At least three of the apostles have entered new polygamous relations since the manifesto of President Woodruff," while cohabitation with plural wives "is almost universal," at least six of the apostles having had children born to plural wives since the manifesto. However, any mention of such matters "is regarded as evidencing the greatest hostility to the Mormon people," and "subjects the persons so offending to practical ostracism in any Mormon community."[11]

Charles Mostyn Owen had said he was after only big game. The attempt to stop him once again brought war between the LDS Church and the United States. For three years the Senate would have the church on the rack, with one of the most exhaustive hearings in the nation's history. Ostensibly, the investigation was to determine whether Reed Smoot, a Mormon apostle, would be by his church office unfitted to retain his seat in the Senate. But church president Joseph F. Smith declared that the church, not Smoot, was on trial. Smoot did retain his seat, but at great cost. "Although Smoot's vindication might be interpreted as a victory for the Mormons," Klaus J. Hansen commented wryly, "the church leaders would not have been able to survive many such victories."[12] Following the Smoot investigation the fire would rage through the trust-busting and muckraking periods, with the church a prime target.

When at last the fire burned itself out, after almost twenty

11. SI, 1:1–26.

12. *Quest for Empire: The Political Kingdom of God and the Council of Fifty in Mormon History* (Michigan State University Press, 1967) (hereafter, "Hansen").

years, nearly every vestige of the pioneer concept of Mormonism, which had made the Saints a Peculiar People, was in ashes. The phoenix which arose from the fire was "yet another American success story in a society that measures success largely by material standards: Mormons have become eminently adept at imitating and assimilating American middle-class values; therefore, Mormons are okay," Klaus Hansen pointed out in the LDS literary quarterly, *Dialogue*. He quoted social historian Christopher Lasch:

"As long as the Mormons were different from their neighbors, their neighbors hounded them mercilessly," Lasch said. "Only when they gave up the chief distinguishing features of their faith" did the Latter-day Saints become "another tolerated minority."[13]

As the arsonist who struck the match, Charles Mostyn Owen must have watched the fire with exultant joy.

13. *Dialogue, a Journal of Mormon Thought,* Spring 1969.

2

The Devil's Deal

HAD IT BEEN PLANNED, the arrival of Charles Mostyn Owen at Salt Lake couldn't have been better timed for his indoctrination into the conflict. Before the engineer had finished his first glass of valley tan at the bar of the Walker House, he found it necessary to declare himself for one side or the other.[1] It was 1887, and two events made that year the turning point of the war which had raged for half a century between the Mormons and the United States government. First was the passage by Congress that spring of the harsh Edmunds-Tucker Act, which finally cornered the church. Second was the death of the church president, John Taylor, who had refused all compromise, and the decision of new leadership to capitulate.

Since the first law against polygamy in 1862—twenty-five years previously—Congress had been trying to contrive legislation that would stop the practice in Utah. Aided by Supreme Court rulings— one of which declared the Mormon Church to be an organized rebellion, justifying any measures necessary to quell it—it at last had found the answer. With the Edmunds-Tucker Act:

· Adultery was a felony.

· A wife could testify against her husband in polygamy cases.

1. The condition still exists. Fawn Brodie, author of the definitive biography of Joseph Smith, *No Man Knows My History,* made the cogent observation during a talk at Salt Lake that "In Utah, everyone must wear a label."

· It was a felony to perform a marriage ceremony that was not a matter of public record.

· Children of plural marriages were disinherited.

· Female suffrage was abolished.

· A test oath disfranchised all polygamists, and prohibited them from jury service "or to hold any office."

· The legal entity of the church as a corporation was dissolved.

· All church property in excess of $50,000 was forfeited and escheated to the United States government.

Owen was amazed at the exactly opposite reactions to this punitive legislation. Members of the so-called Utah Ring, who had been in Washington lobbying for more repressive measures, were disappointed. The church, in an *Epistle* issued from the underground,[2] declared that "The Edmunds [-Tucker] law, instead of appeasing the anti-Mormon appetite for power, only whetted it." The *Epistle,* read to the assembled Saints at April conference, said that "to find its parallel one must search the records of medieval times."

After "Falsehood . . . mob violence, fire, fetters, the rifle and the sword, wholesale expulsion and military force" had failed, "a new crusade has been inaugurated in the form of judicial tyranny, prompted by Satan and carried on by cunning adventurers and reckless fanatics." Although unlawful cohabitation was merely a legal misdemeanor, "All other offenses, however gross and horrid, appear to sink into insignificance in the eyes of the federal officials." The excesses employed in enforcing the Edmunds-Tucker act, "will yet be read with surprise and wonder."

The *Epistle* promised the Saints that, if faithful, "They who fight against Zion shall be destroyed; and the pit which has been digged shall be filled by those who digged it."[3]

However, this proved to be the last of the thundering messages

2. John Taylor, president of the church, had been a fugitive for the past two and a half years, together with his counselors, George Q. Cannon and Joseph F. Smith.

3. For this and other official communiqués, see James R. Clark, *Messages of the First Presidency,* vols. I–V. Salt Lake: Bookcraft, 1965–71. Hereafter "MFP."

of defiance that John Taylor had hurled against the awesome might of the government during his ten years as leader of the church. His health had broken in the confinement of the underground; when he died in late July, surrender began.

During his terminal illness appeasers already were negotiating in Washington as to what would satisfy Congress and the nation. The price of statehood, they found, would come high: the complete abolition of the Principle. This, to Taylor, had been the Devil's deal; he'd had no truck with similar propositions.

He was spared the humiliation of seeing the doctrine for which he had fought so long repudiated at the polls by his own people. At an election held three days after his funeral, citizens of Utah voted overwhelmingly in support of a proposed constitution, to be submitted with yet another petition for statehood, that would prohibit polygamy forever.

Whatever was done officially, there was every determination to continue the Principle underground. "Yes, I accept the self-imposed conditions of Statehood," Apostle Erastus Snow wrote to a wife, Elizabeth, from a Mormon settlement in Mexico. However, that applied strictly to the United States, "and any who, living in the State of Utah, desire to marry other wives can bring them for me to marry in Mexico cheaper than to pay the fine."[4]

John Taylor had rejected this attempted appeasement, predicting that Congress would throw it back in the faces of the Saints. This proved to be the case. In Washington, Senator Edmunds declared, "I do not favor the admission of Utah upon any terms; it might result in the establishment of a Mormon hierarchy. Neither a Mormon executive nor Mormon courts would enforce the law prohibiting polygamy, though they might pretend to."[5]

The Gentiles of Utah had scornfully refused to attend the convention that drafted the proposed constitution or to vote on the matter. The anti-polygamy provision was "exquisitely absurd, from premises to conclusion," the *Tribune* declared. "Does this article actually abolish polygamy? It does not. It simply declares—in obscure words—bigamy and polygamy to be a misdemeanor." The real issue was "the absorption of the State in the Church here, . . .

4. July 22, 1887.
5. *Tribune*, November 16.

the complete dominance of the priesthood in everything—religion, politics, business, and social relations."[6]

The outside world echoed the *Tribune*'s charge that the proposed constitution was merely a device to attain statehood, after which polygamy would be reinstated.[7]

The Utah Commission, a carpetbag board appointed to oversee political affairs in the Territory, was frankly skeptical of the anti-polygamy provision. In its annual report to the secretary of the interior, September 29, 1887, it declared itself "unable to understand how the great body of the people could undergo an overnight conversion on the subject," except that it was a ploy to attain statehood "with the hope of escaping from the toils" of federal pressure. "A republican form of government has no existence in Utah," the Commission warned. The Saints would never obey the laws "until the political power of the Mormon Church is destroyed."

The *Deseret News* declared that the Saints "have entered into no compacts, formulated no agreements, made no compromises of a religious or any other nature," in framing the proposed Constitution.[8] The *Tribune,* however, was scornful.

"No honest man, knowing what obligations every Mormon is under to support polygamy, could for one moment believe that an assemblage of Mormon priests would dare pass a resolution proclaiming that tenet of their faith a misdemeanor," the *Tribune* commented acidly, "except they were ordered to do so, . . . knowing the whole movement was an intended fraud."[9]

In this atmosphere, the fifth petition of Utah for statehood over a period of thirty-seven years was again rejected by Congress, which reported that Utah should not be admitted to the Union until it was certain that polygamy had been entirely abandoned.

As he traveled about Mormon country attending to his engineering business, Charles Mostyn Owen kept his ears open. He heard

6. July 21.
7. Apostle John Henry Smith wrote to his cousin, Joseph F. Smith of the First Presidency, regarding securing statehood: "It looks to me as if the only chance on that score is to give the whole business [of plural marriage] away, renouncing our faith say for five years and then taking it up again when once inside the great government fold." (Letter, April 3, 1888.)
8. July 6, 1887.
9. October 11, 1887.

enough to make a deal with the *Tribune* and began his career as a snoop, reporting new plural marriages and swearing out complaints of unlawful cohabitation.

Church officials, on the other hand, began claiming that polygamy was a thing of the past, with no new plural marriages being performed. This was part of a concerted policy of appeasement, as the government showed its muscle. U.S. District Attorney George S. Peters began to escheat church property, taking possession of the Gardo House, used as official residence of the church president; the Tithing Office; the Church Farm; the Historian's Office; stocks in various business enterprises, including the Deseret Telegraph and the Salt Lake Theater; coal mines; and herds of livestock accepted as tithing, consisting of cattle, horses, and 30,000 sheep. Gentiles grinned and Mormons glowered at the sign tacked to a door of the tabernacle: "FOR RENT. SEE U.S. MARSHAL."[10]

On a night in the spring of the following year a carriage pulled by a matched team drove at a smart clip north from Salt Lake City. At the reins was the massive figure of Charles Wilcken, veteran of the Prussian army and former bodyguard of President John Taylor. Since Taylor's death he had been on duty at the underground hideout of George Q. Cannon, first counselor of the new church leadership. In the rear seat were two of Cannon's sons, Frank J. and Abraham H. Both were in the publishing business, Frank as editor of the Ogden *Standard,* Abraham as business manager of the periodical, the *Juvenile Instructor.* Abraham was a member of the First Council of Seventy,[11] and had served a term of six months in the penitentiary for u.c. Frank, a brilliant orator and writer, held no church office, and, in fact, he had a drinking problem, which might not have been worthy of mention, except in Utah. The two young men had an appointment to consult with their father regarding a possible solution to the desperate plight of the Saints. "A more despairing situation then theirs, at that hour, has never been faced by an American community," Frank wrote.[12] Virtually every promi-

10. The church became tenant of the properties. It galled the Saints to be paying high rentals on their own hard-earned possessions. Another result of the escheatment was that work ceased on the unfinished temple at Salt Lake.

11. The following year Abraham became a member of the Council of the Twelve.

12. *Under the Prophet in Utah* (Boston: C. M. Clark Publishing Co., 1911); written with Harvey J. O'Higgins.

nent Mormon was in prison, had served a sentence, or was a fugitive. "Hundreds of Mormon women had left their homes and their children to flee from the officers of the law; many had been behind prison bars for refusing to answer the questions put to them in court; more were concealed, like outlaws, in the houses of friends. Husbands and wives, separated by the necessities of flight, had died apart, miserably."

After a 9-mile trip the carriage stopped at an adobe farmhouse on the outskirts of Bountiful, where guards admitted the two young men to see their father, white-haired, with blue eyes and a short beard running in a straight line below the ears and mouth. They sat in the horsehair chairs of the parlor, furnished in black walnut, with an organ, marble-topped bureau, a "store" carpet on the floor, walls hung with walnut-framed lithographs of church authorities and with a picture of the angel Moroni holding the golden plates containing the text of the Book of Mormon.

"I have sent for you," George Q. Cannon said to Frank, "to see if you cannot find some way to help us in our difficulties. I have made it a matter of prayer, and I have been led to urge you to activity." Frank had never served a mission for the church, nor "obeyed the celestial covenant" of marriage; but this, his father said, "may have been a providential overruling" in preparing him to deal with the Gentiles. Frank could meet them on equal footing, talk their language, understand their viewpoint, match them drink for drink in good fellowship. "I have talked with some of the brethren, and we feel that if relief does not soon appear, our community will be scattered and the great work crushed," Cannon said. "Can you see any light?"

Frank replied that he already had been to Washington twice, talking with friends in Congress whom he had known while secretary to Utah Delegate John T. Caine. "I am still of the opinion I expressed to you and President Taylor four years ago. Plural marriage must be abandoned or our friends in Washington will not defend us."

Frank's plan had been that every male polygamist would surrender to the law with the plea that he had entered the covenant of celestial marriage as the law of God and now offered himself for whatever judgment the courts might impose. His father had believed that this would vindicate the sincerity of the polygamists and that "the world would pause to reconsider its judgment upon us if it saw thousands of men—the bankers, the farmers, the merchants, and all the religious leaders of a civilized community—marching in a mass to perform such an act of faith."

President John Taylor had vetoed the plan at that time; but now Taylor was dead and new leadership might adopt it. With his father's approval, Frank counseled with other church officials, and with their blessing took a train to New York, where he saw Mayor Abraham S. Hewitt, telling him "I hoped to have some man appointed as Chief Justice in Utah" who would begin the solution of "the Mormon question" by giving merciful sentences when the community leaders gave themselves up.

"The man you want," the mayor said, "is here in New York— Elliot F. Sandford. He's a referee of the Supreme Court of this State—a fine man, great legal ability, courageous, of undoubted integrity. Come to me, tomorrow. I'll introduce you to him."

In the interview with Sandford, Frank Cannon told him that the Mormons were becoming more desperately determined in their opposition because of feeling persecuted. The district attorney and the courts were "harsh to the point of heartlessness"; nearly every federal appointee "had taken a tone of bigoted opposition to the people"; until among the Saints "the law was detested and the government despised because of the actions of the federal carpet-baggers.

"I did not really reach his sympathy until I spoke of the court system of Utah—the open venire, the employment of 'professional jurors,' the legal doctrine of 'segregation' under which a man might be separately indicted for every day of his living in plural marriage —and the result of all this: that the pursuit of the defendants and the confiscation of property had become less an enforcement of law than a profitable legal industry."

Sandford pointed out regretfully that to accept an appointment in Utah would mean the sacrifice of his professional career in New York. To let Cannon down gently, he suggested that his wife, who was waiting in the outer office, should offer her opinion.

Mrs. Sandford proved to be handsome, expensively gowned, "a woman of the smiling world." Convinced of failure, Frank nonetheless repeated to her the Utah situation. She didn't seem to have been reached, until she unexpectedly turned to her husband and said, "It seems to me that this is an opportunity—a larger opportunity than any I see *here*—to do a great deal of good."

When Sandford learned that the salary of the chief justice of Utah was only about $3,000 a year, he smiled at his fashionably groomed wife. "How many bonnets would that buy?"

"If *that's* been the cause of your hesitation," she said, "I'll agree to dress as becomes the wife of a poor but upright judge."

It was "in such a happy spirit of good-natured raillery," Frank recorded, "that a decision so momentous in the history of Utah . . . was confirmed with a domestic pleasantry."

After considerable string-pulling, Frank Cannon gained an audience with President Grover Cleveland and succeeded in persuading him to try a change of tactics in solving the knotty Mormon problem.

"He told me, at last, that he was going to appoint Mr. Sandford chief justice of Utah," Frank wrote. "He was appointed chief justice on the 9th day of July, 1888, and—as the Mormon people expressed it—'the backbone of the raid was broken.' "

Three weeks after Sandford arrived in Salt Lake City, George Q. Cannon surrendered to him and pleaded guilty of unlawful cohabitation. The sentence of $450 fine and seventy-five days in jail was indeed merciful, considering that Cannon was a fugitive who had jumped $45,000 bail and had a price on his head. Other prominent Saints followed his example. As another gesture of cooperation, President Wilford Woodruff ordered demolition of the Endowment House, where many plural marriages had been performed. "Many of the non-Mormons, who had despaired of any solution of the troubles in Utah," Frank recorded, "now began to hope."

Charles Mostyn Owen was puzzled. In the new climate of amnesty and cooperation, as hundreds of polygamists followed the example of Cannon and other church leaders by surrendering, the official posture professed strict obedience to federal law. In explaining the destruction of the Endowment House, Woodruff said it was because it had been discovered that a single plural marriage had been performed there, without his knowledge or consent.

To Owen there was something definitely strange about the new façade. In his travels as an engineer, he was uncovering evidence of new plural marriages all over Mormon country. He dug up cases of men who had a legal wife in Salt Lake, a recent plural in Canada, another in Mexico, and two more posing as widows at various locations in the Great Basin. How could this be? Certainly the Mormon Church leaders were honorable men of honesty and integrity. With the tight LDS organization, they would simply *have* to know what was going on. How, then, could they deny it?

Owen was baffled, until an evening at St. George, where after sharing a jug of good Dixie tithing wine with an informant, the man opened up with the great secret. The brethren were telling the strict truth, the informer said, if you knew how to interpret what they meant. The *church* had indeed quit sanctioning polygamy; however, the *priesthood authority within the church* was keeping it alive.

Owen was boggled. His informant reminded him that in the beginning Joseph Smith received priesthood authority from heavenly beings. With this authority, Joseph organized the church. The priesthood authority and the church organization were thus two separate entities and could act independently.

Within a year after the church was founded, Joseph received a revelation authorizing polygamy.[13] It was a dozen years later that he received a second revelation on the subject,[14] and nine more years were to elapse before polygamy was officially acknowledged as church policy. During this entire period of twenty-one years the church emphatically denied the practice of plural marriage, while the priesthood authority within the church fostered it as absolutely essential to attainment of the celestial glory in the hereafter. And now, the informant told Owen, the Principle simply had gone underground again, as in the days of Kirtland, Missouri, Nauvoo, and early Utah.[15]

13. This revelation of 1831 has never been given to the body of the Saints. Scholars, however, are aware of it. One of its provisions gives practical advice on how the Lamanites were to become "a white and delightsome people"—by Mormons taking Indian maidens as plurals.

14. This subsequently became Section 132 of the D&C.

15. See the author's *The Kingdom or Nothing* (New York: Macmillan, 1976). Briefly, the steps in taking polygamy underground again were these: In 1882 President John Taylor issued an *Epistle,* "On Marriage," authorizing church marriages outside the Endowment House and temples. Two years later he admitted in court testimony that he had authorized hundreds of men to perform secret marriages at any place convenient. Two revelations of John Taylor pertain to the situation. One of June 27, 1882 is directed to the secret Council of Fifty, who evidently were directed to take charge of the Principle on the underground. A

With a gleam in his eye, Charles Mostyn Owen renewed his valiant efforts to prove what he now knew.

Frank J. Cannon accepted the official posture at face value. Though dealing with men in the highest church echelons, he wasn't a member of the hierarchy, nor was he privy to the big secret. He had been entirely sincere in assuring President Cleveland of complete capitulation in Utah. Other Mormons in Washington backed him. When the Mormon-eating congressman from Idaho, Fred T. Dubois, charged that Cleveland was defeating the purposes of the Edmunds-Tucker Act by pardoning large numbers of polygamists, the Utah delegate, John T. Caine, refuted the "stale slanders" in "the intemperate remarks of the gentleman from Idaho." Polygamy, he declared, was a dead issue which "has ceased to exist."[16]

Caleb W. West, carpetbag governor of Utah, was of different mind, claiming that "the avowal of a renunciation of polygamy" was only a ploy in the church's struggle for political control. The union of church and state was "perfect and indissoluble," he declared, "emanating immediately from God, in all things secular as well as spiritual."[17]

In his annual message to Congress, December 3, 1888, President Cleveland happily reported that due to the "firm and vigilant execution" of the Edmunds-Tucker Act there had been nearly 600 convictions of polygamists (voluntary surrenders) and that "polygamy within the United States is virtually at an end."

"The President is satisfied that polygamy is virtually dead in Utah," the *Tribune* said scornfully two days later.

---

revelation of September 27, 1886, a few months prior to Taylor's death, emphasized that "the law" never would be revoked. At a meeting the following day he completed the organization to continue the Principle underground.

Despite every effort of the modern church to squelch polygamy—and sweep the entire subject under the rug—it is thriving today as never before. In 1976, according to a reliable source, the leader of the major branch of the Fundamentalist faction claims membership of 35,000 for his flock alone.

For the Council of Fifty, see Klaus J. Hansen, *Quest for Empire* (East Lansing: Michigan State University Press, 1967); Norman C. Pierce, *The 3½ Years* (Salt Lake: The author, 1963); Lynn L. and Steven L. Bishop, *The Keys of the Priesthood Illustrated* (Draper: Review and Preview Publishers, 1971); James R. Clark, "The Kingdom of God, the Council of Fifty, and the State of Deseret," UHQ, April 1958.

16. *Congressional Record,* August 13, 1888.
17. *Annual Report,* October 27, 1888.

What has satisfied him? His assertion simply proves what atmosphere is around him. Has one sign been given that polygamy is dead, or that the chiefs who rule here have surrendered one point? We defy him to supply one iota of proof that will justify his belief.

Later that same month Wilford Woodruff recorded in his journal that the Quorum of the Twelve, in the privacy of such meetings, thoroughly considered the proposition of renouncing polygamy to secure statehood, and unanimously rejected it.[18]

Cleveland's attitude actually meant little at the time. He was a lame-duck president, having been defeated by Benjamin Harrison in the Republican victory of 1888. Upon assuming office the following March, Harrison left no doubt that he was returning to the harsh policy that had spawned the Edmunds-Tucker Act.

Frank J. Cannon was outraged when the U.S. attorney general requested Chief Justice Elliot Sandford's resignation. Sandford had held the position for a period of only nine months. His attempt "to administer justice and the law impartially to all men" had drawn furious complaints from the Utah Ring that he was coddling polygamists.[19] In his place the attorney general reinstated the dreaded Charles S. Zane, characterized by the *Herald* as "a bitter enemy of Utah" who hated the Saints with the intensity of a fanatic. During the "four years he sat there breathing hate and employing his power to oppress and persecute," he had "struck poor Utah a blow from which she will be long years in recovering"; while out of office he continued to breed trouble as a "social and political firebrand."[20]

The newly appointed governor, Arthur L. Thomas, warned the secretary of the interior against "any temporizing policy" regarding church political control and advised "that future legislation should be aimed at the political power of the church." Mormons "put the church first, the country second." As for polygamy, the Saints would never renounce it "until they are convinced that God has commanded them to do so" and that hadn't happened.

The *Deseret News* claimed that the governor's report "falls into

18. *Journal,* December 20, 1888.
19. However, while his term of office was short, it was of profound importance in shaping Utah history. Also, his wife didn't have to deprive herself of new bonnets very long.
20. March 28, 1889.

the sloughs of error and folly which engulfed so many of his predecessors."

He repeats the stories invented by so-called "liberals," with whose aims and schemes he shows himself to be associated. Much of what he offers is anti-Mormon gossip.[21]

The report "is frank and truthful," the *Tribune* countered next morning. It "shows the old spirit rules, the old assumptions are maintained in the councils of the hierarchy."

The official position was given by President Woodruff when interviewed by the St. Louis *Globe Democrat:*

Q. What is the church attitude toward the law prohibiting polygamy?

WOODRUFF: We mean to obey it. We have no thought of evading or ignoring it. We recognize the laws as binding upon us. I have refused to give any recommendations for the performance of plural marriage since I have been President.[22]

The Mormon world was falling apart. Even within Utah, the Saints were losing political control. In February 1889 the Liberal (Gentile) Party swept the municipal election at Ogden, the state's second-largest city. True, Ogden was a railroad town, with many Gentiles; true, there were accusations of trainloads of transients being imported for voting purposes—but then in the August municipal election the Liberals took control of Salt Lake City itself.

"Hurrah! Hurrah, Tiger!" the *Tribune* exulted. "A mighty victory has been won! The city is redeemed from the hands of the Mormon Church that has squatted like a blight over his fair land for 40 years."

In preparing for the county elections in February, both parties campaigned to have every eligible voter registered, making house-to-house canvases. The crux of this effort centered on the admission of new citizens, the People's (Mormon) Party being anxious to naturalize the large number of foreign converts gathered in Zion.

21. Report published by *Deseret News*, November 5, 1889.
22. Quoted by *Herald*, October 27, 1889. Perhaps it should be noted that Woodruff actually had been church president only since the previous conference in April. Prior to that time, since the death of John Taylor in July 1887, Woodruff had led the church as head of the Quorum of the Twelve.

In the test case of John Moore, he passed the requirements for naturalization, but was challenged with having taken an oath against the government in the Endowment House.

"If any organization requires an oath against the government," ruled Thomas J. Anderson, associate justice of the Utah Supreme Court, "we have the right to get at it."

In the emergency, the Lord spoke to Woodruff by revelation:

I, the Lord, will hold the courts . . . and the nation, responsible for their acts toward the inhabitants of Zion. . . . Fear not, little flock, it is your Father's good pleasure to give you the Kingdom. . . . The wicked are fast ripening in iniquity, and they will be cut off by the judgments of God. Great events await you and this generation, and are nigh at your doors.[23]

Despite the Lord's reassurance and a spirited defense by church attorneys in court, denying that any oath of vengeance was taken during the endowment ceremony, that there had ever been a policy of killing apostates, or that there was any "doctrine, tenet, obligation, or injunction" hostile to the government, Judge Anderson ruled that "an alien who is a member of the church is not a fit person to be made a citizen of the United States."

"There never was a time probably in our history when the Latter-day Saints needed more than they do at present the assistance which God has promised," the First Presidency declared on December 2, two days after the decision, in a letter to the stakes. The twenty-third of the month, birthday of Joseph Smith, was designated "as a day of fasting and of solemn prayer unto the Lord," at a time when "there appears no earthly help of which we can avail ourselves."

This document, seeking the Lord's aid in confounding the plots and schemes "of robbing us of our civil and political rights," and in softening the hearts of the nation, was hailed by the Saints as their "bill of rights." Among his associates on the *Tribune,* however, Charles Mostyn Owen found skepticism that it would soften the government attitude. Washington wouldn't forget that despite fervent avowals of patriotism, the Saints had for years flouted the

23. November 24, 1889.

laws of the land, which had been upheld as constitutional by the Supreme Court. Congress now had the church pressed against the wall and was determined to settle the Mormon question once and for all.

The error in the work of apologist historians is that they have written Mormon history from hindsight. The image of Mormons leaving the United States in order to set up an independent kingdom of God [in Utah] conflicts with the subsequent self-conscious Mormon view of themselves as loyal citizens of the pluralistic twentieth century. What these writers fail to acknowledge, simply, is that a transformation has taken place in the attitude of the Mormons toward the United States. This shift, while patently apparent, has in fact served to obscure Mormon understanding of their own past.

—KLAUS J. HANSEN, Quest for Empire

3

Beat the Devil at His Own Game

ON DECEMBER 12, 1889, ten days after its issuance, the church buttressed the bill of rights with an *Official Declaration* refuting Gentile charges of blood atonement, ecclesiastical domination of political, judicial, and business affairs, and of disloyalty. This epistle was exceptional in that it was signed not only by the First Presidency, but by the Council of Apostles, which emphasized its importance.

Although the *Trib* crowd and the Utah Ring delighted in picking it apart, informants with good connections convinced Charles Mostyn Owen that while some of the statements might not have been watertight historically, they were highly significant as indications of future policy. Only two years after President John Taylor's death, the church was being diverted into different channels. Seen in this light, the *Declaration* was a landmark document, detailing the abandonment of pioneer concepts and the adoption of new values.

"We solemnly make the following declarations," the epistle stated:

That this Church views the shedding of human blood with the utmost abhorrence. . . . Notwithstanding all the stories told about the killing of apostates, no case of this kind has ever occurred. . . .

26

More exactly, Owen was told, no case was ever acknowledged by official church sources. All evidence pertaining to such cases simply was rejected.[1]

That we regard the killing of a human being, except in conformity with the civil law, as a capital crime which should be punished by shedding the blood of the criminal after a public trial before a legally constituted court of law.

This was true at the time the *Declaration* was issued. However, Owen knew, long before he arrived in Utah, of the past attitude, which had resulted in the butchery of all adult members of a wagon train at Mountain Meadows in southern Utah. More than 120 men and women were slaughtered, the only ones spared being young children. The massacre had been planned and directed by the highest church officials of the region, and some fifty-five loyal Mormons participated. Mountain Meadows could only be understood by realizing that it was the culmination of an attitude that had sponsored many lesser events of violence. The horror of the massacre effectively stopped further practice of "blood atonement."[2]

We declare that no Bishop's or other court in this Church claims or exercises the right to supersede, annul or modify a judgment of any civil court. Such courts, while established to regulate Christian conduct, are purely ecclesiastical, and their punitive powers go no further than the suspension or excommunication of members from Church fellowship.

As a matter of practice, church courts settled all types of litigation between church members, temporal as well as spiritual. John Taylor had declared, "It is expected that the Saints will adjust any matter of difficulty or dispute that may arise among them before those courts, and that they do not go to law before the ungodly."

1. This attitude is typified by Roberts in the CHC, 4:494, where he brushes off affidavits and confessions in one case by stating that "Such evidence as is cited in the case is purely circumstantial, or it rests upon the testimony of very questionable characters, who themselves were implicated in the murders." Certainly if testimony of people involved cannot be accepted, if evidence considered unfriendly is rejected as untrue, there is little hope of ascertaining facts from official sources.
2. See Juanita Brooks, *The Mountain Meadows Massacre* (Stanford: Stanford University Press, 1950). Only one man was ever brought to trial for the event, John D. Lee, though the church had a complete record of others involved. This record is still suppressed.

He affirmed this as God's law, warning that those disobeying would be deprived of temple blessings, and, "I will promise them, in the name of the Lord God of Israel, that they will be destroyed by the ungodly."

The scope and power of the church courts was tremendous. As to punitive power, disfellowshipment or excommunication could shatter a man's life and destroy his ability to make a living in Utah. Moreover, if he was a polygamist, he couldn't move away, for where else would he be accepted?

Although the district courts were under federal control, Mormons ran the probate courts of Utah (making them, in effect, church courts), expanding their powers until Congress acted to restrict their jurisdiction.

That this Church, while offering advice for the welfare of its members in all conditions of life, does not claim or exercise the right to interfere with citizens in the free exercise of social or political rights and privileges. . . . No man's business or other secular affairs are invaded by the Church or any of its officers.

Certainly the *Tribune*, the Utah Commission, governors of the Territory, and the Utah Ring had stated exactly the opposite, time after time, year after year.

Free agency and direct individual accountability to God are among the essentials of our Church doctrine. All things in the Church must be done by common consent, and no officer is appointed without the vote of the body.

Such was doctrine. Policy was another thing. Owen had attended services at local wards, and conference in the Salt Lake Tabernacle, observing what the democratic form meant in actual practice. All decisions came from above. There was no opportunity for previous discussion nor of discussion when decisions were announced from the pulpit. The congregation simply "sustained" the *fait accompli* by uplifted hand. Although a perfunctory request was made to "make manifest by the same sign" if in disagreement, to do so was considered a serious sign of being out of harmony. On the rare occasion when a brave soul raised a negative hand, he was called on the carpet to explain his contumacious attitude and counseled to repent.

28

The congregation had no voice whatsoever in the selection of officers. In fact, there were strict precautions to prevent any leak of information regarding appointment of officials until announced from the stand.

In other matters, such as adoption or revision of church Scripture, the literary work—which the people had had no chance to examine—was simply announced from the rostrum and automatically sustained.[3]

We declare that there is nothing in the ceremony of the endowment, or in any doctrine, tenet, obligation or injunction of this Church, either private or public, which is hostile ... to the Government of the United States. . . .

Utterances of prominent men in the Church at a time of great excitement have been selected and grouped, to convey the impression that present members are seditious. Those expressions were made more than thirty years ago. . . .

At that time excitement prevailed and strong language was used; but no words of disloyalty against the Government or its institutions were uttered. . . .

It was a matter of record that the previous president, John Taylor, defied the United States government to his last breath and in consequence died on the underground with a price on his head just two and a half years previously. "The people of the rest of the country are our enemies," he thundered. "God is greater than the United States. And when the Government conflicts with heaven, we will be ranged under the banner of heaven and against the Government. . . . We want to be friendly with the United States; . . . but not one jot nor tittle of our rights will we give up to purchase" such friendship. "I defy the United States. I will obey God."[4]

While the constitution was revered "as a heaven-inspired document," the church had continued to flout, for a period of eleven years, the Supreme Court decision of 1879 affirming the constitu-

3. An example is *The Pearl of Great Price.* The first American edition of 1878 was adopted as one of the four Standard Works of Scripture (others are the Bible, Book of Mormon, and *Doctrine and Covenants*). Subsequently, in 1902, there was a major revision of this work, which already had been accepted as the word of God. This revision was routinely sustained at conference by the people, who had had no opportunity to examine it.

4. *Tribune,* January 6, 1880.

tionality of anti-polygamy legislation. Thus to Congress, Mormon professions of patriotism and loyalty had a hollow ring. And the Supreme Court itself, in its decision upholding the Edmunds-Tucker Act, declared that the church was

an organized rebellion, a contumacious organization, the distinguishing features of whose creed were polygamy and the absolute ecclesiastical control of its members. It wielded by its resources immense power in Utah, and employed whose resources . . . in constantly attempting to oppose, subvert, and thwart the legislation of Congress and the will of the Government.[5]

Owen's informants claimed that the most significant departure from pioneer values in the *Declaration* was the statement that

We also declare that this Church does not claim to be an independent, temporal Kingdom of God, or to be an *imperium in imperio* aiming to overthrow the United States or any other civil government. . . . It proclaims that "the kingdom of heaven is at hand." Its members are commanded of God to be subject unto the powers that be until Christ comes, whose right it is to reign.[6]

From old-timers who had known Joseph Smith, Owen learned that the expectation of the Mormon kingdom, rolling forth like the little stone of the prophet Daniel to overwhelm the earth, seemed so imminent to Joseph that he designated men to political office for the expected takeover. Joseph himself would be king of the world, Brigham Young president of the United States, John Taylor vice president; other Mormons would fill Cabinet positions, occupy the Supreme Court, be governors of the various states, senators, congressmen, and, in fact, hold all offices of importance.

When Joseph was martyred, and the Saints were forced to evacuate Nauvoo, their intent was to leave the United States and set up their own independent kingdom. Only the coincidence of the Mexican War brought Utah under United States jurisdiction.[7]

5. Whitney, 3:740.
6. There is most abundant evidence that "the kingdom of God and the church were separate organizations," Klaus J. Hansen says in his *Quest for Empire*. Further, "a political kingdom of God, promulgated by a secret 'Council of Fifty,' is by far the most important key to an understanding of the Mormon past."
7. The Saints even had their own flag. See "The Flag of the Kingdom of God," by D. Michael Quinn, *BYU Studies*, Autumn 1973; also *The 3½ Years*, by Norman C. Pierce (Salt Lake: Published by the author, 1963).

The disavowal of the concept of an *imperium in imperio* certainly was exactly opposite to the pioneer goal visualized by Woodruff's predecessor. John Taylor's motto was "The Kingdom of God or Nothing."[8]

To Charles Mostyn Owen, another remarkable statement of the *Declaration* concerned separation of church and state.

Church government and civil government are distinct and separate in our theory and practice, and we regard it as part of our destiny to aid in the maintenance and perpetuity of the institutions of our country.[9]

Most certainly the church from its beginning had been deeply involved in politics and other temporal affairs. It was this, and not religious belief, that invited trouble at Kirtland, caused the expulsion of the Mormons from Missouri, and forced them to abandon Nauvoo. At the time of his death, Joseph Smith was candidate for president of the United States. This same involvement in temporal affairs precipitated the long Mormon-Gentile war in Utah. It was a power struggle, not polygamy, that brought the church into conflict with the nation. Gentiles in Utah at first considered plural marriage in the nature of a ribald jest, before they utilized it as a most effective weapon in the bitter fight for political and economic control.

As for separation of church and state, during the recent administration of John Taylor he routinely approved bills of the territorial legislature before they were acted upon.[10]

8. In his article, "The Kingdom of God, the Council of Fifty, and the State of Deseret," UHQ, April 1958, James R. Clark says, "The basic ideas for the government of the State of Deseret were not worked out after the Mormons arrived in Utah, but in meetings of the Council of Fifty in Nauvoo before the westward migration. The State of Deseret was the planned result of the doctrine of the Kingdom of God. . . . This Kingdom of God was to be a religio-civil government and is not to be confused or identified with the Mormon Church as such. . . . The insistence of the Mormon leaders on this concept of the Kingdom of God was largely instrumental, along with the practice of polygamy, in delaying statehood for Utah for half a century. A careful consideration of the Kingdom of God concept as the basis for the societal pattern—economic, educational, and political—may well cause Utah history, at least for the territorial period, to be re-valued and rewritten."

9. The intimate relationship of church and state in Utah was to occupy a large portion of the Senate hearings in the Smoot case, 1903–1907. See SI, vols. 1–4.

10. See letters to Taylor from his son, John W., who was a member of the legislature, regarding the submission of proposed legislation to the church president for approval, particularly letters of February 5 and March 1, 1886. Copies at Church Historical Department and University of Utah.

The *Tribune* scorned the *Official Declaration* as "a confession of a band of desperate priests," who "assume the right to defy the laws, to enslave a people, degrade the American home, and outrage civilization." As for trouble, "There has never been a day" when perfect peace could not have been achieved simply by obeying "the laws that all other Americans accept."

However, the *Trib*'s pipeline to the inner circle made it apparent that while the *Official Declaration* might be derided for its misstatements of prior policy, it must be considered seriously as the pattern of future attitudes. It was a blueprint of the metamorphosis of the pioneer faith into the modern culture.[11]

Frank J. Cannon characterized Wilford Woodruff as being "as helpless in the political world as a nun."

He was a gentle, earnest old man, patiently ingenuous and simpleminded, with a faith in the guidance of Heaven that was only greater than my father's because it was unmixed with any earthly sagacity.

Upon this venerable man, who never "showed the slightest bitterness to anybody," rested the responsibility of ushering in the inevitable capitulation to the overwhelming might of the United States government. On his shoulders, bent with the weight of eighty-three years, was the decision to cut the church away from the past and direct it into new and uncharted directions.

"The crisis was precipitated by a movement that had begun in the territory of Idaho," Frank wrote, "where the Mormons had been disfranchised by means of a test oath."

Anyone registering to vote in Idaho was required to swear that he was not "a member of any order, organization, or association which teaches, advises, counsels, or encourages its members, devotees, or any other person to commit the crime of bigamy or polygamy."[12]

11. Modern Mormonism, Hansen indicates in *Quest for Empire*, "differs fundamentally from the Mormonism of 1890, even though no theoretical change in doctrine may have occurred. Yet it is a fact that doctrines such as plural marriage, economic communitarianism, and the political kingdom of God are either totally ignored or else 'held in abeyance'—doctrines which throughout the nineteenth century were considered part of the very fibre and essence of Mormonism by the hierarchy. . . ."

12. To meet the situation, large numbers of Idaho Saints officially "withdrew" from church membership in order to vote, while the church contested the test-oath in the courts.

Idaho was at this time seeking statehood with a constitution disfranchising all Mormon citizens. During the debate before the Senate Committee on Territories, Idaho Delegate Fred T. Dubois charged that the Mormon Church was a criminal conspiracy, and that the only way to handle it was to destroy its political power. The Supreme Court upheld the legality of the Idaho test-oath, and the Senate approved the application for statehood.[13]

The Supreme Court decision spurred the Utah Ring to foster similar legislation in Congress. The Cullom-Struble bill, designed to disfranchise Utah Mormons, was actually written by ardent ringite R. N. Baskin at his Salt Lake office. Baskin carried it to Washington, accompanied by Governor Thomas and ex-Governor West. As an indication of increasing Gentile strength, the trip was sponsored by the Salt Lake Chamber of Commerce, of which West was president.

Frank J. Cannon went to Washington as an emissary of the church. There, he had an audience with Secretary of State James G. Blaine and with members of the Senate Committee on Territories advising them in confidence "that the Mormon Church was about to make a concession concerning its doctrine of polygamy. . . . Finally I appeared before each committee and argued our case at length."[14]

"You punished our fathers for an act," he said, "and now you punish us for a thought." Frank admitted that he believed in the revelation regarding plural marriage; however, "in obeying the law of Congress which forbids the practice," he said, "I believe I am not violating the creed of the church."

The real motive of the Utah Ring, he emphasized, was not to suppress polygamy but to gain political control of Utah. Flushed by Liberal victories at Ogden and Salt Lake, the Gentiles next planned to take control of Logan. This Mormon stronghold, fourth largest city of Utah, contained only fifty Liberal voters.[15]

13. Idaho was admitted to the union in July 1890.

14. Whitney says, "A brilliant speaker, well informed on local and national affairs, Mr. Cannon made a stirring appeal in behalf of 'Young Utah'" (Whitney, 3:732).

15. "It was proposed," Whitney comments, "to strip the majority of the franchise and hand them over bound hand and foot to be tyrannized over by fifty petty rulers." A previous example was provided by Tooele, where Gentiles took control by importing trainloads of voters, and for a period maintained the notorious "Tooele Republic" (Ibid., 3:733).

Frank J. Cannon returned to Salt Lake, after having gained the promise of a rehearing of the Cullom-Struble bill. In reporting to President Woodruff, "I warned him that the passage of the measure of disfranchisement had been no more than retarded. I pointed out the fatal consequences for the community if the bill should ever become law." It had only been held back because of Frank's promise that polygamy would be abandoned.

"Brother Frank," Woodruff said, "I have been making it a matter of prayer. I have wrestled mightily with the Lord. And I think I see some light."

"To be very plain with you, President Woodruff, our friends expect, and the country will insist, that the Church shall yield the practice of plural marriage."

After a long moment of reflection, "I hope," the old man said at last, "the Lord will make the way plain for his people."

In the midst of such negotiations, Charles Mostyn Owen remained busy. As a result, the Utah Commission charged in its annual report in August 1890 that it had information of "41 male persons who, it is believed, entered into the polygamic relation" since June of the previous year.

The commission urged passage of the Cullom-Struble test-oath bill, "believing that it would do more to put an end" to polygamy than anything else.

The *Herald* called the report "a most despicable slander for political purposes," while the *Deseret News* declared "There is no language strong enough to characterize the ineffable meanness of the cunningly devised and unsupported story." But Charles Mostyn Owen and the *Trib* crowd were happy, and the outside world believed the commission.

Frank J. Cannon returned to Ogden after the interview with Woodruff and resumed editorship of the *Standard* during "the anxious days that followed." He knew that Washington would "demand some evidence of our good faith before Congress should reconvene." Finally his father sent word that President Woodruff wished to see him. Frank hastened to Salt Lake where "President Woodruff took me into a private room and read me his 'manifesto,'" which officially set aside the practice of plural marriage by the church.

"Here, shaking in the hand of age, was a sheet of paper by which the future of a half million people was to be directed, and that simple old man was to speak through it, to them, with the awful authority of the voice of God."

Addressed "To Whom It May Concern," the statement refuted press dispatches "sent for political purposes" by the Utah Commission concerning charges of polygamy.

> I, therefore, as President of the Church of Jesus Christ of Latter-day Saints, do hereby, in the most solemn manner, declare that these charges are false. We are not teaching polygamy or plural marriage, nor permitting any person to enter into its practice. . . .
>
> Inasmuch as laws have been enacted by Congress forbidding plural mariages, which laws have been pronounced constitutional by the court of last resort, I hereby declare my intention to submit to those laws, and to use my influence with the members of the Church over which I preside to have them do likewise. . . . And now I publicly declare that my advice to the Latter-day Saints is to refrain from contracting any marriage forbidden by the law of the land.[16]

Frank Cannon found the statement "disappointingly mild." He wondered "whether the nation would believe that such an equivo-

16. The authorship of the Manifesto remains controversial. Frank Cannon says, "He told me he had written it himself, and it certainly appeared to me to be in his handwriting. Its authorship has since been variously attributed. Some of the present-day polygamists say that it was I who wrote it. Chas. W. Penrose and George Reynolds have claimed they edited it."

At the Smoot investigation, George Reynolds testified before the Senate committee that he helped write the Manifesto. "President Woodruff wrote it in his own hand—and he was a very poor writer, worse, I believe, than Horace Greeley— and he gave it into the hands of three of the elders to prepare it for the press, . . . C. W. Penrose, John R. Winder, and myself. . . . We transcribed the notes and changed the language slightly to adapt it for publication."

Thomas J. Rosser stated that, when a missionary to Wales in 1908, he asked the mission president, Charles W. Penrose, during a missionary conference, if the Manifesto was a revelation from God. "Brethren, I will answer that question, if you will keep it under your hats," Penrose said. "I, Charles W. Penrose, wrote the Manifesto with the assistance of Frank J. Cannon and John White. . . . Wilford Woodruff signed it to beat the devil at his own game."

HP 4:67 states that the Manifesto then "was submitted to a committee of non-Mormons, Judges Charles S. Zane, C. S. Varian, and O. W. Powers, none of whom were well known for their friendship for the Mormons. . . . A change of wording was insisted upon in the Manifesto, and the document was recopied by a clerk named Green. It would seem very unusual that the Lord would dictate a statement to His mouthpiece upon the earth that required a committee to render it intelligible."

cally worded document meant an absolute recession from the practice of plural marriage." He asked Woodruff "point blank, whether it meant an absolute recession from polygamy," and also whether it put an end to living with plural wives.

"Why, of course, Frank," Woodruff said. "You know they didn't get our brethren in prison for polygamy, but for living with their plural wives."

Inasmuch as the felony of polygamy was almost impossible to prove, because marriage records were secret, the entire government thrust had been against unlawful cohabitation, a misdemeanor. "It was part of President Woodruff's unworldliness that he did not see the satire of his words," Frank said, "and I was the more convinced of his good faith."

A few days later Frank "was summoned to attend a meeting of the Church authorities in the president's offices, and I knew the test had come." He subsequently wrote the only published account, in detail, of that historic meeting which altered the course of church history as no other before or since.[17]

The meeting was attended by the First Presidency and Council of the Twelve, "with two or three of their most trusted advisors." President Woodruff stood under the oil portraits of former presidents and prophets, looking "so old and other-worldly that he seemed already of their circle rather than ours."

"We have sought," he said, "to live our religion—to harm no one—to perform our mission in this world for the salvation of the living and the dead. We have obeyed the principle of celestial marriage because it came to us from God. We have suffered the rage of the wicked; we were driven from our homes into the desert; our prophets have been slain, our holy ones persecuted—and it *did* seem to me that we were entitled to the constitutional protection of the courts in the practice of our religion."

But the courts had decided "against us." The church attorney, Franklin S. Richards, had advised that the last legal defense had fallen. "In broken and contrite spirit" Woodruff had sought the will of the Lord, and the Holy Spirit had revealed to him that it was necessary to relinquish the practice of the principle for which the brethren had been willing to lay down their lives.

17. Minutes of such meetings are kept in a safe from which very little emerges, even of events of the previous century.

The Manifesto was read during "a sort of ghastly stillness." Then Woodruff said, "The matter is now before you. I want you to speak as the Spirit moves you." There was discussion as to the meaning of the document. Did it pertain only to future plural marriages or did it also require a man to set aside plural wives already members of their families?

When Woodruff "answered, firmly, that it did . . . the storm broke. One after another they rose and protested, hoarsely, in the voice of tears, that they were willing to suffer 'persecution unto death' rather than to violate the covenants which they had made 'in holy places' with women who had trusted them. One after another they offered themselves for any sacrifice but this betrayal of the women and children to whom they owed an everlasting faith."

First Counselor George Q. Cannon reviewed again the long but futile efforts "to resist what we believed to be unconstitutional measures to repress our practice of a religious faith." However, as citizens they were required to obey the law. They had the alternative either of defying the power of the United States government or submitting to its authority. For his part, he was willing to do the will of the Lord.

Woodruff called on Frank J. Cannon, who arose "knowing that I must urge these elders to sacrifice themselves and their families . . . but sustained by the remembrance of the solemn pledge which I had been authorized to give in Washington. . . .

"I reminded them that the sorrow and the parting, at which they rebelled, could only be for a little breath of time; . . . that by the celestial covenant, into which they had entered, they were assured that they should have their wives and children with them throughout the endless ages of eternity."

One by one the brethren rose to accept the Manifesto "as a revelation from God." Second Counselor Joseph F. Smith was one of the last to speak.

"With a face like wax, his hands outstretched, in an intensity of passion that seemed as if it must sweep the assembly, he declared that he had covenanted, at the altar of God's house . . . to cherish the wives and children whom the Lord had given him. . . . He would rather choose to stand, with them, alone—persecuted, proscribed, outlawed—to wait until God in His anger should break the nation with His avenging stroke. But . . .

"He dropped his arms. He seemed to shrink in his commanding stature like a man stricken with a paralysis of despair. The tears came to the pained constriction of his eyelids.

" 'I have never disobeyed a revelation from God,' he said. 'I cannot—I dare not—now.' "

The vote for acceptance was, as was customary, unanimous.

"In any discussion of the public affairs" of Utah, Frank J. Cannon stated, "a line of discrimination must be drawn at the year 1890. In that year the Church began a progressive course of submission to the civil law, and the nation received each act of surrender with forgiveness. The previous defiances of the Mormon people ceased to give grounds for a complaint against them."

But he could look into the ground no further than the next man, as he was soon to discover.

From the beginning, ambiguity and controversy accompanied the Manifesto, which persists to the present day. Ordinarily, a revelation would come to public attention when presented at conference and accepted by the congregation. Yet the Manifesto was first issued as a press release from Washington by Utah delegate in Congress John T. Caine, September 25, 1890. As such, it was signed only by Woodruff, not by the First Presidency as an official declaration ordinarily would have been. "We cannot resist the thought that this was not prompted by President Woodruff at all," the *Tribune* commented next morning, "but that it was prompted by shrewd men in the Church, and that the object is purely political."

The *Trib* charged that George Q. Cannon persuaded Woodruff to issue it as a smokescreen, urging him to announce "something which would give the country an idea that we had abandoned polygamy because of our respect for the laws."

As a press dispatch, it would not be an edict from the church, Cannon said, but "merely gives your personal, individual, human advice to the Saints, and which, of course, does not count any more than the advice of any other man."

Governor Thomas was dubious, the *Deseret News* reported that afternoon. "The general sentiment is a hope it is in good faith," he said, "but many things lead to doubt." He noted that "it does not come in the usual channel," that while submission to the law is advised, "there is no injunction to obey the laws," that nothing was said about unlawful cohabitation nor "that polygamy is wrong or the law is right."

"We believe," the *Tribune* concluded after considering things overnight, "that his manifesto was not intended to be accepted as a command by the President of the Church, but as a little bit of harmless dodging to deceive the people of the East."

In contrast, the *Deseret News* quoted Congressional Delegate John T. Caine, in Washington: "The practice of polygamy has entirely ceased in Utah," and, furthermore, "I do not personally know of a single case in which a man is now living with more than one wife."

The *Trib* characterized Caine's statement as an effusion from "The Mormon literary bureau in all its glory."[18] With Woodruff's letter the cue, "Eastern papers are being filled at the usual column rates" by apologists and Jack Mormons, the propaganda being managed by John T. Caine.[19]

"The history of the Latter-day Saints has demonstrated," the *Deseret News* countered, "that it is useless for them to attempt to please the world or satisfy the demands made upon them by their enemies." Certainly this was prophetic of events during the next three decades.

At October conference, Bishop Orson F. Whitney read the Manifesto from the stand. Lorenzo Snow, president of the Twelve, moved that the congregation accept Woodruff's "declaration concerning plural marriages as authoritative and binding." The people sustained this, and, officially, the church abandoned the Principle.

Gentile skepticism remained strong. Charles Mostyn Owen remained active. Three months after the Manifesto was issued, President Benjamin Harrison in his annual message to Congress said that while he "hoped" that the "recent letter of Wilford Woodruff" would be "beneficial in restraining infractions of the laws," that "the doctrine of the church remains unchanged," and the Manifesto

18. As the Smoot investigation was to prove, Mormon polygamists had absolutely no intention of putting aside plural families. Joseph F. Smith, president of the church at that time (1903), testified that his five plural wives all had borne children since the Manifesto of 1890.

19. The term "Jack Mormon," here used as a Gentile friendly to the Saints, has come to mean in modern usage an inactive member of the church, particularly one who breaks the Word of Wisdom. A Jack Mormon has also been defined as a Saint with a sense of humor, and as "a seagull who won't eat crickets."

39

merely "advises against the practice of it" because it was illegal.[20]

"The only safe thing," Harrison concluded, "is to deal with the Territory of Utah so that those who believe polygamy to be rightful shall not have the power to make it lawful."[21]

The specter of disfranchisement still hung over Utah.

---

20. Joseph Smith's revelation on plural marriage still remains in the D&C. See Section 132.

21. *Herald,* December 2, 1890.

I would say to the political world ... that the opposition they are so anxious to promote [with the two-party system] contains the seeds of the destruction of the government that we live in. ... Every government lays the foundation of its own downfall when it permits what are called democratic elections.

—BRIGHAM YOUNG, Journal of Discourses, 14:93

There have been times in the past when the church ... has completely swallowed up the state, even to the literal putting of the foot of the ecclesiastical ruler upon the necks of kings. At other times, ... the state has absorbed the church, and ecclesiastical dignitaries are shuffled about as mere puppets of regal power. In such cases church and state occupy but a single sphere. The lion and the lamb lie down together, it is true, but the lamb is inside the lion.

—CALVIN REASONER, "Church and State; The Issue of Civil and Religious Liberty in Utah"

4

Out of Harmony

FOR YEARS, both in public and during stormy sessions of the Quorum of the Twelve, Moses Thatcher had advocated complete separation of church and state. Although Apostle Thatcher was a wealthy man, influential and enormously popular, he found solid opposition within the quorum. Ever since the first days of the church, it had been vigorously active in politics; such a policy was not easily relinquished.

However, Congress and a hostile carpetbag judge made it plain that change was necessary, if Utah was ever to obtain statehood. Despite the Manifesto on plural marriage, Congress was debating bills to disfranchise all Mormons, while Judge Thomas J. Anderson's decision, that a foreign-born Saint "is not a fit person" for citizenship, was entrenched as Gentile policy.

Washington was suspicious that the Manifesto was nothing but a ruse to attain church domination of Utah. "The purpose is merely to secure Mormon statehood, to be ruled by the creed," the *Tribune* warned. Within six months after admittance to the Union, "The whole machinery of government would be turned over to the Saints," the paper claimed.

From the first, the dream of the chiefs has been to secure statehood, behind the lines of which the real government would be the rigid edicts of the creed, a mere priestly despotism.[1]

Reporting on anti-Mormon measures before Congress, the *Herald* correspondent wired:

Of these bills, the more important were the Stewart bill, restricting the rights of the Mormons, which was drawn by "Judge" Baskin and sent on here; and the Struble disfranchisement bill; Paddock's bill, authorizing the governor to appoint certain county officials; the Cullom disfranchisement bill; Platt's substitute for Cullom's bill prescribing the Idaho anti-Mormon test oath for voters, and the Edmunds bill, reported as a substitute for Paddock's bill.[2]

Although none of these measures was passed before Congress adjourned March 4, 1891, it was all too obvious that further repressive legislation was in the offing, unless there was convincing evidence of the separation of church and state in Utah.

And then, to Thatcher's delight, the church advocated dissolution of the People's (Mormon) Party and the Liberal (Gentile) Party, urging both factions to join the national Republicans or Democrats as they might choose. In the case of the Republicans, official approval was implied by the fact that a giant mass meeting was held in the church-owned Salt Lake Theater. The following week Franklin S. Richards, church attorney and chairman of the People's Party in Salt Lake County, submitted a resolution that the party disband "and its members left free" to join the national parties.[3]

Thatcher became a Democrat, along with several other promi-

1. September 26, 1890 and February 24, 1891.
2. March 6, 1891.
3. *Herald,* May 30.

nent Saints, notably B. H. Roberts, the eminent historian, and Charles W. Penrose, editor of the *Deseret News*.[4] Most of the hierarchy became Republicans. For the first time in the sixty-one years of the church's existence, the Saints weren't expected to vote as a unit. Mormon could run against Mormon for political office.

Predictably, the *Trib* suspected the worst. "A few men, backed by all the power of the Mormon Church, are trying to carry the Liberal Party off its feet," it charged, "trying to dissolve the organization which was made necessary here because of the tyrannies, superstitions and the slavery engendered by the Mormon creed, and to undo the work of a quarter of a century." However, after it became apparent that the Liberal Party was a lost cause, the *Trib* capitulated.

Another Gentile paper, the Salt Lake *Times,* interviewed Wilford Woodruff and his first counselor, George Q. Cannon.[5] "The only reason put forward in opposition to the organization of parties on national lines in Utah," the *Times* said by way of introduction, was that the whole thing was a plot "by which the Liberals are to be divided and the political control of Utah placed in the hands of the Mormon people."

In brief, it had been claimed that the purpose of the church was to secure statehood for Utah, then "seize all the offices and carry on the government in the interests of Mormons" to Gentile disadvantage. "It is held that the church claims the right to exercise absolute authority over its members in all matters," including "direct dictation as to whom they should vote for."[6]

The paper repeated Gentile claims that "polygamy has simply been suspended, to be re-established in the future under the protection of state laws enacted by Mormon legislatures," and that other laws would be passed "intended to oppress Gentiles and work virtual confiscation of their property."

4. Democrats included Apostles Brigham Young, Jr., and Heber J. Grant, John R. Winder of the presiding bishopric, together with sixteen other well-positioned Saints.

5. June 23, 1891. Roberts notes in the CHC, 6:302, that "a list of very carefully prepared questions," was submitted, which were "carefully considered and written answers made thereto, for which reason the '*Times* Interview' became a somewhat noted and official document in political controversies in Utah." He digests it in the CHC. For complete interview see MFP 3:211.

6. During Brigham Young's time, the numbered ballot guaranteed correct voting, for each person's ballot could be checked.

In answer, the First Presidency made blanket denial of the charges contained in the introduction.

Q. Does the Church claim the right to dictate to its members in political matters?

A. The Church does not claim any such right. . . . We disclaim the right to control the political action of the members.

Several questions centered on whether candidates would be supported because they were Mormons and discriminated against if Gentiles. The presidency declared that "we would consider it the height of folly" to do so; adding that, "If statehood should ever be obtained, all the influence we could use to break down the distinctions which have created such bitterness in the past would be exerted."

A number of questions concerned separation of church and state and persistent reports of the continued practice of polygamy. The presidency squarely upheld the first and vehemently denied the second. It also refuted the charge that Mormon leaders "are now engaged in a political conspiracy to secure political power for the church," stating that "We see nothing to be gained for the Church in this way."

Q. The Opponents of party division on national lines declare that they want evidence of the sincerity of the Mormon people. The *Times* would ask you to state whether the declarations of sincerity on the part of those leaders who have been before the public reflect your views and meet your approval.

A. Those declarations express our view and meet our entire approval. What greater evidence can be asked than those which have already been furnished?

The presidency pointed out that the Manifesto showed sincerity in curtailing polygamy, while the dissolution of the People's Party disproved the charge of priesthood political control. "If the elements of sincerity were wanting, such a movement would result in entire demoralization."

Despite the *Times* interview, Thatcher reserved judgment. With his access to the inner circles he knew that the church had been deeply involved in politics. With a Republican, Benjamin Harrison, in the White House, party leaders had convinced church authorities that only a Republican Utah could obtain presidential amnesty for convicted polygamists, the return of church property escheated to the government, and statehood. Judge M. M. Estee, who had been chairman of the Republican national convention that had nominated Harrison for president, was in Salt Lake expediting matters at the time the People's Party disbanded. And it was at this time, during a meeting in the Gardo House of the church hierarchy, stake presidents, and others of influence, that the worm crawled out of the apple. Those present adopted as a policy "that men in high authority who believed in Republican principles should go out among the people" and campaign for Republican candidates. However, those "who could not endorse the principles of Republicanism should remain silent."[7]

Thatcher hadn't attended the Gardo House meeting. He was incensed on learning that not only were he and fellow Democrats counseled to "remain silent," but that the church presidency had appointed a committee to promote Republicanism. In fact, Apostle John Henry Smith received an appointment to a roving mission as campaigner among the Saints for the GOP.

When Thatcher publicly denounced John Henry's mission, together with church involvement in politics, the fat was in the fire. Apostle Franklin D. Richards warned the hierarchy that church involvement in politics would, if proved, result in passage by Congress of the impending disfranchisement legislation. Church policy proved stronger than political affiliation, and "counsel was obeyed by all the apostles and high authorities except Moses Thatcher, who talked to the people contrary to the wishes of his brethren," A. H. Cannon recorded.[8] This put Thatcher "out of harmony" with the brethren and, in particular, with Joseph F. Smith of the First Presidency and his cousin, Apostle John Henry Smith. Being out of harmony was a most serious situation, for despite differences of

7. See A. H. Cannon journal; also Calvin Reasoner, "Church and State; the Issue of Civil and Religious Liberty in Utah," pamphlet (Salt Lake, 1896). Utah politics of the period are well treated by Gustive O. Larson, *The Americanization of Utah for Statehood* (San Marino: Huntington Library, 1971).

It has been said that the Gardo House decision is reminiscent of the statement in George Orwell's *Animal Farm,* that everyone is created equal, but some are more equal than others.

8. Quoted by Larson.

opinion within the council, it was essential that final voting always be unanimous and considered the will of the Lord.

Thatcher continued displaying his contumacious spirit by political speeches contrary to official posture. This buttressed the annual reports of the Utah Commission and of Governor Arthur L. Thomas, which again were skeptical of polygamy having been abolished and of the church getting out of politics. The commission listed eighteen alleged plural marriages "during the past year, notwithstanding the 'manifesto,' " and stated that "In the light of history no one can doubt the power of the Church to control" the vote "for the furtherance of its ends."

The following month at October conference the church denounced the Utah Commission for "many untruthful statements." The congregation sustained an official resolution which denied recent plural marriages and also "most emphatically the assertion of the Commission that the Church dominates its members in political matters and that the Church and State are united."

"Our Saintly friends somewhat overdid the business," the *Tribune* commented next morning. "Their declaration that the Church has never interfered with politics will strike the whole people of the United States as about as preposterous and gally a declaration as ever emanated from the Lord's anointed." Joseph Smith founded the church as the "Kingdom of God on earth," with the Saints to rule forever. "Did not the air of Utah ring for 40 years with defiance of the laws—such laws as did not suit the Saints?"

In January 1892 the Territorial Legislative Assembly addressed a memorial to the U.S. Congress, seeking home rule under "new conditions," being now "free in the full sense of American constitutional freedom, . . . which consists in civil and political rights absolutely guaranteed." Later in the year at the Democratic national convention in Chicago, the Utah delegation stated that the "sole objections" against the Saints, "to wit: polygamy and Church dictation in politics," had been "entirely removed."

Thatcher, however, found things different in official circles. Frank J. Cannon was Republican candidate for delegate to Congress, and a campaign brochure called "Nuggets of Truth" went out together with a letter from the chairman of the Republican Committee, Charles Crane, urging that a copy should "reach the home of every man in the Territory." Crane added helpfully, "I would suggest the Sunday School, or the elders' meetings, or church meetings, as the best means of attaining the desired result."

The *Herald* protested the use of church assemblies "to advance the cause of a political party," adding that such use "has been permitted to pass unrebuked by those in authority." The "celebrated circular" contained pictures of Joseph Smith, Brigham Young, John Taylor, and Wilford Woodruff, the four presidents of the church, of Joseph F. Smith of the First Presidency, "and upon the last page a large picture of Frank J. Cannon, the Republican candidate for Congress."[9]

During the 1892 campaign, Ivins states, Republicans of high church office stumped the state; but when Thatcher, Roberts, and Penrose campaigned for the Democrats, "The three brethren . . . found themselves in trouble."[10]

The work of Roberts and Penrose was particularly effective in the campaign, for they were on the editorial staff of the *Herald,* and were determined that this should be a free election. In fact, Penrose had left the editorship of the *Deseret News,* after twelve years in that position, in order to be free to express his political convictions. Both men were popular speakers, powerful writers, and of good church position; and, incidentally, both had proved their dedication by taking plural wives.

In April of that election year Thatcher spoke at Logan on "Evils Resulting from the Union of Church and State," and again at Ogden the following month. This called forth a letter to the Ogden *Standard* by Joseph F. Smith and John Henry Smith, which was "a quiver full of arrows," Reasoner states, aimed at Thatcher. Now the disagreement was out of the quorum and into the newspapers. Inasmuch as the *Standard* was edited by a Republican candidate, Frank J. Cannon, Thatcher replied to the letter in the *Herald.* Answering the charge of discussing theology in a political speech, he suggested that "theological discourses ought to deal in theological matters solely and ought to leave political matters alone."

9. October 22. In his book, Cannon repudiated "Nuggets of Truth" as being circulated during his absence and without his permission. However, Roberts points out in the CHC that "nothing was heard in Utah" about this until publication of Cannon's book, "nineteen years after the election."

10. "The Moses Thatcher Case," pamphlet (Salt Lake: Modern Microfilm, n.d.).

Thatcher said "I fully recognize" the right of "my Republican friends, Joseph F. and John Henry, . . . to criticize anything that I may politically say or do; but I do not accord them a higher right in that respect than that accorded to the humblest Republican in the rank and file."

Certainly this public example of lese majesty did Thatcher no good with his quorum; and it was a shock to the Saints, accustomed from long tradition to belief in perfect harmony among the Lord's anointed.

Despite pressure from on high, Utah went Democratic in 1892. So, also, did the nation, Grover Cleveland making a comeback for a second term. Among Republican casualties was Frank J. Cannon, despite "Nuggets of Truth." Ironically, he was defeated by Joseph L. Rawlins, who had been publicly branded an apostate.

The church had suffered a defeat. At meetings of the Quorum of the Twelve for several months following, the "subject of Apostle Moses Thatcher, B. H. Roberts, and C. W. Penrose was discussed at length; they all went in direct opposition to the First Presidency policy in the last fall political campaign," Apostle Marriner W. Merrill recorded. Most of one meeting was devoted to "grievances against Apostle Moses Thatcher in the recent campaign." Then in April, just three days prior to the scheduled dedication of the Salt Lake Temple, "It was agreed that the Brethren above named should not attend the dedication of the Salt Lake Temple until they made matters right."

The dedication of the temple was the greatest spiritual event since the Saints had arrived in the Salt Lake valley forty-six years previously. Brigham Young had designated the site by inspiration. Truman O. Angell became the architect. After preliminary excavation, the four cornerstones were laid "with impressive ceremonies, amid great rejoicing of the assembled multitude," in 1853 on the birthday of the church, April 6. Brigham declared, "This temple will be known as the first temple built in the mountains by the Latter-day Saints." But circumstances dictated otherwise. Temples were completed at St. George, Logan, and Manti while the one at Salt Lake was under construction.

Inasmuch as the structure was designed to last through the millennium, only the most enduring materials could be utilized. Source of the gray granite for the walls was at Little Cottonwood canyon, 20 miles away and a four-day trip for ox teams hauling the huge blocks. During the Utah War of 1857, work stopped and the foundation was covered over. Several years after work resumed, Brigham ordered the foundation torn up and replaced, upon discovering that the footing was of "chinky, small stones." The second time, footings were 16 feet thick and 8 deep, basement walls 8 feet thick and those above ground 6.

The enormous amount of stone required caused the Saints to begin digging a canal from the mouth of Little Cottonwood across the benchland to an outlet in City Creek. Before it was finished, however, twenty years had elapsed with the building project and the railroad had arrived. It was simpler to run a spur to the quarry. The canal was completed for the city water supply.

In the temple walls were fifty carved "Earthstones," fifty "Moonstones," and fifty "Sunstones"; while "Starstones" formed the keystones of most windows and also were in the walls.[11]

The day of dedication was April 6, 1893, just forty years after the cornerstones were laid.[12] The zeal of those seeking to qualify for a "recommend" to attend was intense. The three Democrat rebels learned to their dismay that, despite their church positions, unless they repented they wouldn't be allowed to be there. Under the circumstances, Thatcher, Roberts, and Penrose capitulated. "But I want to tell you," Joseph F. Smith subsequently informed a congregation at Logan, "that Moses Thatcher was only admitted to the dedication of the Salt Lake Temple after long hesitation. He only got in by the skin of his teeth."[13]

In his dedicatory prayer Wilford Woodruff said,

We pray thee to bless, that they decay not, all the walls, partitions, floors, ceilings, roofs and bridging, the elevators, stairways, railings and

---

11. These "are allegorical emblems of the conditions to which the resurrected souls of mankind will be assigned when all are judged 'according to their works,'" explains N. B. Lundwall in his *Temples of the Most High* (Salt Lake City: Bookcraft, 16th printing, 1968).

12. Some scholars trace the modern emphasis on the Word of Wisdom to the fact that Brigham exhorted the Saints to forgo their tea, coffee, tobacco, and liquor during construction and donate the money saved to the project. After forty years, advice had hardened to commandment.

13. *Tribune,* May 10, 1896.

steps, the frames, doors, windows, and other openings, all things connected with the lighting, heating, and sanitary apparatus, the boilers, engines, dynamos, the connecting pipes and wires, the lamps and burners, and all utensils, furniture and articles used in or connected with the holy ordinances administered in this house, the veils and the altars, the baptismal font and the oxen on which it rests, and all that pertains thereto, the baths, washstands and basins. Also the safes and vaults in which the records are preserved, with the records themselves, and all books, documents, and papers pertaining to the office of the recorder, likewise the library, with all the books, maps, instruments, etc., that may belong thereto. We also present before thee, for thine acceptance, all the additions and buildings not forming a part of the main edifice, but being appendages thereto; and we pray thee to bless all the furniture, seats, cushions, curtains, hangings, locks, and fastenings, and multitudinous other appliances and appurtenances found in and belonging to this Temple and its annexes, with all the work of ornamentation thereon, the painting and the plastering, the gilding, bronzing, the fine work in wood and metal of every kind, the embroidery and needlework, the pictures and statuary, the carved work and canopies. Also the materials of which the buildings and their contents are made or composed—the rock, lime, mortar and plaster, the timbers and lath, the woods of various trees, the gold and silver, the brass and iron, and all other metals, the silk, wool, and cotton, the skins and furs, the glass, china and precious stones, all these and all else herein we humbly present for thine acceptance and sanctifying blessing.

"Obviously," M. R. Werner commented in quoting this excerpt of a prayer detailed enough to fill ten printed pages, "the President was determined to leave nothing to the Imagination."[14]

As excursion trains converged from the four corners of Deseret, the dedicatory service was repeated twice daily to capacity congregations for seventeen days, with one night service. At a "thoroughly conservative calculation," the *Deseret News* reported that the services "have been attended by 75,000 people."[15]

The following January, President Harrison rewarded the attempt to swing the Republican vote in Utah by proclaiming "full amnesty and pardon" to polygamists

14. *Brigham Young* (New York: Harcourt, Brace & Co., 1925).
15. May 6, 1893.

who since November 1, 1890, abstained from such cohabitation, but upon the express condition that they shall in the future faithfully obey the laws.[16]

The Democratic victory had other beneficial results. The new Congress passed legislation putting an end to carpetbag government in Utah. Federal officials would henceforth be selected from residents of the Territory. President Grover Cleveland signed legislation restoring church property which had been escheated to the federal government. Congressional Delegate Joseph L. Rawlins introduced an Enabling Act in the House for Utah's admission as a state.

"Utah is very little better prepared for statehood now than it was 10 years ago," the *Tribune* protested. "It is not true that polygamy has been given up." During debate, Congressman Elijah A. Morse of Massachusetts made a caustic attack on the Enabling Act, claiming that "The history of Mormonism is a history of superstition, licentiousness, murder, and crime that is a disgrace to civilization and one of the foulest, blackest blots on the pages of history." With Utah a state, he feared that the church president "will have another revelation re-establishing the 'destroying angels,' the 'blood atonement,' the 'endowment house,' and polygamy."

Rawlins turned the tide with his retort to the esteemed Congressman from Massachusetts:

"Who was responsible for the education of the men who established polygamy in Utah? . . . [They] were born, bred, and educated under the system of civilization of New England, . . . which in some of its excrescences burned witches, persecuted Quakers, drove out Roger Williams, and later produced the gentleman from Massachusetts. (Laughter and applause.) . . . There is less polygamy . . . in proportion to population [in Utah] than there has been . . . in the State of Massachusetts. (Great laughter and applause.) And when a gentleman rises upon this floor . . . and makes the assertion with respect to the people of Utah, that they are murderers, polygamists, thieves, and is not able to produce one syllable of evidence to justify his statement, he ought to hang his head in shame. (Applause.)[17]

16. Church leaders and the Salt Lake Chamber of Commerce had petitioned Harrison for amnesty, but, Larson says, "The President, unwilling to risk alienation of any support for reelection, procrastinated." After his defeat he had nothing to lose, and when "Republican leaders pressed him to vindicate their party's promises to the Mormons before his term expired," the lame-duck president complied.

17. *Deseret News,* December 19, 1893.

As Rawlins spoke, "the lobbies and cloakrooms were deserted and a large audience was gathered around the speaker," the *Tribune* reported. "Delegate Rawlins covered himself with glory with his magnificent speech."[18]

A mellowed House ended a filibuster against the bill, and passed it the following day. At long last, Utah was scheduled to become a state. Rawlins as a result received the remarkable distinction of being praised by the *Deseret News,* the *Herald,* and the *Tribune.*

"We rejoice," the *Herald* declared upon passage of the Enabling Act, "that this is a Democratic measure." However, church political support was potent, and the Republicans won control of the Utah legislature by a narrow margin in 1893, then the following year elected a majority of delegates to the convention that would write a constitution for the state of Utah. The Democrats in turn, "with the approach of the 1895 election, which was to choose the first state officials," Ivins states, "decided that they would use the church a little," by nominating B. H. Roberts for Representative to Congress and announcing that if they won control of the Legislature, Utah's first two senators would be Moses Thatcher and Joseph L. Rawlins. "But this action backfired on them."

In recounting what happened, B. H. Roberts issued a statement, in the form of an interview, which was distributed by state Democratic headquarters.[19] Though out of harmony politically, "I have always regarded myself as properly respectful and attentive to church authority," he stated. All manuscripts of his tracts and books "have been invariably submitted" to the presidency for approval.

This was hardly news in Utah, where Roberts, of the First Council of Seventy, was well known as a powerful speaker as well as perhaps the best and most prolific author in defense of the faith.[20] Both Saint and Gentile recognized his opening statement as the obligatory "bearing of testimony," the affirmation of faith and the

18. December 13.
19. *Tribune,* October 14, 1895; also SI 1:751.
20. His works include *Ecclesiastical History, New Witness for God, The Missouri Persecutions, The Rise and Fall of Nauvoo,* and *The Life of John Taylor,* as well as many tracts and lesson manuals. He edited the 7-volume *History of the Church* (commonly known as the "Documentary History"), covering events up to the settlement of Utah, and climaxed his literary career with *A Comprehensive History of the Church,* in 6 volumes, covering the first century, 1830 to 1930. An extremely skillful author, Roberts was able to treat "sensitive" material as no one else before or since. Even so, his work was subjected to merciless censorship.

respect for authority which is an absolute must, for otherwise there is grave risk of being accused of apostasy, which means automatic rejection of everything said.

Roberts' credentials were top hole. He grew up at Centerville, a few miles north of Salt Lake, and at age seventeen became a blacksmith's apprentice. He attended Deseret University at Salt Lake, and upon graduation taught school and also did part-time blacksmithing.

On an early mission to Tennessee a fellow elder was killed by a mob. Roberts disguised himself as a ruffian, penetrated hostile territory, secured the body, and returned it to Utah.

Roberts displayed his zeal by entering the Principle, for which he was arrested on the charge of u.c. and released on $1,000 bond. On the same day he was called to serve a mission in England. He jumped bail and remained overseas nearly two years, working as assistant editor of the *Millennial Star,* learning the facility of his pen. On returning, he joined the Salt Lake *Herald,* rising to editor-in-chief.

Roberts had "a long-standing intention to enter into the study of law," but before beginning he "submitted the proposition" to the church presidency. On learning that "they considered it would interfere with my labors in the church, I gave up what had been with me, up to that time, a life purpose."[21]

"But," the question came, "have you been likewise attentive to their wishes in political affairs?"

"I think I have, within proper limits." When the church had issued the statement of policy counseling authorities to abstain from political activity, "I accepted it with pleasure."

However, as prominent church officials continued to campaign for the Republican party, it was evident that the prohibition against political activity applied only to Democrats. Even so, Roberts declined the importunities of Democrats to engage in political affairs, until, in his absence, the Democratic convention of Davis County nominated him as delegate to the constitutional convention. He was

---

21. Roberts accepted counsel on this personal matter, even though, he said, "I receive no regular salary from the church." When engaged in church projects, "I have, from time to time, had appropriated to me varying sums to aid me in meeting my current living expenses; . . . but the sums appropriated have come nowhere near meeting my wants, and I have had to depend upon my own exertions to make up the very large balance."

told the "strings had been taken off." Roberts immediately sought counsel from a member of the church presidency, who "said it would be all right," and so had "been active in politics ever since," without any complaint from church authorities.

At the State Democratic convention at Ogden, Roberts was nominated for Congress by acclamation. There had been no word of warning, and in fact after the meeting several of the brethren congratulated him on the nomination. A week or so later he consulted with the First Presidency on other matters, where "No complaint was then made ... though ... both time and opportunity conjoined to give a chance to correct me if I had made an error."

However, at October conference, Joseph F. Smith of the First Presidency "strongly rebuked Thatcher and Roberts" from the rostrum, Ivins states, for accepting political nomination without church permission. Wilford Woodruff and George Q. Cannon of the presidency endorsed Smith's stand. With the church officially opposed to the Democratic ticket, party leaders prepared an eight-column "Address to the People," published in the *Herald*,[22] protesting the union of church and state. The campaign became a contest between the Democrats and the church.

"Though I know the impulsiveness of the gentleman," Roberts said of Smith's public attack, "I was surprised that anything should be said there, when such excellent opportunities for complaint had before existed."

Did he think "that the Republicans will use it against you and the party?"

"You might as well ask me if water will run downhill," Roberts replied. "They are already using it." The day after conference rumors were afloat that "B. H. Roberts was out of favor with the presidency of the church, likely to be disfellowshipped; therefore must be defeated in the election."

Similar statements "came from all over the Territory," Roberts said, giving the Democrats "just cause of complaint."

All this, however, was "preliminary to what is really the chief issue," the questioner said: "Do you recognize the right of the church to dictate what a member's politics shall be?"

"No; the church has no right to dictate what a man's politics

22. October 22, 1895. See also SI 1:820–53.

54

shall be," Roberts said. However, it did have the right to prohibit political activity by high officials; but if permitted to enter politics at all, "these men ought to be absolutely free" to choose their political affiliation.

In the crisis, Roberts offered either to resign his nomination, "Or, if the Democratic party, responsive to that noble spirit of democracy which ever rises higher as difficulties increase, wants me to meet and crush this church influence," he declared, "then I stand ready still to be their standard-bearer."

"I do not know what the result will be to my religious standing," Roberts admitted in conclusion, "but in this supreme moment I am not counting costs."

Thatcher took a similar stand, insisting upon complete separation of church and state. When he and Rawlins appeared at a Democratic rally in the Logan Opera House, the charge was openly made that Rawlins shouldn't be elected because he was an apostate. "I stood before a very large audience," Thatcher said, and told them that if Rawlins was to go down for that reason, "I would take him by the right hand and go down with him, although I was an apostle."[23]

With two rebels and an apostate on the Democratic ticket, the weight evidently sank the boat; Thatcher and Rawlins did go down, as Utah went Republican in the election.

On January 4, 1896 the *Deseret News* for the first time in its history used a three-column headline on a story. Dedication of the temple had merited only two columns. But the story was worth the space. Utah had become a state.

At 9:13 this morning the usual early morning serenity of East Temple street was decidedly disturbed owing to the fact that Superintendent Brown of the Western Union Telegraph company was observed to rush frantically out of the office armed with an old reliable shotgun, the contents of which belched forth in two resounding reports. A small boy in the near vicinity dived for an adjacent doorway, his juvenile

23. SI 1:1047. See also MFP 3:272, where Clark points out that the political controversy of that campaign "still seems to be (1966) a part of the political scene in Utah seventy years later. In the most recent general election in Utah, the First Presidency . . . again issued a 'Manifesto' reiterating the stand taken seventy years ago that the Church has no official candidates for political office. Such repeated announcements made by the First Presidency over a seventy year period . . . have still not prevented 'whisperings' that the Church supports this or that candidate."

brain having grasped the idea that a holdup or bank robbery was in progression.

After the excitement had subsided somewhat it dawned on the rapidly accumulating crowd that the chief Magistrate in Washington had signed the Statehood Proclamation, who showed their appreciation of the fact by giving vent to a cheer. The news spread like wildfire and on all sides merchants proceeded to decorate their stores and buildings with national emblems, bunting and Old Glory. Messrs George M. Scott and Cunningham & Co. erected some temporary but effective steam whistles outside their respective places of business. The stars and stripes were strung across the east and west towers of the Temple.

"Bedlam broke loose," the *Herald* reported next morning. "To the happy acclaims was soon added the tooting of whistles, bells rang everywhere, the swarming crowds filled the streets shouting and laughing." And in Washington, it reported, "Frank Cannon was given the coveted pen" which the president had used in signing the historic document.

Certainly statehood was a goal sought desperately for more years than most of the celebrants had been alive. Very few at that time stopped to reckon that, to achieve it, the Saints had bartered away values which to the pioneers had been basic and unalterable laws of God. Yet even these few refused to acknowledge the price which had been paid. God didn't change his mind. They clung to the futile belief that, once again, it had been a trick to beat the Devil at his own game.[24]

It might seem that defeat of the Democratic ticket at the polls would have settled matters for Roberts and Thatcher. Such was not the case for the two "out of harmony." Shortly after the election, the *Deseret News* ran a long editorial, "Application of Church Discipline," stating that members must be subject to discipline in temporal affairs, and that those critical of this policy were in rebellion against divine authority.[25]

---

24. It is ironic that the people in general had come to accept the changed values. "Utah's achievement of statehood was due in part to deliberate change of the unpopular stereotype of the Mormon of the 1850s to that of the solid, energetic, conservative American citizen of the 1890s," points out Howard R. Lamar. "While the church revision of the Mormon image may have begun cynically or to escape persecution," by the time statehood was achieved "the Saints had convinced themselves of their own true Americanism." See UHQ, Fall 1971, "Statehood for Utah: A Different Path."

25. November 9, 1895.

During the winter Thatcher was felled by a serious illness; doctors feared he was at death's door. Meanwhile, the brethren labored with Roberts. On February 13, 1896 he was on the carpet before the First Presidency, Council of the Twelve, and First Council of Seventy regarding his "conduct in the last fall's political campaign." Roberts adamantly upheld his course and refused "to make reconciliation." The brethren gave him until March 5 to think things over; by which time, however, his heart was still "like stone." For five hours they "prayed with him and wept over him, but without avail." Then they lowered the boom. Roberts was "dropped from his Quorum," with the stipulation that unless he repent, "the action of the Presidency and Apostles and the six Presidents [of Seventy] is to be final in his case."

Apostles Heber J. Grant and F. M. Lyman labored with the rebel. "Day after day and night after night they went to him and wept and prayed, and he wept and prayed," until after nine weeks "he yielded." Roberts appeared before the brethren, where he "made a full confession" of his errors, was forgiven, "and a time of tears and rejoicing was indulged in by all."[26]

Meanwhile, "a document, which came to be called a political manifesto, had been prepared," Ivins states. It denied that the church had ever interfered with affairs of state and said that "it had always been understood that men holding high church positions should not accept political office without first obtaining approval."[27]

Even though Roberts had repented, he refused to sign this manifesto as a member of the First Council of Seventy. Once more the brethren wrestled with his soul, this time for two weeks, before he capitulated.

In the case of Thatcher, however, he never saw the proclamation until about noon of the opening day of April conference, when Lorenzo Snow and Brigham Young, Jr., brought it to his sickbed. They told him to sign it before 1:30, for it was to be presented that afternoon for sustaining as the word and will of the Lord. The sick man felt he needed more time to study what, to him, appeared to be not a separation of church and state but exactly the opposite. "He saw it as a misleading statement of the past and present attitude of church leaders in political matters, and as a step toward giving

26. See Ivins and Reasoner.
27. For text of political manifesto, see MFP 3:271.

those leaders more political power," Ivins says. "When his time was up, he returned it, with a written statement that he did not feel that he could sign it without 'stultifying' himself."

"The session of the Mormon Church conference yesterday afternoon produced a stupendous political and religious sensation," the *Tribune* reported next morning. The political manifesto in itself excited "the most profound interest," but the fact that B. H. Roberts endorsed it "was sensational." But more was to come. "When the names of Apostles were called in the conference, that the people might vote to sustain these officials, that of Moses Thatcher was not announced." This deliberate omission "excited the most intense interest" in the great congregation assembled in the tabernacle.[28]

"A great moral question is involved," a letter from an unidentified "prominent churchman" stated in the *Tribune*.[29] Although church authorities "claim that Church and State have been divorced," an examination of the manifesto would "convince one that Moses Thatcher is right when he says it might be the means of making the Church a great political machine."

When Thatcher remained unrepentant, the rift between him and the brethren deepened. At October conference the congregation witnessed a concerted attack from the rostrum on a member of the Quorum of the Twelve.[30] Wilford Woodruff declared that "The First Presidency and the Twelve Apostles were never more unified as a body than they are today." However, "That is the case with all of us, with one exception. That exception is Moses Thatcher." Lorenzo Snow and Brigham Young, Jr., told of vainly laboring with the "spirit of darkness" in Thatcher's heart. John Henry Smith said that "except for his physical condition," Thatcher would have been dealt with within three days after refusing to sign

28. Ivins adds, "This unorthodox, and rather underhanded, punishment of Thatcher was unfavorably looked upon by many of the Saints, as shown by the reception given the political manifesto when it was presented to the different stakes and wards. At the Cache Stake conference, three members of the High Council refused to approve it. When it was presented at the morning session of the Tooele Stake conference, it received three negative votes. One of them was cast by J. C. De La Mare, an alternate member of the High Council. At the afternoon meeting, Apostle Francis M. Lyman declared the manifesto to be a revelation, and asked the congregation to vote to suspend Elder De La Mare from his church position. Between 20 and 25 voted for suspension and 8 or 10 against it, but most of the 250 to 300 who were present refused to vote."

29. November 21, 1896.

30. Quotations from *Deseret News*.

the manifesto. It was a question, Joseph F. Smith said, whether people would unite with the priesthood, "or whether they will be misled by one man." He counseled the people to guard against unwise sympathy for a rebel.

George Q. Cannon declared that not since the apostasy at Kirtland, Ohio, in the early days—at which time the infant church was brought to the brink of extinction—had there been such criticism of church leadership. He warned that the furor over the Thatcher case was a sign of apostasy, and exhorted the Saints "not to speak evil of the Lord's anointed."

Following conference, Thatcher decided to attend the regular meeting of his quorum, "desiring, if possible, to be in harmony," he wrote Lorenzo Snow; "but upon appearing at the door of the Temple, was denied admittance."[31]

Later in the day he was handed an official notice by the First Presidency, which said, "It having been reported to us that Brother Moses Thatcher has on three different occasions addressed congregations of the Saints" in Cache valley, people were notified that inasmuch as he had not been sustained in conference as an apostle, such action suspended him from "preaching the Gospel or administering any of the ordinances thereof," until "by making satisfactory amends" he was restored to fellowship.

"In Cache Valley, at least, Moses Thatcher will receive full credit for sincerity," a letter to the *Tribune* stated.[32] Special efforts had been made to discredit him here, "probably because here he was best known and loved." It was here that Joseph F. Smith "publicly rebuked Bishop B. M. Lewis for praying for Moses Thatcher during our recent quarterly conference." This displayed a spirit so "contrary to the teachings of the Savior," that many who had considered Thatcher's opposition to the political manifesto wrong "wondered whether, after all, some strong personal feeling did not underlie the pressure brought to bear on him."

Meanwhile national politics ironically wrote the final chapter of Moses Thatcher's struggle against church and state. He had been a delegate to the Democratic national convention at Chicago the previous June, where William Jennings Bryan hypnotized the audience with his famous "Cross of Gold" oration. Three years previ-

31. Letter, October 16, 1896.
32. November 21, 1896.

ously, Congress had repealed the law providing for free coinage of silver at a ratio to gold of 16 to 1. As a result, the bottom dropped from the price of silver. Utah, which produced nearly nine million ounces a year, was hard hit; and, in fact, the nation was precipitated into the Panic of 1893.

Now, at the Democratic convention of 1896, "Ten acres of people saw the silver-helmeted gladiator of the area overpower the gold phalanx and plant the banner of silver upon the ramparts of Democracy," the *Herald* reported.[33]

In the election on November 3, Utah went solidly Democratic. This meant that the Senate seat which would become vacant the following March 3 would be filled by vote of the Utah legislature.[34] The *Tribune* asked Thatcher if he was a candidate. He said that if "young Utah" felt that his election would vindicate his stand and help "prevent the forging of chains upon the people," he was willing to be.

On November 19, four days later, the ax fell:

Hon. Moses Thatcher, City:

Dear Brother:—It becomes my painful duty as the President of the Twelve Apostles to inform you that, at a meeting of that body, held today, . . . it was decided, after a full consideration and individual expression of everyone present, to sever you from the Council of the Twelve Apostles, and deprive you of your Apostleship and other offices in the priesthood. I remain, your brother,

Lorenzo Snow.

Then came a concerted effort to defeat Thatcher's candidacy for the Senate. For five days the *News* ran violent anti-Thatcher editorials, declaring his candidacy an assault upon the doctrines and the very existence of the church. The *Trib* declared that "The people are growing very tired of this perpetually recurring interference of the church in political affairs," and predicted that "this people will not stand for that sort of tyranny."

The *News* denied it was threatening Thatcher, insisting that his candidacy was not a political question but a religious one. Part of the *News'* ire was that Thatcher had published his correspondence

33. July 9.
34. Utah's first senators were Frank J. Cannon and Arthur Brown. To stagger future elections, one was to have a short term. It was decided by lot, Brown drawing the short term.

with Lorenzo Snow concerning his case in the *Tribune*. This violated the iron-clad rule that all discussion within the quorum—and particularly controversy—must remain private.

A Gentile, P. L. Williams, charged in the *Tribune* that the action against Thatcher "makes clear the purpose of the church to visit upon Mr. Thatcher political disabilities for ecclesiastical offending," and that it "insists that no party shall elect a candidate for office who is objectionable to it."[35]

Before the legislature convened in January, "Even Thatcher's friend, B. H. Roberts, now came out against him," in the *Deseret News* of January 8, Ivins reports. "He took nearly 7,000 words to explain his position," which was, in a nutshell, that the election of Thatcher to the Senate "would be a gross insult" to all Mormons.

The other major candidate for the position was Joseph L. Rawlins, who as delegate to Congress had perhaps done more than any other single individual to achieve statehood. But the church didn't want Rawlins, either, and threw its support to a Gentile, Judge Henry P. Henderson. Better an unbeliever than an apostate. With two highly popular candidates and a third having church backing, the legislature deadlocked, and remained so after fifty-two ballots.

Opposition to Rawlins was basically the same as with Thatcher —he had rebelled at church domination of temporal affairs. When Rawlins was a boy his father had twice been called away on missions, leaving the wife with three small children to run the farm as best she could. The boy acquired a deep resentment against "the religious system that sent men off to bring more converts to Zion instead of taking care of the ones who were already there."[36]

His first conscious break with the church came when, after attending the University of Deseret, he set out for Indiana University to broaden his education. This was a bold step in 1871, because of Brigham Young's fears that Mormon scholars would be corrupted by the teachings of the wicked outside world.

By the time he returned two years later, his attitude had crystallized to the worldly conviction that Utah must abolish polygamy and eliminate church involvement in politics.

After studying law, he was "astonished" when Brigham spon-

35. November 22.
36. Joan Ray Harrow, "Joseph L. Rawlins, Father of Utah Statehood," UHQ, Winter 1976.

sored him for the office of city attorney despite his unorthodox
views. After serving two terms his firm remained on a monthly re-
tainer to represent the city in the courts, and he also was an attorney
for church affairs. In 1892 he defeated Frank J. Cannon as delegate
to Congress, where his work in having escheated church property
restored, and in shepherding the Enabling Act, won high praise at
home. However, he was branded an apostate, and the church opposed his appointment to the Senate.

Thirty-two votes were needed. After fifty-two ballots the legislature was deadlocked, Thatcher 28, Rawlins 21, Henderson 14.
Ivins states that:

Finally it was apparently decided that Rawlins was not quite as objectionable as Thatcher. Henderson's supporters were released, and on
the 53rd ballot, all but 3 of them switched to Rawlins. He received the
necessary 32 votes, with Thatcher getting 29. . . . All of the 11 who
switched from Henderson to Rawlins were Mormons, including two
Stake Presidents and two Bishops.

"Although he had now been deprived of his church position and
politically destroyed," Ivins says, "the case of Moses Thatcher was
not forgotten." Wealthy, enormously popular, and now considered
by many as a martyr to the cause of liberty, Thatcher remained a
thorn in the church's side. On July 30, 1897 he was formally
charged with "apostasy and un-Christianlike conduct . . . such as to
forfeit his right to fellowship and standing in the church."

Thatcher was well aware that the verdict was made before the
trial began. Although he would be tried by the High Council of his
stake, the complaint came from higher authority and was signed by
three apostles, Brigham Young, Jr., Francis M. Lyman, and Heber
J. Grant. That the stake High Council wouldn't sustain the charges
of the Council of the Twelve was unthinkable. Still, Thatcher did
appear for the ordeal (many, knowing the futility, don't). The
hearing continued a week, during which "Great plainness of language
was used in presenting to Brother Thatcher the position in which
he stood." The High Council found thirteen instances where he
"exhibited an apostate spirit," and it delivered a decision containing
sixteen retractions he must make to retain church membership.

Crux of the complaint evidently was point number 12, his
"course on the public mind:

"That he was the champion of freedom as against the chains which the church was forging to bind them; . . . that the leaders of the church had promised political liberty to the people in order to obtain statehood, and then had changed their policy and promulgated a new rule to dominate them and restrict their political liberties, and were thus guilty of double-dealing and punic faith.

"This was shown by . . . the rallying around Brother Thatcher of the enemies of the church; the endorsement of the hostile press, and the cheers of the multitude who were antagonistic to the church leaders."

Essence of the decision was that he must confess that he had been "in error and in the dark"; and "That he was mistaken in conveying the idea that the church authorities desired and intended to unite church and state or to exercise undue influence in political affairs. . . . That he has obtained light wherein he was in the dark, . . . and desires the fellowship of the church, and humbly asks forgiveness for all his faults."

Thatcher endorsed the decision "without qualifications or mental reservations," and while shorn of office retained his church membership.

Though I speak with the tongues of men and of angels, and have not money, I am become as sounding brass, or a tinkling cymbal. And though I have the gift of prophecy, and understand all mysteries, and all knowledge; and though I have all faith, so that I could remove mountains, and have not money, I am nothing. . . . Money never faileth; but whether there be prophecies, they shall fail; whether there be tongues, they shall cease; whether there be knowledge, it shall vanish away. . . . And now abideth faith, hope, money, these three; but the greatest of these is money.

—I CORINTHIANS 13, as adapted by
George Orwell

5

Richest of All People

FRANK J. CANNON returned from Washington with the historic pen used to sign the proclamation of Utah's statehood. At Salt Lake he found that "the Church, freed of proscription, with its people enjoying the sovereignty of their state rights," had only one further freedom to desire, "and that was its freedom from debt." After a half century of conflict with the federal government, Utah was drained white.

Making matters worse was the severe financial depression afflicting the nation in the 1890s. The Provo Woolen Mills, a church enterprise, stayed open during the early years of the panic only by paying wages in cloth and produce. Later it paid part cash and part scrip good for trade at the local tithing office. The *Deseret News* accumulated a debt for back wages of more than $14,000 during these hard times. John A. Evans, who took charge of the paper in 1896, sometimes drew from his personal savings account to meet the payroll, and, when that was exhausted, tapped the savings of his children. Base pay for reporters was $10 a week, partly in tithing scrip.[1]

---

1. Wendel J. Ashton wrote the story of the *Deseret News* in his *Voice of the West* (New York: Duell, Sloan & Pearce, 1950). See also J. Cecil Alter, *Early Utah Journalism* (Salt Lake: Utah State Historical Society, 1938).

If times were hard, prices were low: bread sold for 5¢ a loaf, eggs 15¢ a dozen, butter 20¢ a pound. At the tithing stores, 25¢ in scrip would get two pounds of steak, while the church barber would cut hair for a 10¢ coupon.

Early church-sponsored projects included the Iron Mission, the Sugar Mission, the Lead Mission, the Cotton Mission, the Wine Mission, the Silk Mission, the Flax Mission, and the Wool Mission. Members were called to these labors just as missionaries were called to labor with the Gentiles in the Lord's vineyard. The prime purpose of the industrial missions was to prosper for the welfare of the Saints.[2] "The Lord designs to make the Saints rich," Brigham Young had declared. The riches of the earth were there for the taking. "The Lord has done His share of the work," he said. "He has surrounded us with the elements containing wheat, meat, flax, wool, silk, fruit, and everything with which to build up, beautify, and glorify the Zion of the last days. It is now our business to mould these elements to our wants and necessities. . . . In this way will the Lord bring again Zion upon the earth, and no other."[3]

With the tightly knit organization of the church, with the belief in a communal type of living known as the United Order—which actually was the first law of the gospel—wherein all wealth would be pooled and shared under direction of church authorities, and with the remarkable cooperative effort characterizing the people, the Saints considered the temporal enterprises as part of the warp and woof of the Mormon way of life.

The church had borrowed heavily to finance water power and irrigation projects, railroad building and manufacturing, to support

2. "These were not," Leonard J. Arrington points out, "the isolated and desultory efforts of private individuals experimenting, as Americans have always experimented, with new products; but part of the calculated campaign to achieve self-sufficiency in order to prepare for the Millennium." *Great Basin Kingdom; An Economic History of the Latter-day Saints* (Cambridge: Harvard University Press, 1958).

3. Arrington comments that to the outsider, the most startling aspect of Mormonism was not the former practice of plural marriage, not the belief in a personal God, not even the restoration of biblical Christianity, nor the Book of Mormon or the belief that Joseph Smith received visitations from heavenly beings, but the exaltation of economic welfare into an important, if not indispensable, element of religious salvation. Quoting the *Deseret News*, October 29, 1877, he notes that the Mormons believed religion to be not only "a matter of sentiment, good for Sunday contemplation and intended for the sanctuary and the soul," but also had to do with "dollars and cents, with trade and barter, with the body and the daily doings of ordinary life."

enterprises designed to relieve unemployment and sustain the welfare of the hard-pressed Saints. The specter of debt haunted Wilford Woodruff. "The Presidency of the church are so overwhelmed in financial matters it seems as though we shall never live to get through with it, unless the Lord opens the way in a marvelous manner," he confided to his journal in 1896. "It looks as though we shall never pay our debts."

At a special priesthood meeting held during October conference that year, Woodruff asked all bishops to canvas their wards for men willing to make personal loans to the church, to be repaid with interest. Among those responding was Jesse Knight, one of the richest men of the state, with a loan of $10,000. The church sugar plantation at Laie in Hawaii also contributed $20,000.

The temporary meeting of short-term obligations did not settle the basic problem. "There has never been a time since we have been in these mountains that we have had such things to contend with," George Q. Cannon said at April conference in 1898. "In the early days there was scarcity of comforts and of money; but there was no debt. Now the great bulk of the people—that is, the leading people—are in debt. The most prudent among us have got entangled."

Cannon devised a plan to finance the church by issuing bonds as "a normal investment for eastern capital," Frank stated. "I was asked to draw up the plan in detail."

After Woodruff "eagerly accepted the plan," Frank and his father took train to New York to sell eastern capital on the proposition of investing in Mormonism as a business deal.

"It was interesting to watch the encounters between the Mormon prophet and some of these astutest of the nation's financiers," Frank related, as they interviewed Judge John F. Dillon and Winslow Pierce, attorneys for some of the Union Pacific interests; also Edward K. Harriman, George J. Gould, and members of the firm of Kuhn, Loeb and Company. "It was as if one of the ancient patriarchs had stepped down from the days of Israel to discuss the financial problems of his people with a modern captain of industry."

Cannon "was listened to, with the interest of curiosity, as the chief living exponent of the Mormon movement;... and I was impressed by the fact that these men of the world had a large and splendid sympathy for any wholesome social effort designed to abolish poverty and establish a quicker justice in the political affairs of the race," Frank wrote.

"Your clients make their investments frequently in railroad stocks and bonds," Cannon said to Judge Dillon. "What are the underlying bases of the values of railroad securities? Largely the industry and stability of the communities through which the railroad lines shall operate. Then, in reality, the security is valuable in proportion to the value of the community and in its steadfastness, its prosperity and the safety of its productive labor. In your railroad investments you are obliged to take such considerations as a secondary security. In negotiating this Church loan with your clients, you can offer the same great values as a primary security."

Confronted with this novel proposition, Judge Dillon asked for a balance sheet. This showed a total cash indebtedness of $1,200,-000. Revenues from tithes for the previous year were slightly over $1 million, being low because of the financial depression. Disbursements were chiefly for interest on debt, maintenance of temples and tabernacles, for educational and charitable work, for missionary headquarters, and for the return of released missionaries.[4] The church business enterprises had an estimated value of from $4 to $6 million.

However, it was not the balance sheet on which the loan was to be based, but rather on the people themselves. "Probably nowhere else in the world is there a people at once so industrious and so stable as ours," George Q. Cannon told Dillon. Frank wrote:

"It was the boast of the Mormons that there had not been an almshouse nor an almstaker in any of their settlements, up to the time of the escheat proceedings by the federal officials; and this was literally true. Every man had been helped to the employment for which he was best fitted. If an immigrant . . . had been a silk-weaver, efforts were made to establish his industry and give it public support. If he had been a musician of talent, a little conservatory was founded, and patronage obtained for him. When the growth of population made it necessary to open new valleys to agriculture, the church, out of its community funds, rendered the initial aid; in many instances the original irrigation enterprises of small settle-

4. Frank notes: "The missionaries themselves received no compensation; they were supposed to travel 'without purse or scrip;' their expenses were defrayed by their relatives, and they had to pay out of their own pockets for the printed tracts which they distributed."

ments were thus financed; and the investments were repaid not only directly, by the return of the loan, but indirectly, many times over, by the increased productiveness and larger contributions of the people. Cooperation, in mercantile, industrial, and stock-raising undertakings, assured the support and patronage of each community for its own particular enterprise.

"It was the First Councillor's theory that when people contributed to a common fund they became interested in one another's material welfare," Frank said of the tithing system. "The man who paid less in tithes this year than last was counselled with as to why his business had been unsuccessful, and the wise men of his little circle aided him with advice and material help. The man who contributed largely was glad of a prosperity from which he yielded a part in recognition of what the community had done for him and in a reverent gratitude to God . . . —but he was anxious that his neighbor also should be a larger contributor each year."

All civil disputes were heard and settled by church courts, thus avoiding expensive litigation. In many counties no lawyer could be found, and "it was considered an act of evil fellowship, amounting almost to apostasy," for a man to go to law against his brother.

"In short—as my father pointed out—Utah, at that time, expressed the only full-bodied social proposition in the United States," Frank related. "There never had been in America another community whose future, in the economic aspects, offered so clear a solution of problems which still remain generally unsettled. It was as if a segment of the great circle of modern humanity had been transported to another world, otherwise unpopulated, and there— with the experience gained through centuries of human travail— had attempted the establishment of a just, beneficent and satisfying social order."

Such was the Utopian proposition presented by the Mormon salesmen to eastern capitalists. The plan was aborted, however, by the death of Wilford Woodruff, on September 2, 1898. His successor to the presidency, Lorenzo Snow, withdrew the bond issue. Thus no one will ever know what might have happened, had the church gone into bondage to the Gentiles.

Lorenzo Snow was a tall, stately man with a full white beard. Elegant and courtly, he prided himself on his manners, culture, and appearance, in a day when great store was placed on the qualities associated with the word "gentleman." He spoke in quiet and well-modulated tones, walked with an unhurried and measured stride. But while he was the Lord's choice as prophet, seer, and revelator, there was apprehension that at the age of eighty-four he wouldn't have the necessary vigor and initiative to cope with the critical problems of a society threatened with bankruptcy.

Despite his age and the polished gentility of his manner, however, Lorenzo Snow proved to have a firm mind and a will of his own. He canceled the bond issue against the advice of his counselors. "No good, he said, could come of publishing the affairs of the community," Frank recorded. "Those affairs were purely the concern of the prophets."

George Q. "necessarily bowed to" Snow's decision. "It is within the authority of the Prophet of the Lord," he told Frank, "to determine how he will conduct the business of the church."

Frank admired such dedicated obedience; however, having no church office himself, he wasn't ready to accept what he felt was a serious mistake. Snow's administration "marked the change from the old to the new regime in Utah," he believed. It also marked the decline of his father's influence, and of Frank's participation in it. In fact, this proved to be the turning point of Frank J. Cannon's attitude that eventually resulted in complete alienation from the church.

Again ignoring advice of his counselors, Snow called in the leading businessmen of the state for financial discussion. Two of the most prominent were Jesse Knight and David Eccles. They proposed that the church bond itself to its own members to pay off current debts and meet impending obligations. This resulted in a bond issue of $1 million, which was taken largely by the men Snow had assembled. This met the emergency, but did nothing toward solving the problem, which was that with its multitudinous enterprises essential to the welfare of the people, the church was spending more than its income. Thus the bond issue had its ironic aspect: by long tradition the Saints were advised to be thrifty and frugal, to make do or do without, to abhor debt; yet the church itself had adopted a policy of living on borrowed funds and beyond its means.

The winter passed, and at April conference the talks by the

brethren were all sweetness and light. There was no mention of the financial pinch, with the church committed to deficit spending. In fact, "I have been very much pleased with what has been said," President Snow said in his closing remarks. "We certainly have had a very excellent time."

The curiously remote attitude of the speakers seemed to ignore the ominous apprehension in some quarters that the church was on a collision course with disaster. In addition to the financial situation, trouble again was brewing with politics, polgamy, and the union of church and state.

B. H. Roberts, with the necessary official sanction, had been elected to Congress the previous fall, "despite the protests of my father and many others who foresaw the evil results of electing a polygamist," Frank says. His father previously had been denied a seat as delegate to Congress because of having plural wives, and, Frank says, "I accepted Roberts' nomination as proof that this question must be settled anew at Washington," where, he predicted, the House would "forever dispose of these ecclesiastical candidacies of which Utah refused to dispose for itself."

While Roberts claimed to have married his plurals before the 1890 Manifesto, one of them had recently presented him with twins—rather convincing proof of unlawful cohabitation—and the day following the election the *Tribune* published a cartoon showing the babies, in swaddling clothes, saying good-bye as daddy left for Congress:

> Ha! Ha! Ha!
> There's my Pa,
> He'll go to Washington,
> But he won't take Ma.

The Roberts case brought simmering Gentile discontent to a boil. The Utah Presbytery made formal protest that the church "has returned to politics," that "more than 1,000 polygamous children have been born in Utah since statehood was granted," and "that the old ostracism is practiced toward those who speak of these things."[5]

Summarizing the resolution, the *Trib* said, "The Presbytery simply assail the Saints with the charge that they are breaking their word."

5. *Tribune,* September 2, 1898.

Presbyterian opposition led to an alliance of local Gentile ministers who drafted a memorial asking the loyal citizens of America to help fight the seating of a polygamist. With the help of the national press, this resulted in petitions flooding Congress bearing an estimated seven million names.

A Gentile lawyer of Salt Lake, Theodore Schroeder, who was also a busy free-lance writer, whipped up sentiment in the anti-Roberts campaign. In his own journal, *Lucifer's Lantern,* and in national periodicals, Schroeder lambasted Roberts as symbolizing Mormon polygamy, and he went to Washington to appear before Congress as an attorney for the opposition to the seating of Roberts.[6]

Mormons had shown by their votes that they wanted Roberts in Congress. One, however, Eugene Young, a worldly grandson of Brigham, declared in a New York speech:

"Mr. Roberts is an instrument, a representative of mighty forces. . . . Through his election a people of 300,000 strong have turned from American liberty and morality, and have taken the initial step toward the establishment of a hierarchy foreign to our institutions and our social laws."[7]

"I declare most solemnly and emphatically that the statements which are being published to the effect that the Mormon Church is encouraging and teaching polygamy are utterly untrue," Lorenzo Snow wired the New York *World* in reply. "Ever since the issuance of the Manifesto on this subject, polygamy has entirely ceased in Utah." The election of Roberts "was an entirely secular affair," Snow stated. Church and state in Utah were "entirely distinct and separate." "He was not a church candidate in any sense of the word. The church had no candidate."[8]

It was inevitable that Roberts, like George Q. Cannon before

6. An agnostic, Schroeder for awhile had been friendly to the Saints; but his attitude curdled because of church-state involvement, together with the underground continuation of polygamy. His pamphlet, "The Gospel Concerning Church and State," was ostensibly a defense of the Saints by quotations from past church publications; however, his purpose was to damn church leaders by their own words. David Brudnoy says, "Schroeder attempted to show that the Saints had often lied in the past in order to justify their actions, that they lied now, and that they were particularly culpable in regard to matters of church-state separation." See "Of Sinners and Saints: Theodore Schroeder, Brigham Roberts, and Reed Smoot," *Journal of Church and State,* Spring 1972.

7. *Herald,* December 28, 1898.

8. Ibid., December 30.

him, would be rejected by Congress. His candidacy had achieved nothing except to arouse again the national hysteria about polygamy.[9]

Such was the situation of a badgered and impoverished church with its back against the wall, during the conference of April when, from what was said by the brethren, everything was peaches and cream. Snow didn't seem worried at all.

However, the following month, while on a tour of southern Utah, Snow seemed to take fire. It was as if he had been waiting for inspiration. Now he knew the will of the Lord concerning the financial plight of the church. The solution could be summed up in one word—tithes. About one-quarter of the Saints paid no tithes at all, while the offerings of many others were of a token nature. Payment of a full tithe obviously would solve the church's financial plight—yet, how to tap this vein? Year upon year the people had been exhorted to tithe, asked, begged, threatened, and even excommunicated for refusal. Tithing had been dinned into the people until they were heartily sick of the subject. Yes, it *was* a duty; yes, it *was* the Lord's will; yes, it *was* a law of the gospel— but they had financial problems of their own. Besides that, there were other portions of the gospel where they weren't perfect, either, and for which the striving for betterment wouldn't cost so much.

Lorenzo Snow had the answer at St. George, where his tithing sermon electrified the audience. As his party moved northward, tithing was the theme at every stop. At the Mutual Improvement Association conference in May he preached tithing. He sent missionaries with the message into every ward of all the stakes. He called a great fast meeting and solemn assembly in the Salt Lake Temple devoted to the subject. And at October conference he discussed tithes in the new concept: payment of the Lord's share would not only bring spiritual blessings, but—and here was the added dimension that brought money in the till—it would protect against disaster. The Saints must either give the Lord his due, or suffer Divine wrath for cheating him.

Why had the Saints been driven from Jackson County, Missouri, in the early days, then expelled from the entire state? Why had they been mobbed and plundered at Nauvoo, until forced to

9. See "The B. H. Roberts Case of 1898–1900," by R. Davis Britton, UHQ, January 1957.

leave Illinois? Why had the U.S. Army marched against Utah in 1857? "Our enemies are upon our path," Snow warned. "If we are unfaithful in this matter the same results will follow us as followed the people in Jackson County." It was wiser, simpler and cheaper, he declared, to give the Lord his tithe and let him take care of the battles. "It is not our business to fight our enemies," he said. "It is our business to do what the Lord requires of us, and he will protect us."[10]

"The lines are being drawn," warned Elder Rudger Clawson. Retribution would follow even in the hereafter for those shirking their tithes in this life. "Those whose names are not found recorded in the book of the law of God shall have no inheritance in Zion" when the day of reckoning comes.[11]

Joseph F. Smith expounded on the positive rewards of tithe-paying. It was the purpose of God "not only to benefit mankind spiritually, but also benefit them temporally." The Lord, he said, "designed that His people should become the richest of all people. And this not only means the richest of all people in heavenly gifts—in spiritual blessings and riches—but it also means that the people . . . shall be the richest of all people with regard to temporal matters.

"If faithful we have a right to claim the blessings of the Lord upon the labor of our hands. . . . The farmer has a right to ask the Lord for blessings upon his farm, . . . upon the animals, . . . [upon] the grain that he sows and the seeds of the fruit that he plants in the soil. It is his right and privilege to receive blessings . . . upon all that he puts his hand unto in righteousness."

But, as in ancient Israel, the Lord's wrath awaited the wayward. "When they forgot their tithes and their offerings, when they forgot their prayers, and became rebellious and disobedient, . . . then were the rains withheld, and the earth became dust beneath their feet; their vines cast their fruit before their time; they were cursed with the blight, and with the mildew, and with the rust, and with the grasshopper, and with the devouring insects, until they were brought down low in poverty and distress."[12]

Smith told of his boyhood, when his mother, a widow with a

10. CR, October 1899.
11. CR, April 1900.
12. CR, April 1898.

large family to support, delivered a load of her best potatoes to the tithing office. The clerk, William Thompson, shook his head, saying it was a shame that she should tithe, when others—strong and able to work—were supported by the tithing office.

"My mother turned upon him and said, 'William, you ought to be ashamed of yourself. Would you deny me a blessing?' She had just as much right as a rich man to receive the Lord's blessing."[13]

Receipts picked up dramatically. At October conference, 1899, Lorenzo Snow reported that for a three-month period, July to September, tithing receipts were $134,200, which was more than three times the amount received for the corresponding months of the previous year, $44,100. Through the device of bootstrap finance, Lorenzo Snow had found the key to freeing the Saints from the bondage of debt and putting them on the road to becoming the richest of all people.

Just five years later, on March 2, 1904, the first witness at the Smoot investigation revealed the amazing increase of church wealth and business influence. He was a lean man of sixty-six with rimless glasses and a benign expression, who wore a beard reaching almost to his waist. "My principal business," testified Joseph F. Smith, "is that of president of the Mormon Church."

Robert W. Tayler, counsel for the Senate Committee on Privileges and Elections, glanced at his notes, then asked, "In what other businesses are you engaged?"

Smith hesitated. The business interests of the church were a matter of sinister accusation at this time, as the U.S. Senate opened hearings on the question of whether Reed Smoot, elected to the Senate from Utah, should be denied his seat because of his church office as a member of the Council of the Twelve. A committee of eighteen Utah Gentiles—ministers, businessmen, the editor of the *Tribune,* and the mayor of Salt Lake City—had protested the seating of an apostle, claiming that Smoot would represent "the ruling authorities of the Mormon Church," rather than the United States. It also was charged that there was a union of church and state "in all matters whatsoever, civil and religious, temporal and

13. CR, April 1900.

spiritual," and that after being officially abolished fourteen years previously polygamy was still thriving.

Similar petitions of protest poured in from every state and from almost every city of the nation. Mormonism had been a political whipping boy for more than a half century. Now the church was on the rack of a formal Senate investigation, being tried by its avowed enemies. Small wonder that its president testified with caution.

In reply to the question, Joseph F. Smith admitted to being president of ZCMI, the department store and the largest retail and wholesale mercantile business in Utah; president of two banks; president of Utah Sugar Company; president of Consolidated Wagon and Machinery Company; "and there are several other small institutions with which I am associated."

When reminded by Senate counsel, Smith admitted that he was president and director of the Utah Light and Railway Company, which furnished electricity, gas, and streetcar service to Salt Lake City.

"Had you this in mind," Tayler asked, "when you classified the others as small concerns?"

"No, sir," Smith admitted. "That is a large concern."

Further questioning brought out that Smith also was president and director of the Salt Lake and Los Angeles Railroad; and of the Saltair Beach Company, a popular pleasure resort built over the briny waters of Great Salt Lake. And that was all, he testified, that he could recall at the moment.

Tayler glanced at the members of the Senate committee seated along the table, then asked, "What relation do you sustain to the Idaho Sugar Company?"

"I am a director of that company and also president of it."

"Of the Inland Crystal Salt Company?"

"Also the same position there."

"The Salt Lake Dramatic Association?"

"I am president of that and also a director."

"Are you," Tayler asked, "president of any other corporations there?"

"I do not remember any more just now."

Tayler prodded the memory of the witness. "What relation do you sustain to the Salt Lake Knitting Company?"

"I am president of it, and also a director."

When reminded, Smith also recalled being a director of the Union Pacific Company; vice president of the Bullion, Beck and Champion Mining Company; and editor of two church magazines, the *Improvement Era* and the *Juvenile Instructor*. While he had no personal connection with the *Deseret News*, "I presume," he said, "the present ownership is the church."[14]

To next day's newspaper readers across the nation, the "Mormon menace" had been established beyond doubt. The tithe, wrote Richard Barry in *Pearson's* magazine, "under the name of Joseph F. Smith as trustee in trust, flows into the most substantial investments," controlling or owning principal industries in Utah, Idaho, and Wyoming. "And in Wall Street, Joseph F. Smith, 'trustee in trust,' sits as one of the select little group of millionaires which directs the affairs of the Union Pacific Railroad Company.

"A river of gold! A great thunderbolt of financial power, with which the wielder may have his will. . . . How much money is there? No Gentile knows. . . . For there is never any accounting to the membership of the Church for a single penny taken in through the tithing office!"

"The reason that Joseph F. Smith is found to be the president of so many great corporations," Barry explained, was that the Saints supported "only those enterprises which are stamped with the trademark of the leader of the Church."

Smith, he said, "knows little about banking, nothing about farm machinery, nothing about department stores or drugstores, nothing about railroading, and nothing about the salt industry beyond the fact that it produces enormous profits; . . . to the knitting trade he is a stranger and to the theatrical and recreational business a rank outsider. But his name goes as the head of the leading institutions in these lines in Mormon country. Therefore all such institutions are patronized exclusively by all good Mormons."

Smith's name "is the brand under which the Church strives to effect its purpose of controlling all governments, business as well as religious," Barry said.

"The tithing system is a tremendous drain on the community,

14. SI, 1:79–83.

as it takes out of circulation a very large sum of money, the most of which does not return to circulation locally. What the tithing system leaves, the various branches of 'church' investments get. Thus individual effort is crushed, and all business is diverted into Church channels."[15]

Writing in *Collier's* of "The Great Mormon Conspiracy," Alfred Henry Lewis said: "Mormonism is now brought face to face with Americanism at the bar of the Senate Committee on Privileges and Elections. Nominally the issue is whether Apostle Reed Smoot shall take his seat in the United States Senate. The real issue is . . . that the Mormon hierarchy, . . . as has been indicated by the astounding testimony of President Joseph F. Smith, . . . is, in fact, a practical conspiracy against the United States Government."[16]

As Mormon wealth and influence continued to grow, Lewis saw in 1911 the colonization of the West as part of a vast plan to gain control of the region. A cartoon illustrating one of his three articles in *Cosmopolitan* showed Smith holding aloft Reed Smoot in his grasp, while Smoot in turn held strings attached to western senators which ran from them to the House of Congress.

"Consider what money must have been paid in tithes into the hand of the Mormon Church during the sixty years past! . . . It was, every dollar, invested the moment it came in; and its profits have been invested and reinvested ever since as fast as they accrued. Sixty years of investment and reinvestment! What would a Rockefeller or a Rothschild say to that? . . .

"And where is it to end? Prophet Smith and the church intended it shall end in a practical Mormon conquest of the country.

"Twenty years more of tithes, of profits on investments, of speculation, of an Apostle Smoot in a Senate seat, of [tariff] rapine under the specious pretext of 'protection,' will behold Mormonism the overpowering money-force of the country, indeed, of the world," Lewis predicted.[17]

Exactly the same lurid charges, arousing the same fears and apprehensions, had, though expressed in different words and under different conditions, resulted in mob attacks, arson, rapine, and beatings throughout the violent history of the church. These fears

15. "The *Mormon* Method in Business," November 1910.
16. March 26, 1904.
17. "The Viper on the Hearth," "The Trail of the Viper," "The Viper's Trail of Gold," March, April, May, 1911.

had aroused their neighbors to drive the Saints from Ohio, Missouri, and Illinois. And as the long war with the world reached a climax during the administration of President John Taylor, he had seriously considered another exodus, scorching the earth behind him, leaving Utah the desert as the Mormons had found it, and taking his people to a refuge in Mexico or the islands of the Pacific.[18]

The intimate interplay of the spiritual and temporal is part of the Mormon way of life and always has been. The founder of the church, Joseph Smith (uncle of the Joseph F. who testified before the Senate committee), was active in real estate, banking, printing, construction, and other business enterprises. He was mayor of Nauvoo, Illinois, largest city of the state; he was judge of the municipal court, active in politics, commander of the local militia (the largest armed force in the nation except for the U.S. Army), and at the time of his death was candidate for the presidency of the United States. This set the pattern for church authorities from that day to this. If it arouses antagonism from the outside world, and unrest among Mormon intellectuals and competing businessmen, there doesn't seem to be much to do about it.

While Jesus warned that "No man can serve two masters: . . . Ye cannot serve God and mammon"; and Paul the Apostle declared that "the love of money is the root of all evil"; the Mormons added a new dimension to the pursuit of the buck. It was not money that was bad, in this concept, but the love of it. "The man who cannot become rich without apostatizing is a disgrace to his fellow man," millionaire Brigham Young declared. The worthy Saint would remain uncankered by riches. Thus, among the Mormons the ability of a man to get ahead in the world is highly admired. Although they would be quick to deny a correlation between a man's wealth or prominence with his opportunity to advance in church office, certainly this would never *hinder* his advancement, as any investigation of the backgrounds of the general authorities would confirm. The other side of the coin is that because of the church's vast business enterprises, any poor man who becomes a general authority automatically will die wealthy, because of his participation in them.[19]

18. See the author's *The Kingdom or Nothing* (New York: Macmillan, 1976). Also see John Taylor correspondence at the Church Historical Department, and copies at University of Utah.

19. Inasmuch as the church is extremely reticent to discuss its financial situation, such information is circulated through the thriving underground press of Zion.

The vow of poverty simply has no place in the doctrine or practice of the Saints. In fact, to renounce the good things of material well-being would boggle the mind of a Mormon as sheer foolishness. Wealth, with its attendant responsibilities and temptations, is thus a test of a man's character and genuine spirituality, for it may cause him to forget the source of all blessings.

The marriage of God and Mammon has caused concern among intellectuals. "Some LDS businessmen link the money-success pattern to church doctrine by reducing Mormon concepts such as free agency, recompense for paying tithing, the law of consecration, and eternal progression to some kind of related *business* meanings," Joseph H. Jeppson stated.[20]

"For instance, they believe that 'eternal progress' consists essentially of learning 'leadership' skills in this life which can be utilized in the next. Knowing how to run a ship-shape used car lot should train men to organize galaxies as Gods. . . .

"If there is a theme about riches which runs through the Book of Mormon," he pointed out, "it is that there is a tendency for riches to turn men's hearts away from God," and this is confirmed by the Bible.

"It is not wicked to be wealthy, but it is easy to covet riches. It is not evil to rule, but it is tempting to worship power. It is not difficult to persuade oneself that the worship of riches and of power is really the worship of God or of things holy. In the LDS Church, where the great majority of Ward leaders (and higher) are both lay preachers and businessmen, it is too easy for such leaders to pass off their weekday philosophies as Sunday fare and their success philosophy as 'true religion.' . . .

"The spirit of God unfolds in the opening of a human heart, not in the building of a success-oriented 'character' which will pass muster either at Rotary or at the Pearly Gates," he concluded. "All too often that kind of 'character' is merely another name for an unyielding posture that makes it easy for men to be self-righteous, unforgiving, and fatalistic."

A mimeographed sheet stated that "we in the LDS Church have the dubious distinction of having the highest paid ministry on the face of the earth." See *Mormonism—Shadow or Reality,* by Jerald and Sandra Tanner (Salt Lake: The authors, 1964).

20. "Merging Business and Religion," *Dialogue, a Journal of Mormon Thought,* Autumn 1966.

The tendency to equate spirituality with money rubbed a California Mormon the wrong way. On being interviewed as to his worth to be advanced to the office of elder, he was asked if he would promise to pay a full tithe. "Do you mean I can buy advancement?" he asked, and flunked the interview. The two primary questions asked an applicant for a temple "recommend," the holders of which constitute an elite spiritual group, are whether he observes the Word of Wisdom and the law of tithing.

The faithful Saint who suffers misfortune is wont to search his soul for the cause. What has he done wrong to incur Divine wrath? "Things began going bad for me," a good member of the author's ward confided. "My wife got sick. One of my kids broke his arm. I lost my job. A friend I'd loaned money to went bankrupt. I didn't know which way to turn.

"So I'll tell you what I did," he said. "I went to see my bishop, and settled up back tithing!" And *then*, he said, he confidently expected a change for the better. "I'd done my part, and the Lord was *bound* by his promise to bless me for it."

*It is hardly conceivable that one can under-
stand the history of the LDS Church for this
first part of the twentieth century [1901–15]
without becoming familiar with the testimony
offered by President Joseph F. Smith at the
Smoot hearings in Washington, D.C., early in
March, 1904.*

—JAMES R. CLARK, Messages of the First
Presidency, 4:XI

*The world understands that polygamy is an
enslavement of women. The ecclesiastical authorities in Utah today [1911] have discovered
that it is more powerful as an enslavement of
men. Once a man is bound in a polygamous
relation, there is no place for him in the civilized world outside of a Mormon community.*

—FRANK J. CANNON, Under the Prophet
in Utah

*...It was shown by the testimony...that
a majority of those who give the law to the
Mormon Church are now, and have been for
years, living in open, notorious, and shameless
polygamous cohabitation.*

—Final REPORT, Smoot investigation,
June 11, 1906, SI 4:480

6

The Principle

THE CHILD awakened. All was quiet in the night, except
for the regular breathing of Deli beside her and the ticking of the
grandfather clock in the hallway below. Then came a muffled sob.
A man's low voice tried to give comfort. Lillian slipped from the
bed and went to the window. Below, moonlight made black shadows across the front lawn from the row of tall Lombardy poplars
lining the street, the shadows shimmering as the new leaves danced
in the spring breeze. Mama and Bishop Manwaring were standing
by the gate of the picket fence. Mama was crying, face in her
hands. The bishop gently patted her hunched shoulder.

81

"It will be all right, Sister Nettie," he soothed.

"I don't understand," Mama sobbed. "How could they do this to John?"

"The Lord's purpose is sometimes difficult to understand, Sister Nettie."

"John did no more than *they* did!" Mama cried. "The only difference is that he was caught at it. The others went into hiding. John's case became public knowledge in Washington."

"Hold the faith, Sister Nettie. It will be all right."

When Mama turned and came into the house, Lillian got back into bed, snuggling close to Deli to get warm. Mama's steps came up the stairs, then the door opened as she came in to check the two children and tuck in the covers. Lillian kept her eyes closed until Mama went out to visit the other upstairs bedrooms, where Joseph, Rachel, and Ruth were asleep. Then from below came the baby's wail, and she hurried downstairs to take care of Raymond.

Lillian lay awake, a lump in her throat. What had they done to Father? What had happened would be because of that subpoena by the Senate committee in Washington, which Father had been avoiding for so long. Where was he tonight? She didn't see much of him, and when he did visit he arrived at night, didn't appear on the streets, and she'd been taught to call him "Uncle Mose." The five families were scattered, with the investigation on, and Mama took an underground name. Aunt May, the first wife, lived at Salt Lake. The second wife, Aunt Nellie, had a home at Raymond, in Alberta, Canada. Mama, the third, had just moved to Provo. The two last wives, Aunt Roxie and Aunt Rhoda, were at Colonia Juarez, Mexico.

Lillian was six now—six and a half, really—and ever since she was three, Father had been in trouble, because the church wanted Apostle Reed Smoot to be a senator.

They lived at Farmington then, and Mama was supervising the remodeling of the big red-brick house, taking charge because Father was away so much. He was establishing the Mormon colonies in Alberta, laying out towns, stocking the prairie with livestock, supervising irrigation projects, fostering industry. Whenever he was home, men called around to discuss big projects—dam building, mining, timbering.

It was a happy time. Lillian knew that she was someone special. Mama was proud that the very choicest spirits from heaven were privileged to be born in the Principle. In the hereafter, Mama would be queen of her own world, and Father the god of that world, as a reward for entering celestial marriage. Lillian also was special because she was the daughter of an apostle; John W. Taylor was known as the prophet of the quorum. It seemed that everyone loved Father and was especially nice to Mama and the family.

Lillian was the baby of the family then, and with construction underway Mama would have one of the Welling girls over, Roxie or Rhoda, to tend the children. Lillian loved them both, Roxie soft-spoken, sweet, and gentle, Rhoda with her rollicking good humor. Before long Lillian felt a tension in the air whenever Father was home. Mama was under some sort of strain. One night she heard voices through the wall in argument.

One Sunday Brother Cowley spoke in church, then came to the house. Matthias F. Cowley was Father's great friend and a fellow member of the Quorum of the Twelve. A stocky man of medium height, with close-cropped beard and moustache, he was gentle and soft-spoken, but, like Father, a tiger in defense of the Principle. On that afternoon Lillian was supposed to be taking her nap; but she heard through the doorway, left partly open so that Mama could listen for the child to awaken. And Lillian learned that Father planned to marry both Roxie and Rhoda.

Mama was firmly opposed. The Manifesto, she said, had prohibited further plural marriages eleven years ago. Father said scornfully that the Manifesto was only a trick to beat the Devil at his own game. It had been necessary to secure statehood for Utah. And as Mama well knew, he said, there had been many plural marriages since that time.

Mama said that before she would consent, she would have to know that the marriages of Roxie and Rhoda were approved by President Joseph F. Smith himself. "That," said Brother Cowley, "is why I am here, Sister Nettie." He explained that President Smith did not want to *know* about such things. If called to testify under oath, he wished to be free to declare that he had no personal knowledge of such matters. If a worthy man went to him for permission to take a plural wife, the president would tell him the church forbade such marriages. Subsequently, a man of high priesthood ranking would visit him and give permission.[1]

Not *church* sanction, Father said, but by authority of the *priesthood*. Plural marriage hadn't ceased, it simply had gone underground, as in the days of Nauvoo during Joseph Smith's time.[2] His own father as president of the church, Father said, had before his death formed the organization to continue the Principle underground when the church should set it aside.

"What can I say, when I know you will do as you please?" Mama said in a voice so barren and forsaken that Lillian burst into tears. Mama hurried in to pick her up.

Father arranged things in the customary manner. Roxie and Rhoda went through the temple by themselves, and then on a hot afternoon, August 29, 1901, Brother Cowley married them to Father. None of Mama's family attended the ceremony; it was best not to *know* about such things.

Mama was busy that fall, getting the remodeling done before Christmas. Following the holidays on February 15 she presented Father with a valentine, a baby girl. He was not only delighted but grateful. At last he had paid off the liabilities of a previous ill-fated business venture and was free from the bondage of debt. In recognition of the Lord's help he christened the baby Deliverance.[3]

Roxie stayed at the house, posing as a domestic, after the marriage. In the fall she left, supposedly to teach school at Grantsville; actually she went to the Mormon colonies in Mexico to have her baby outside the country. In December, Father took Mama and the family to Mexico, Rhoda going along ostensibly to help with

1. For this type of arrangement, see author's interviews with Nettie M. Taylor and Roxie W. Taylor. A typical example is related in B. Harvey Allred's *A Leaf in Review,* regarding his marriage of a plural wife in 1903, thirteen years after the Manifesto. The story of the wife was published in "The Star of Truth," November 1954: *A Biographical Sketch of the Life of Mary Evelyn Clark Allred.* See also Kimball Young, *Isn't One Wife Enough?* and Frank J. Cannon, *Under the Prophet in Utah.*

2. At Nauvoo, the church officially denounced plural marriage, while the priesthood authority within the church fostered it as essential to celestial glory. The Fundamentalist bibliography on this subject is enormous. See also the author's *The Kingdom or Nothing* (New York: Macmillan, 1976), and his *Nightfall at Nauvoo* (New York: Macmillan, 1971).

3. Always sensitive about her name, she went by the diminutive Deli. When as an adult she moved to California, and the bishop of her ward read her name as a new arrival, she refused to acknowledge that she was "Deliverance Taylor." "If I go to hell," she said afterward, "you can blame Father."

the children. They arrived at Colonia Juarez to find Roxie with a week-old baby, which Father christened Emma.

The big guessing game at the colonies was to match up the pregnant girls who arrived with absent husbands. Roxie had joined a dozen other girls in her condition, known as the "Salt Lake colony." She hadn't revealed the identity of her husband until Father arrived.

Lillian never forgot a chilly day when the family was away, and she huddled behind the stove of a Mexican woman who was tending her. As the woman poked the first vigorously the high stovepipe jarred loose. She screamed. Lillian ducked, and the sharp edge of the pipe cut through her heavy hair and into the scalp. It took weeks to heal and left a life-long scar.

Father bought a cottage of white stone for the new wives and immediately began drawing up plans for "remodeling" that would dwarf the original structure. He always had to have the finest house in town. It took the girls (as Mama called the sisters) awhile to get used to his habit of arriving for supper with up to a dozen unannounced friends. Mama of course knew what to expect. She told the girls that she never had had a meal with John alone.

Talk among the guests was primarily about two things: the Principle and the political situation in Utah. It was vital to gain a majority of Republicans in the state legislature, which in turn would elect Apostle Reed Smoot to the U.S. Senate, in place of Joseph L. Rawlins, whose term was expiring.

Smoot's candidacy stirred up a storm in Utah. "Would Mr. Smoot be considered seriously as a candidate if he held no high ecclesiastical office?" the Salt Lake *Herald* demanded,[4] while "Throughout the campaign," Frank J. Cannon charged, "the inspired order was given the faithful that they must vote for the legislators who could be relied upon to do the will of the Lord." Even Senator Rawlins' mother was counseled to vote against her own son, "and it was 'at the peril of her immortal soul' that she disobeyed the injunction."[5]

While most of the Saints in Mexico were jubilant at the Republican landslide, Mama had forebodings of trouble, and, true enough, soon after the election the Salt Lake Ministerial Association pro-

4. November 2, 1902.
5. *Under the Prophet in Utah.*

tested Smoot's impending nomination "because he is one of the Quorum of Twelve apostles, who, with the First Presidency, rules that church as with a rod of iron." Smoot's election "would force upon the citizens of Utah a union of church and state."[6]

Father and his guests chuckled over an interview by a *Trib* reporter with President Joseph F. Smith, who said, "It is not true that Smoot has been put forward by the church as a candidate for public office, but he has the same right as any other American citizen enjoys to accept any office which his fellow citizens may elect him to occupy."

When Mama asked, "How about Moses Thatcher?" Father just grinned.

"Does the Mormon Church solemnize or permit plural marriages?" the *Trib* reporter asked. President Smith said,

Certainly not. The church does not perform or sanction, or authorize, marriage in any form that is contrary to the laws of the land. The assertion that prominent Mormons practice polygamy is evidently done to mislead the public.[7]

This showed the wisdom of Brother Smith's policy of not *knowing* about such things, Father declared. With a laugh he added, "But he *understands* that things are different."

Thomas Kearns, the Gentile senator from Utah, added to the furor by claiming that President Theodore Roosevelt had declared that the election of an apostle to the Senate would "be very unwise," and "would work great harm to the State."[8] While the *Deseret News* was astonished that "the President would attempt to intervene in a matter that belongs only to the legislature of a sovereign State," the nation's press endorsed Roosevelt's position, the New York *Mail* declaring that "The sentiment of the country will sustain him in protesting . . . this new outrage on public decency."

The *Tribune* warned that the election of an apostle "will reopen the old rancorous faction fight which prevailed for a generation, and which we had all hoped was done with."[9]

Mama felt that other men, equally well qualified to represent

6. *Tribune,* November 25, 1902.
7. December 3, 1902.
8. *Tribune,* January 9, 1903.
9. January 22, 1903.

the state, could have been elected, without pulling the world down over the heads of the Saints.

Smoot went to the Senate, and petitions of protest deluged Washington from every state and almost every town in the nation, largely through the efforts of the Women's Christian Temperance Union, the International Congress of Mothers, and the Interdenominational Council of Women. The petition of most telling effect came from eighteen prominent "citizens and qualified electors of the State of Utah."[10] They included four ministers, three lawyers, a banker, the *Tribune* editor, the mayor of Salt Lake City, two businessmen, a real estate man, and five mining executives, one of whom was Utah's first congressman. The man who wrote the petition was a prominent attorney and former assistant U.S. attorney for Utah and state legislator, E. B. Critchlow.[11]

Despite the brouhaha, however, there was no opposition on the floor of the Senate to Smoot taking the oath of office. There was jubilation in Colonia Juarez. "The entire west," the *Deseret News* declared, "will hail with pleasure the triumph of Americanism over religious intolerance."[12]

Since things had settled down, Father took Mama and the family back to Farmington in August, leaving the girls in Mexico. Mama was appalled by the lack of care by the renters of her big house; but she and the children pitched in to get it cleaned up. Now she was settled again in her own home, she declared, and she would stay there the remainder of her life.

The Senate Committee on Privileges and Elections changed all that by scheduling hearings on whether Reed Smoot was entitled to retain his seat. Father arrived from Canada to warn Mama that all plural wives must go underground. He was taking Aunt Nellie to Canada with him. He told the children that Mama would be away for awhile; only Joseph would know where she was. Meanwhile, he'd visit when he could, but when he did they must call him "Uncle Mose," pretending he was his brother.

Phoebe Welling, a widow, came to the house after Mama left with Deli. Each afternoon Joe would ride off on his pony and return to say that Mama and the baby were fine. Generally Mama sent

10. SI 1:1.
11. The petition is summarized in chap. 1.
12. March 5, 1903.

something—cookies, apples, an apron she'd made, or stockings she'd darned. Then in late fall Joe stopped the visits, because Mama had moved out of town.

Lillian was overjoyed when a neighbor, John Walsh, helped them pack up and took them to Salt Lake, where Mama was living in a cottage on 7th Street near the LDS Hospital, under the name "Nettie May."[13] A subpoena was out for Father to appear as witness at the Smoot investigation, so he remained in Canada except for secret visits.

With the fate of the family in the balance, Mama closely followed events in Washington. Robert W. Tayler, attorney for the Senate committee, charged that

The president of the Mormon Church and a majority of the twelve apostles now practice polygamy and polygamous cohabitation, and some of them have taken polygamous wives since the manifesto of 1890. These things have been done with the knowledge and countenance of Reed Smoot.

Smoot issued a statement, saying

I deny that either the president or any of the apostles of the church has taken a polygamous or plural wife since the manifesto of 1890. I deny that either the president or any of the twelve apostles has at any time practiced polygamy or polygamous cohabitation . . . since the manifesto. . . .

Summing up the statements, Senator McComas said that if it could be proved that any apostle or member of the First Presidency had married a plural wife since the Manifesto, had authorized or performed such a marriage, or had lived with a plural wife to whom he had been married before the Manifesto, "that is a ground of disqualification in the Senator."

Little wonder Mama was worried. All of her five children had been born since the Manifesto, and her belly was big with a sixth.

When hearings began the morning of March 2, 1904, President Joseph F. Smith was the first witness. "I am not aware that the church practiced polygamy, or plural marriages, at least, after the Manifesto," he testified, and he even said that "I do not know"

13. She became so well known by her underground name that she retained it the remainder of her life, as "Nettie M. Taylor."

of any such marriages since the Supreme Court decision upheld anti-polygamy laws in 1878, twelve years before the Manifesto.

Mama was aghast. "How could he say *that?*"

"He said he doesn't *know,*" Joseph reminded her.

"Well, he knows *me;* he knows my children."

"You are *reputed* to be Father's plural wife. He has no personal proof of it."

"How in the world do they expect to cover it all up?"

"Father was sent to Canada, Apostle Heber J. Grant to England, Brother Cowley to Mexico; others are either too sick to testify or are out of reach of the law. Only witnesses who will not betray us will testify for the church in Washington."[14]

The following day, President Smith's testimony was a bombshell for the nation's press. Smith admitted to having five wives, and living with all of them. After a flurry of objections by Smith's lawyers, the prosecution was allowed to ask:

MR. TAYLER: Mr. Smith, how many children have been born to your several wives since the manifesto of 1890?

There were more objections. The chairman ruled that "the question is competent."

MR. SMITH: I have had eleven children born since eighteen ninety.

MR. TAYLER: Those are all the children that have been born to you since eighteen ninety?

MR. SMITH: Yes, sir; those are all.

MR. TAYLER: Were those children by all of your wives; that is, did all of your wives bear children?

MR. SMITH: All of my wives bore children.

MR. TAYLER: Since eighteen ninety?

MR. SMITH: That is correct.[15]

With this admission by the president of the church, the Senate committee could have closed its case by disqualifying Smoot. In-

14. Quotations from hearings are from SI. Family details are from notes of interviews and letters over a period of thirteen years by this author with members of the John W. Taylor family and acquaintances. Copy at BYU, Special Collections; also copies at University of Utah and Utah State.

15. SI, 1:133. The *Tribune* published a cartoon showing Smoot in an attitude of consternation, knees bent as from a blow, clapping his hand to his forehead, beads of sweat running down his face and his hair standing on end, with the caption, "Senator Smoot hears President Smith's testimony."

stead, the testimony was a taste of blood, and the committee continued in full cry, not in pursuit of Smoot's seat in the Senate, but
of the real quarry, the church itself.

"Who is John W. Taylor?" Tayler asked. Smith identified him
as an apostle.

"Is he a polygamist?"

"Well, now; he is reputed, I think, to be a polygamist. . . .
Of my own knowledge I could not say that he is."

"Have you the slightest doubt of it?"

"I have not very much doubt of it," Smith admitted.

"Where is he now?"

"I do not know, sir."

Tayler asked about others of the quorum, Marriner W. Merrill,
Heber J. Grant, John Henry Smith, Matthias F. Cowley, Rudger
Clawson, Francis M. Lyman, George Teasdale, and the late Abraham H. Cannon. Smith admitted that all had been polygamists.
Crowding him, Tayler asked how Teasdale could have married a
plural wife before 1890 when she hadn't met him or been in
this country before 1893. Smith denied having married Abraham
H. Cannon to a plural wife, Lillian Hamlin, during a boat ride to
Catalina in 1896. He knew nothing about the marriage, he said,
until accused of having performed the ceremony "through the
public prints."[16]

President Smith further testified—and Mama gasped when she
read it—that "If any apostle or any other man claiming authority"
should perform a plural marriage, he would "be subjected to discipline and excommunication from the church."

"I believe Mr. Smith, when he says plural marriages have
stopped, is using the words in a sense different from that in which
those words would be understood by yourself or myself or anyone
else," E. B. Critchlow testified. When Smoot's attorney asked him
if he was accusing Smith of not speaking the truth, Critchlow said,
"I believe he is not speaking the truth, if you wish me to say it. He

16. Frank J. Cannon repeated this charge in his *Under the Prophet in Utah*,
claiming that his father told him of the matter in Smith's presence. "Smith could hear
every word that was said. My Father had included him in the conversation, and he
was listening. He not only did not deny his guilt; he accepted it in silence. . . . He did
not deny it later, when the whole community had learned of it. He went with Apostle
John Henry Smith to see Mr. P. H. Lannan, proprietor of the Salt Lake *Tribune,* to
ask him not to attack the Church for this new and shocking violation of its covenant."

is not speaking the truth with regard to conditions as they exist in Utah. . . ."[17]

President Smith returned from Washington amid a furor in the local and national press. Salt Lake Gentiles held a mass meeting to protest his assertion that the people of Utah "are broad-minded enough to consent to the shocking violations of law and public decency which he confesses to have committed. We protest that we are not deserving of this sort of praise."

The protest asserted that polygamists had "surrounded themselves with an impenetrable wall of secrecy," had suppressed records making it impossible to gain legal evidence, and that "the power and control of the polygamous hierarchy" made it "a matter of discipline" to keep silent "about polygamous relations and to deny knowledge of the same." At the Smoot hearing "the veil has been lifted" for the first time, "and nowhere in the whole country did this testimony occasion so much astonishment and humiliation as in Utah."[18]

The League of Women's Organizations denounced the "Mormon monster," and called "the preachers of this country in aid of their battle in defense of the home, on which the safety of the nation rests."[19] The *Literary Digest* reported:

The New York *Globe* is shocked at "the cool effrontery and callous immortality" of the man who owns up to having led such a life; and the Springfield *Republican* thinks that "the least that can be said" is that the Mormon Church "needs a new head, who will obey the laws of the land, rather than insolently defy them." . . .

"Does not Mr. Smoot's representative relation to a band of confessed outlaws disqualify him in good conscience from membership in the Senate?" asks the Philadelphia *Ledger*. The Norfolk *Pilot* refers to

17. Wayne Stout says that President Smith's denial of plural marriages since 1890 "profoundly shocked public opinion. The answer was an honest one but inaccurate. His answer caused tongues to wag in Utah where the truth was known" (*History of Utah,* 2:175). Also, in the CHC, Roberts admits that the Smoot investigation disclosed that the injunction against plural marriages of the Manifesto of 1890 "had not been strictly adhered to even by some high officials of the Church" (6:399). Perhaps it also should be noted that Anthony W. Ivins, president of the Juarez Stake in Mexico, where many plural marriages were performed after the Manifesto, quite obviously acted with official sanction, for he was subsequently rewarded by being elevated to the Quorum of the Twelve and selected a member of the First Presidency.

18. *Deseret News,* March 15, 1904.

19. *Herald,* March 12.

Mormonism as "a conspiracy to commit crime," and it declares that to seat one of its leaders in the Senate "would be nothing less than an infamy and a shame."[20]

Why? Mama asked, why was it necessary that an apostle be in the Senate? Why must such a high price be paid?

She was heavy with child, so couldn't attend April conference, where a "second Manifesto" came as a result of the Smoot hearings:

Inasmuch as there are numerous reports in circulation that plural marriages have been entered into contrary to the official declaration of President Woodruff of September 26, 1890, . . . I, Joseph F. Smith, . . . do hereby affirm and declare that no such marriages have been solemnized with the sanction, consent, or knowledge of the Church; . . . and if any officer or member of the Church shall assume to solemnize or enter into any such marriage he will be deemed in transgression against the Church, and will be dealt with according to the rules and regulations thereof and excommunicated therefrom.[21]

Two weeks later Mama gave birth to a baby boy. Father sent word to name him for the town he was laying out in Alberta, Raymond.[22]

As hearings resumed in Washington, Mama moved again, to a house in Sugarhouse near the penitentiary. When a prisoner escaped, Lillian was terrified until the family moved to the Forest Dale district, renting a house from the brother of Father's attorney and good friend, John M. Cannon.

On arriving, Ruth hurried inside for a drink and said the water tasted funny. Mama warned the others to let the taps run awhile to clean out the pipes. Presently Ruth came down with typhoid. She was sick a long time and pneumonia set in. Mama got a woman to come in as nurse. Ruth's beautiful golden curls were falling out, and each night the nurse would clip off a few locks. Lillian heard a scream in the dark; Ruth had awakened to find scissors in her hair.

Lillian went to Forest Dale school with Joe and Rae. A school-

20. March 12 and 19.
21. This second manifesto is generally credited with ending the underground sponsorship of plural marriage; however, it was subsequently necessary to issue others.
22. At this time John W. Taylor predicted that Raymond would someday be a great oil-producing center, which came true after his death.

girl friend of Rae's got smallpox. Soon there was an epidemic. When Rae became sick, Dr. Richards vaccinated the others of the family; but it was too late. Ruth was recuperating from typhoid when she contracted smallpox. Joe came down with it, then Deli, and Mama also. Dr. Richards told Mama to wean Raymond so he wouldn't catch the disease. She told him she just didn't have time, with four deathly sick children. He warned that if she didn't go to bed herself she would collapse. "How can I?" she asked.

Rae was getting a little better when Mama went dizzy and fell in a heap on the floor. Lillian helped her crawl to the phone, where she called Father's brother, Uncle Frank, and John M. Cannon. A nurse arrived and helped pull the family through. The house was quarantined, with a bright yellow sign on front, SMALLPOX. If anyone opened the door, or even a window, someone would yell to close it. Mama phoned Brother Cannon about groceries, and he would leave them on the back porch. He also brought letters from Father, sent in double envelopes and signed "Carl."

In Washington they were closing in on Father and Brother Cowley. Hulking Ed Abbott, sheriff of Davis County, who had been their neighbor at Farmington, testified that Roxie and Rhoda Welling were Father's wives and that they were about twenty-two and twenty-four years of age.

"If they are only twenty-two and twenty-four years old, he is bound to have married them since the Manifesto," Senator Overman said, because at that time "they could not have been more than ten-years old."

When U.S. Marshal D. B. Hayward of Salt Lake notified the committee that "I have been unable to find in the district of Utah" several prominent churchmen wanted as witnesses, Joseph F. Smith sent the chairman a letter explaining that apostles John Henry Smith, George Teasdale, and Marriner W. Merrill were in "poor health" and unable to leave home. In response to his "earnest desire" that John W. Taylor and M. F. Cowley should testify in Washington, these two had been unwilling to do so. "As this is a political matter, and not a religious duty," Smith said, "I am powerless to exert more than moral suasion in the premises."[23]

Senator Burrows, committee chairman, was definitely skeptical, declaring that church authorities "have succeeded in suppressing a

23. April 15, 1904.

great deal of testimony by which the fact of plural marriages contracted by those who were high in the council of the church might have been established beyond a shadow of a doubt." And, regarding Father: "It is shown that John W. Taylor was sent out of the country by Joseph F. Smith on a real or pretended mission for the church."

As for others beyond the reach of subpoenas, "Every one of the witnesses named left the country at the instance of the rulers of the Mormon Church and to avoid testifying," Burrows declared. "Had those officials seen fit to direct the witnesses named to return to the United States and give their testimony before the committee, they would have been obliged to do so."

On a secret visit to Salt Lake, Father told Mama the real reason why he hadn't gone to Washington. He was staying at Aunt Nellie's home in Raymond when the president of the Twelve, Francis M. Lyman, arrived with the message that Joseph F. Smith wanted him to appear as a witness at the Smoot investigation. Father agreed to obey counsel; but, he told Lyman, he would be under oath and would tell the entire truth. Next morning Father packed up and was on his way to catch the train when Lyman overtook him with new instructions. During the night, Lyman said, the spirit of the late president, Wilford Woodruff, had appeared to him with the message that Father wasn't to go to Washington. Father accepted this counsel from his quorum president and returned to Nellie's house.[24]

Father was in furious disagreement with several members of the Twelve who insisted that Reed Smoot retain his Senate seat at any price. The price, in Father's case, would be to protect the official church posture by putting aside Roxie and Rhoda, denying the marriages (which couldn't be proved), and having nothing more to do with them. He not only refused, but allowed Roxie and Rhoda to come to Utah for a visit.

Mama warned against this. She'd had a dream predicting disaster from such a visit. Father declared that they were his wives just as much as Mama was. They were lonely and homesick in

24. Nellie related this to the author, and also his own mother, Nettie. It has been published several times. See *Truth*, May 1941; also *Supplement to the New and Everlasting Covenant of Marriage*, by J. W. Musser and J. L. Broadbent (n.p., n.d.; published at Salt Lake about 1935).

Mexico; the visit would do them a great deal of good. Anyhow, it would be a secret trip.

When the girls arrived, they found it was not fun being on the underground in Utah, whereas at Colonia Juarez they lived in the big stone house and were accorded recognition as wives of an apostle. Aunt Roxie stayed at Mama's place with her child, Emma. The young woman with the child started whispers again, even as the Senate committee was hearing charges against John W. Taylor. Mama was glad when the girls returned to Mexico; but the visit had added fuel to the fire in Washington. How could Father deny the marriages now, even if he wanted to?

Father visited the girls in Mexico and as house guests entertained his good friend and fellow apostle, Abraham O. Woodruff, who arrived at Colonia Juarez with two wives and several children. Woodruff was keeping under cover because at the time of the Manifesto of 1890 he was but eighteen years old, and he hadn't married his first wife, Helen May Winters, until his return from a mission in 1896. His subsequent plural marriage by no stretch of the imagination could be claimed as being before the Manifesto.

On the evening before Woodruff was to leave for Mexico City, Father had friends in and led the group singing. Woodruff didn't sing, explaining to Father that he was depressed with a premonition of disaster. Father asked if he'd been vaccinated, mentioning the outbreak of smallpox in Mexico City. Woodruff reminded Father of the anti-vaccination campaign in the *Deseret News,* and said he would depend on the Lord's protection. When Father said he didn't believe in asking the Lord to do what a man could do for himself, Woodruff gave him a reproving look.

On the trip south, Woodruff's first wife came down with smallpox. She died, and soon afterward he contracted the disease. On June 20, 1904 he also died.

On returning home, Father told Mama that, aside from losing a friend, Woodruff's death had changed the balance of power in the Quorum of the Twelve. The new member supported abandonment of the underground practice of the Principle; this now became the actual policy as well as the public posture of the church.[25]

25. See author's interviews with John W. Taylor's wives. Also Kimball Young, *Isn't One Wife Enough?* and *Truth,* May 1940 and January 1943. In *A Leaf in*

If the majority of his quorum now favored setting aside the Principle, Mama said, then Father would of course have to go along with them. Never, Father declared. President John Taylor had predicted dire results when the church would abandon the fulness of the gospel for the friendship of the world. There were some, Father said, who must stand and make the good fight.

Lillian saw a haunted look in Mama's eyes from then on. Father was out of harmony with his brethren.

When at last the family was well, the house fumigated, and the quarantine sign taken from the front door, Mama went to the bank to attend to some business for Father. She met President Joseph F. Smith there, who pressed her hand and said he'd shed tears over her travail. Well, she was thankful that everything was all right now, Mama said. He smiled, saying it reminded him of a man who fell off a high building and broke his arms and legs, but was thankful it wasn't his neck.

On a secret visit home, Father likened the Senate committee to wolves in pursuit of a sled. They'd never be satisfied without raw meat, he said. A baby would have to be thrown to the wolves. When Mama asked what he meant, he said that Reed Smoot had demanded his and Matt Cowley's resignation from the Quorum of the Twelve.[26]

Mama gasped, saying that they wouldn't do that. Father said they already had. He and Brother Cowley had been called, as a mission, to step down until things blew over. Thank goodness, Mama said, it would only be temporary, only a mission for the good of the church. For the good of Reed Smoot, Father retorted sharply; and, he said, once out, he and Matt Cowley never would be reinstated. Instead of being honored for their sacrifice, they would be reviled as apostates.

In a quiet voice he said that he and Brother Cowley already had submitted their resignations, to be used in Washington if necessary.

Review, B. Harvey Allred discusses the change in the balance of power at Woodruff's death, and even claims that because of this the Lord withdrew his protection over the colonies in Mexico, with the result that the people were driven out in 1912.

26. SI, 4:440: "... it was charged that Mr. Taylor and Mr. Cowley had taken plural wives since the manifesto. . . . He [Smoot] had requested an investigation be made, and if upon investigation it should turn out the charges were true, he would favor taking action to drop them from the quorum."

There would be a ram in the thicket, Mama said. She'd dreamed of great danger, then being delivered by a sacrifice.

The family moved to Provo, and all during the winter, for a period of five months, Mama clutched at the desperate faith that a lesser sacrifice would be accepted. She went to Salt Lake for April conference, and it was that night that Lillian awakened to hear her crying by the front gate below, with Bishop Manwaring trying to comfort her.

In the morning Mama served breakfast to the family, and then told them that the resignations of Father and Brother Cowley had been announced at conference.

For awhile Mama was shattered. She'd had such a firm sign regarding a ram in the thicket. Then she realized that the dream was correct. The Senate committee wasn't after Smoot; the quarry was the church itself. The baby thrown to the wolves was the Principle.

Through sacrifice of the Principle, the Senate was appeased. It ended the investigation and voted that Reed Smoot should retain his seat.

7

The Little Man Who Isn't There

R E E D   S M O O T   served in the U.S. Senate for thirty years, becoming one of the most powerful men in the nation and in the church. In May 1932, during his final political campaign, Smoot was appraised by syndicated columnist Raymond Clapper:

Utah has fewer inhabitants than Milwaukee. She has two Congressmen against New York's 43. But Utah has Senator Smoot and he has built up a dynasty of appointees which penetrates into a dozen or so of the most important branches of the government. . . .

Ramifications of the Smoot dynasty are intricate enough to provide rich diggings for a political genealogist. Chairman of the mighty Senate Finance Committee, ranking member of the powerful committees on Appropriations, Public Lands, Public Buildings, and Rules, Smoot's influence extends in all directions.

With it all, he is probably the hardest working man in Congress, tireless in dealing with a tariff or tax bill, a demon for efficiency, once described by President Harding as the most valuable public servant in Washington . . . No. 2 man in the Mormon Church and No. 2 man in Washington.[1]

During Smoot's long career in the Senate, Lillian watched, with the keen interest of one who had paid a price to put him there, the repercussions of the Smoot investigation on Mormonism. The hearings had pried open a Pandora's box, releasing powerful forces which demolished pioneer values of her childhood and created the attitudes and program of the modern culture.

The "second Manifesto" of 1904 was followed by others (in fact there were nine more between 1904 and 1921), as the Principle, like the ghost of Hamlet's father, refused to stay dead. Meanwhile on October 5, 1910 the *Tribune* with tongue in cheek helpfully published a list of 220 men who had taken plural wives since 1890, six of them being members of the Twelve. "The list," the *Trib* said, "is steadily growing."

Despite increasingly stiffening opposition, polygamy continued to thrive up through the 1920s, until on April 4, 1931 the church added a new dimension to its campaign to eradicate the practice. In addition to excommunication, which "is the limit of Church jurisdiction," President Heber J. Grant announced that "We have been, and are, willing to give such legal assistance as we legitimately can in the criminal prosecution of such cases."[2]

It was not until June 17, 1933—forty-three years after the original Manifesto—that an *Official Statement* was issued which became known as the "final Manifesto." Then two years later, on March 14, 1935, the Utah legislature passed a bill supporting the

1. Milton R. Merrill, "Reed Smoot: Apostle in Politics," Ph.D. dissertation, Columbia University, 1950. See also Merrill's "Reed Smoot, Apostle-Senator," UHQ, October 1960.
2. MFP 5:292.

complete reversal of pioneer values. Even in the most extreme period of persecution by a carpetbag government prior to the Manifesto—when the church president was driven underground and most high authorities either were on the dodge or in prison—unlawful cohabitation was legally a misdemeanor. The new law, passed by descendants of the persecuted, was:

An Act . . . Making Unlawful Cohabitation a Felony, and Providing That All Persons Except the Defendant Must Testify in Proceedings Thereof.

Perhaps it wasn't a coincidence that the following month the Fundamentalists surfaced from the underground with a monthly periodical, *Truth,* devoted to fervent defense of the Principle. The editor, Joseph W. Musser, filled the columns with speeches and writings of pioneer prophets, and, being the son of a former assistant church historian, he had dug deeply into confidential files for material not intended for the public prints.

Prior to this time, for approximately a half century, those fostering the Principle underground had by and large clung to the belief that despite all official pronouncements to the contrary, they *really* were secret agents on a holy mission during a war with the forces of darkness, and that if exposed they must take their medicine without support of the church.[3] Now, however, the break was clean, battle lines drawn. *Truth* put in cold type what previously had been largely word-of-mouth. It no longer claimed allegiance to the church, asserting that the church had gone astray by rejecting God's law and that authority was held by the Fundamentalists. In issue after issue it presented evidence of plural marriages after the Manifesto with implied church sanction, and it even asserted that the president of the church at the time, Heber J. Grant, was guilty, which, of course, Grant denied.

Truth was such a thorn in the official flesh that there was an attempt in 1944 to get rid of it. Musser was indicted on the charge of publishing an "obscene, lewd, and lascivious" magazine—which the Fundamentalists considered hilarious for a periodical devoted

3. The case of John W. Taylor illustrates this aspect. He accepted entire responsibility for his actions, said nothing of having had what he considered approval, involved no one else. See "Minutes" of meetings of the Twelve, February 28, March 1 and 28, 1911, typescript in author's possession. See also pamphlet, "The Trials for the Membership of John W. Taylor and Matthias F. Cowley," by Fred C. Collier and Robert R. Black (Salt Lake, 1976).

to quotations from pioneer prophets. Evidently the judge saw the irony of the situation, for he threw the case out of the U.S. District Court.

The last great anti-polygamy drive, to date, was the abortive raid on the Fundamentalist colony at Short Creek, which straddled the Utah-Arizona border, on July 26, 1953. Here a few hundred God-seekers scratched out a hardscrabble existence from the desert sand of the red-rock country. Prodded by cattlemen who were taxed to support the Short Creek school, located on the Arizona side, Governor J. Howard Pyle assembled more than a hundred police officers (all but nine of those under his jurisdiction in the entire state), accompanied by newspapermen, cameramen, radio and TV people, and at 4 A.M. descended upon the little community to find the people assembled in the school yard singing hymns. The adults were arrested, their property confiscated, their children taken away and made wards of the state. "Before dawn today the State of Arizona began and now has substantially concluded a momentous police action against insurrection within its own borders," Governor Pyle announced over the radio. "They have arrested almost the entire population of a community dedicated to the production of white slaves," he declared. To "protect the lives and futures of 263 children," under the age of eighteen, the State was "moving at once to seek through the courts" their custody, to protect "the innocent chattels of a lawless commercial undertaking of wicked design and ruthlessly exercised power."

The hyperbole of the raid, the harshness of the treatment of a community that was entirely free of crime or juvenile delinquency, and the violation of civil rights by taking children from their parents because of what they might be taught to think, caused a strongly adverse reaction in the Arizona press. The entire operation was suspected as a diversion to distract public attention from the governor's political problems, and he was savagely ridiculed for the Short Creek fiasco in a series of cartoons by Bud Warner in the Arizona *Free Press*.

In Utah, things were different. In an editorial the day following the raid, the *Deseret News* said:

Law-abiding citizens of Utah and Arizona owe a debt of gratitude to Arizona's Governor Howard Pyle and to his police officers who, Sunday, raided the polygamous settlement at Short Creek and rounded up its leaders for trial. The existence of this community on our border has been an embarrassment to our people and a smudge on the reputations of our two great states. We hope Governor Pyle will make good his pledge to eradicate the illegal practices conducted there "before they become a cancer of a sort that is beyond hope of human repair."

"While I do not share the beliefs of my neighbors," wrote Jonreed Lauritzen, the novelist, to Superior Court Judge Lorna Lockwood, who ruled that the Short Creek children were wards of the state,

I want to testify to you that never in my fifty years experience with people . . . have I seen a more earnest, hard-working, devout, kindly, honest, self-sacrificing, and rigorously moral set of individuals than these of Short Creek. They love their children deeply, and they have worked hard against tremendous handicaps to feed and clothe and shelter and educate them well, and to protect them from vicious and immoral influences. Where else in America would you find dances and entertainments always opened and closed with prayer and decorously conducted? Where else in America would you find people gathered to celebrate or to enjoy a holiday without drunkenness, without necking in parked cars, without smoking, without foul language or lewd jokes, without boisterous or undignified conduct? Where in America will you find a community large as Short Creek which is without divorces, without juvenile delinquency? . . . Nowhere have I seen the moral codes so vigorously enforced as here, and the children so well supervised.[4]

Subsequently the Supreme Court of Utah, in the case of Vera Black, a plural wife of Short Creek living on the Utah side, decided that her eight children were legally "neglected" and should be taken from the parents and placed under the "custody and control" of the Utah State Department of Public Welfare.

The *Deseret News* headlined an editorial on the Black case, "STAMP OUT POLYGAMY."[5]

Separating children from their parents is a heart-breaking and difficult thing to do. The family is the keystone unit of society, and only extreme provocation can justify its dissolution.

4. Lauritzen was a native of Short Creek, and ran a farm there for many years before the town became a refuge for Fundamentalists.
5. January 28, 1956.

But the continued teaching of children to break the law is an extreme provocation. This practice on the part of parents, as much as abandonment or neglect, justifies the state's intervention both for the welfare of the children and of society. . . .

The eminent Mormon author and historian, Juanita Brooks, wrote letters of protest to the *Tribune;* to the justices of the Utah Supreme Court; to the Utah County Welfare Office, which took custody of the Black children; to writer and columnist Frank C. Robertson; and, to the *Deseret News,* she wrote:

I was shocked and saddened by your editorial . . . entitled STAMP OUT POLYGAMY. That the official organ of the Church of Jesus Christ of Latter-day Saints should approve such a basically cruel and wicked thing as the taking of little children and babies from their mother strains the faith of many, many of us. With only one exception, every person with whom I have talked, all members of the Church, feel as I do. . . .

Brethren, this is so deeply wrong that it cannot be carried out to its logical conclusion, at least not in America. . . .

Since the days of negro slavery children have not been torn from parents who loved them and wanted them and provided for them. These are human children, not animals. They are bright, sensitive little people who will compare favorably with your children and mine.

I pray you, see them as children who need their home and mother. In trying to stamp out one evil, let us not commit another so black that it will shame us for ages to come.

Perhaps because of the backlash to the Short Creek affair, there has been an implied truce since that time: The Fundamentalists ceased active proselyting, discontinuing publication of *Truth* and another magazine, *Star of Truth.* Utah authorities in turn ceased active harassment of groups whose members had been excommunicated. This uneasy and unofficial arrangement worked fairly smoothly, all in all. Perhaps it is worthy of note that the church discontinued cutting people off for *polygamy,* as such—now the charge was *bigamy.* Thus *polygamy* no longer existed.

Neat.

But by whatever name, it remained the little man who wasn't there:

> As I was going up the stair,
>   I met a man who wasn't there;
> He wasn't there again today,
>   I wish, I wish he'd go away.[6]

On January 1, 1976 a cloud appeared no bigger than a man's hand. On that date, in California, sex acts between consenting adults became legal. The law had passed despite an impassioned stand by a coterie of Bible-thumping legislators who tried to block it with fulminations about the abominations of Sodom and Gomorrah. Soon after passage, a group called the Coalition of Concerned Christians conducted a statewide drive to repeal the act before it should become law. The San Francisco *Chronicle* reported:

> Churchmen were involved, particularly those in the powerful Church of Jesus Christ of Latter-day Saints and several Fundamentalist creeds.[7]

Despite this, on New Year's day the practice of polygamy was legal in California, which contains more Mormons than Utah. While it was true that the new law did not legalize polygamy as such, it did repeal all penalties for its practice. The marriage ceremony of the Principle was always secret, impossible to prove, and illegal. So the issue always was the relationship, unlawful cohabitation. And cohabiting with more than one consenting adult woman no longer was against the law in California.

Section 132 is still in the *Doctrine and Covenants;* thus a plurality of wives is still part of official doctrine. The practice was discontinued for one reason, and one only: "Inasmuch as laws have been enacted in Congress."

"I wonder what today's Mormons would do if the repeal of sex laws swept away the only reason for not obeying Section 132?" I asked in *Dialogue* (Autumn-Winter, 1971). "Would we, or would we not, embrace the awful responsibilities undertaken by the pioneers?

"While my crystal ball license has expired, I expect that regardless of Section 132 the Saints would put up a ferocious fight against legislation that would result in the right to practice polygamy. My

6. Hughes Mearns, "Antigonish," in *Innocent Merriment,* Franklin Adams, ed. (Garden City Publishing Co. and Blue Ribbon Books, 1945).
7. June 21, 1975.

guess is that if the repeal of sex laws should sweep the country, Utah and a few states of what H. L. Mencken called the Bible Belt would stand firm in clinging to stringent anti-polygamy legislation. And that strange sound you would hear would be John Taylor and other pioneer prophets whirling in their graves."

This hypothesis was subsequently confirmed in Idaho, which passed a law repealing penalties for sex acts between consenting adults, then repealed it, *Playboy* magazine reported, because of pressure from "Mormons and little old ladies in tennis shoes."

Strangely enough, instead of common belief in the Principle unifying the Fundamentalists in a common front against their great enemy, the church, the various groups practicing plural marriage began squabbling over who held the "keys," or authority, and the quarrel became increasingly acrimonious until in the 1970s it exploded into violence. In a power struggle over the "keys" to control of a group in Mexico, Joel LeBaron was murdered in 1972, and his brother, Ervil, convicted of instigating the crime. Two years later Ervil was out of prison and accused of leading an attack on the Fundamentalist community of Los Molinos with firebombs and shotguns, in which two men were killed and nineteen people wounded. Ervil was suspected of being responsible for the mysterious disappearance of Robert Simon of Grantsville, Utah, and for the killing of Grant Vest in San Diego in 1975. Then on May 10, 1977 two women (or men dressed as such) entered the office of Dr. Rulon Allred in Salt Lake, drew pistols, and gunned him down.

Rulon Allred, a naturopathic physician who had delivered some 6,000 babies, was leader of the largest group of Fundamentalists. Shortly before his death he supplied me with an estimate of the size of his own group, giving the figure at 35,000. (Church sources, after his murder, gave the figure of 1,000 to 1,500.)

Ervil LeBaron was suspected of instigating the Allred murder, although at this writing he had not been apprehended.

Anyone who supposed that the Principle was a relic of a past age was in for a rude shock at the arrangements for Allred's funeral. It was held in the auditorium of the Bingham High School, and the house was packed, despite the fact that only people who could afford church displeasure were in attendance. At a previous funeral, of Fundamentalist Ianthus Barlow, several people who attended were called on the carpet and cut off the church. And as people parked their cars at the Bingham auditorium, men were seen busily taking down license plate numbers.

One iconoclast in attendance was a man with two wives who eschewed the power struggle by not belonging to any group at all. "As I watched people coming in I realized there would have been a simple way to settle the hassle," he told me. "All you'd have had to do was to borrow one of those metal-detection devices from the airlines, and you'd find out who had the 'keys.' "

Owen Allred, successor to leadership of the group, conducted the services. Highlights of the ceremony were hymns sung by Rulon's children, one chorus consisting of some twenty sons, the other by a like number of beautiful daughters.

By the time Lillian had become a salty senior citizen, she had lived to see the day when it was unwise, in Utah, to bear witness to "the fulness of the gospel," because that could imply belief in discarded practices. The church not only cut off polygamists, but held the same threat over the heads of those associating with or having sympathy for them. Anyone charged with guilt by association was required to sign a test-oath.[8]

As a living relic of a past age, Lillian received many phone calls. A constant stream of visitors knocked at her door. Writers, scholars, and historians took notes of her memories. But most of those who sought her out were people either living in the Principle or contemplating it.

Lillian gave them no aid or comfort. She pointed out that after growing up in it, not a single one of Father's three dozen children had married into the Principle.[9] And she noted that the prettier the girl, the easier it was for the man to believe in that old-time religion.

At the same time she was proud of her heritage. She never

8. See *Complaint against Ogden Kraut* (Dugway: Pioneer Press, 1972). Kraut was suspected of plural marriage, which he denied. However, he was cut off for refusing to sign the oath.

This loyalty oath requires "sustaining the present day program of the Church." Further: "With respect to the subject of plural marriage, may I say truthfully, wholeheartedly and of my own free will, that ... I do not believe in, nor teach, nor in any way advocate the present day practice of plural marriage."

And just in case someone with loyalty to a dissident sect might sign with crossed fingers, the document in three places identifies the church as being the one "with headquarters at 47 East South Temple Street, Salt Lake City"—which is adequate identification, even though there is no ZIP code.

9. The leader of the largest Fundamentalist sect has a son who is prominent in the Zero Population Growth movement.

apologized for Father, while she held utmost reverence for Mama's dedication to a discredited way of life. Mama had told her that for those entering the Principle there had been a special temple endowment not given to others. Mama had earned the celestial glory. And Lillian cherished the belief that because she was born in the Principle she was one of the chosen few.

Senator Reed Smoot is vindicated. After a searching inquiry conducted by the most skillful inquisitors that immense wealth could buy ... no crime was found against him except his religion. By the vote in the Senate declaring him entitled to his seat in the body, he is completely vindicated.

—DESERET NEWS, February 21, 1907

The Mormons were, in cold fact, systematically opposed ... by their neighbors, by other churches, by rival businesses, and by the national government ... till a typical hotel-room bargain grafted the minority report of the Smoot Investigating Committee on the policy of the Republican Party, and so recognized the importance of the modern Church and ended persecution forever.

—BERNARD DEVOTO, The Centennial of Mormonism"

8

The Great Disturber

AFTER THE FOUR-YEAR CAMPAIGN to unseat Smoot, the Washington *Post* published a cartoon captioned "Smoot's Victory," showing him desperately clinging to an armchair, hands gripping the seat and legs entwined around both the arms and legs of the chair. Another cartoon has him blown heels over head by a bomb labeled "Polygamy Charge," and though his suit is in tatters, collar awry, and shoe soles flapping, he is saying, "Never touched me!"

"For four years turmoil has reigned in Utah," the *Deseret News* stated. "That is enough. Now let us have peace."[1] But Frank J. Cannon, now cast out of the church and a member of the opposition as editor of the *Tribune,* declared that the *News* was guilty of wishful thinking. The "irrepressible conflict" wasn't over, but had merely been brought into national focus by the Smoot investigation. "Smoot and his seat in the Senate are at most a mere incident of

1. February 21, 1907.

108

the great contest here. The issue is between an alien monarchy and this Republic."

"In the hope of correcting misrepresentation," the church issued *An Address* at April conference which denied that "the Church relies on duplicity" and "shuns investigation." It wasn't true that "the Church employs deceptive methods, that she has one doctrine for the Priesthood and another for the people; that she teaches one set of principles to her members in Zion, and another to the world."

This referred to post-Manifesto polygamy which, despite the hysteria it engendered, was after all strictly a religious issue affecting only the Mormons themselves. A much more serious charge was testimony concerning the union of church and state. "These hearings, more than anything else, forced Mormon leaders to come to a decision on church influence in politics," Hansen said, pointing out that Joseph F. Smith's testimony "would have startled Brigham Young," when Smith said church members could reject his counsel as church president with impunity and not be unchurched. "This assertion," Hansen said, "was an affirmation of future policy rather than past practice."[2]

The conference *Address* emphatically denied that "the Church is a commercial rather than a religious institution," that it "dictates to its members," and "aims at absolute domination in temporal affairs."

Temporal advice by church authorities was "counsel and direction," not "the exercise of arbitrary power"; and "both the wisdom of the leaders and the good sense of the people are vindicated in the results achieved."

What would have been equally startling to Brigham Young, who led his people from Illinois to Utah to get away from United States jurisdiction, or to his successor, John Taylor, who went underground the final two and a half years of his life rather than submit to United States tyranny, was the statement that "Neither in mental attitude nor in conduct have we been disloyal to the government."

This assertion of patriotism, Hansen commented, "employed one of the most time-honored uses of history—that of reading the present into the past in order to reshape the future."

The church stood for "the separation of church and state," the

2. Hansen, *Quest for Empire.*

Address declared; "the non-interference of church authority in political matters; and the absolute freedom and independence of the individual in the performance of his political duties."

This "could be interpreted by Gentiles as a Mormon concession," Hansen said; yet actually "it was nothing of the kind." Hansen continued:

> It was, of course, a supreme paradox that the Mormon leaders could apply a theoretical separation of church and state to the very purpose of preventing such a division.

The *Address* was "the same old dry rot," the *Tribune* said, "a defense against the feelings created by its bad faith, broken pledges, defiance of law it doesn't like, and against the inevitable hostility which the treasonable attitude its leaders assume toward the country provokes."

The Salt Lake Ministerial Association called the *Address* "misleading" and claimed the teachings of LDS missionaries "are deceptive." It asserted that "the policy of the Mormon leaders is to keep people in entire subjection to the priesthood" in order "to control political, commercial, and educational conditions in Utah."[3]

In rebuttal B. H. Roberts, known as Utah's Daniel Webster because he could speak as forcefully as he could write, "boldly and brazenly, in the presence of 8,000 wildly applauding Mormons," the *Trib* reported, gave answer at the Relief Society conference, June 9.[4] Roberts' *Answer*, however, being tailored to a highly selective audience, did little except reinforce the convictions of those who needed it least. The charges of the Ministerial Association kept the subject of church and state hot on a national level; and for the next few years, as trust-busting and muckraking became the political and literary fevers of the times, Mormonism was the prime whipping-boy.

In 1909 Reed Smoot broadened his political base by acquiring control of the Salt Lake *Herald,* in association with several prominent men including Governor William H. Spry and the mining executive, D. C. Jackling. The paper became the *Herald-Republican,* which the *Tribune* contemptuously called the "Smoot organ"

3. June 4, 1907.
4. "Recent Discussion of Mormon Affairs; Answer to the Ministerial Association Review," pamphlet (Salt Lake, 1907).

thereafter. "Fulsome praise of Senator Smoot," the *Trib* noted, "appears almost daily."[5]

The political campaign of 1910 was "one of the most bitter," the *Herald* declared, "in Utah history."[6] Frank J. Cannon agreed that the Smoot case had "divided the state again into the old factions" and "involved it in the old war from which it had been rescued."

The Mormons instituted a determined boycott against all Gentiles, and "Thou shalt not support God's enemies" became a renewed commandment of the Prophet. Wherever a Gentile was employed in any Mormon institution, he was discharged. . . . Teachers in the Church would exclaim with horror if they heard that a Mormon family was employing a Gentile physician; and more than one Mormon litigant was advised that he not only "sinned against the work of God," but endangered the success of his law suit, by retaining a Gentile lawyer.[7]

Frank J. Cannon left the *Tribune* for greener pastures in Denver; but with the three-cornered dog-fight between the [Gentile] American, [pro-church] Republican, and [independent] Democratic parties, he arrived in Salt Lake to campaign, charging at an American rally that "The Mormon church is still the chief political power in this State."

When once we break the combine between the prophets and politicians of the church and the interests of the politicians in Washington, all the destiny to which we have a right as American citizens to aspire, is within our grasp.[8]

Politics made strange bedfellows. B. H. Roberts, the keynote speaker at the Democratic rally, made a "blistering" attack on Reed Smoot, the *Tribune* reported, expressing "the hope that the day is coming in Utah when no man could assume by reason of his ecclesiastical eminence to be a political dictator." Smoot's *Herald* claimed the senator was "defamed" by Roberts, whose speech "showed an animosity and bitterness toward Utah's senior senator never before equaled in the history of the state." As for the opposi-

5. J. Cecil Alter, *Early Utah Journalism* (Salt Lake: Utah State Historical Society, 1938).
6. November 9.
7. *Under the Prophet in Utah*.
8. *Tribune*, October 23, 1910.

tion, "The issue at the polls," the Smoot organ declared, was "between the Republican party and the *Tribune* party. . . . There can be no other issue."

Although Republicans were victorious at the polls, this was due to "interference of the Mormon priesthood in the election," the *Trib* charged. "On the night before the election the Mormon Democrats were visited by emissaries of the church and told that it was the will of the Lord that they vote the church Republican ticket."

The *Herald* retorted that "The Salt Lake *Tribune* is the great disturber in Utah. There can be no peace here until that influence is eliminated."

It was during this campaign that the *Tribune* rattled the skeleton in the closet by publication of its famous list of 220 men who had taken wives since the Manifesto. It wasn't a coincidence that eastern magazines joined the fray with hostile articles regarding polygamy, church wealth, and the union of church and state. Richard Barry published three pieces in *Pearson's,* two articles by Burton J. Hendricks were featured in *McClure's,* Alfred Henry Lewis lambasted the church with two tirades in *Cosmopolitan,* and Frank J. Cannon unleashed the big guns in eight issues of *Everybody's.*

Then, a month after the 1910 elections, on December 12, the *Herald* revealed that the magazine campaign had been planned and subsidized by the *Trib,* in cooperation with Fred T. Dubois, former senator from Idaho. Dubois had visited the magazine editors and made personal arrangements for publication. Meanwhile, the *Herald* reported, "Collectors in behalf of the Salt Lake *Tribune* are in New York, prior to a visit to other eastern cities to collect funds for a new fight on Utah and her people."

Dubois was a notorious Mormon-eater who had built his political career on the harassment of Idaho Saints. During the Smoot hearings he had displayed strong antipathy as a member of the Senate committee.

Some of the subsidized articles were so extreme, in particular those of Alfred Henry Lewis in *Cosmopolitan,* "that the writer defeated his own ends," Roberts commented in the *Comprehensive History of the Church,* "for they brought the author and the publisher more censure than praise." However, Frank J. Cannon's series in *Everybody's*—which became the book, *Under the Prophet in Utah*—was another matter. To the national audience, the author's prominence as a former senator from Utah, his association with his father, which allowed him access to the inner workings of the church hierarchy, gave authenticity to his assessment of Mormonism, which covered the spectrum from the resurgence of secret polygamy to church domination of political, financial, business, and commercial affairs.

Within Zion, however, it was an entirely different matter. Cannon's personal vendetta against President Joseph F. Smith caused total rejection of his book by the Saints, for the prophet, seer, and revelator is above criticism among his own people.[9] Cannon had invited his own cutting-off by two editorials in the *Tribune* severely critical of Joseph F. Smith, and by having written the only speech delivered in Washington by Utah's Gentile senator, Thomas Kearns, an attack on the church far too skillfully polished to have originated with the inarticulate senator.[10]

While the Mormons have no collection plate, Cannon detailed the financial drain of church membership. In addition to the tithe, "A score of 'donations' have been added." He listed Stake Tabernacle Donation, Ward Meeting-House Donation, Fast Day Donation, Relief Society Donation, Light and Heat Donation, Missionary Donation, Priesthood Quorum Missionary Donation, Quorum Dues, Nickel Sunday, Dime Tuesday, Nickel Friday, Religious Class Donations, Amusement Hall Donations, Temple Donations, and, "Should a need arise, . . . a special donation is collected to meet it."[11]

Cannon accused Joseph F. Smith of cutting men off the church for opposing him in business dealings.[12] He said that Smith "gives no accounting" of tithes, "is able to use this sum, in bulk, at any given point, with a weight of financial pressure that would over-

9. *Under the Prophet in Utah* was relegated to a position alongside John C. Bennett's *History of the Saints* (1842). Bennett, former assistant president of the church, broke with Joseph Smith at Nauvoo. Despite being almost unique in disclosing high-level workings of the church by insiders, the two books remain in a curious category among Mormon historians: it is necessary to know their contents, but verboten to quote their "sensitive" materials.

10. See CHC, 6:408. The *Tribune* editorials were January 22 and February 1, 1905.

11. While this list no longer is accurate, it is typical of modern offerings. An important contribution which has been added is for support of the church welfare program.

12. An example was Charles A. Smurthwaite. See SI, 4:78.

balance any other single power in the community" and "backs this financial power with his control of legislation" favorable to church monopolies. By announcing the "will of God," he "largely controls the 'labor troubles' of the State," and "He can influence judges, officers of the law, and all the agents of local government by his power as political 'Boss.' " Smith was, Cannon asserted, "at once the modern 'money king,' the absolute political Czar, the social despot, and the infallible Pope of his 'Kingdom.' "[13]

B. H. Roberts refuted the magazine campaign with a statement presented by the First Presidency at April conference, 1911. "Each head of the church, in his turn, has been libeled, lampooned, caricatured, and vilified," the rebuttal stated. It was not strange that Joseph F. Smith should in turn be attacked; yet in view of the fact that the falsehoods "have been repeatedly refuted and exploded, it is somewhat surprising that the old, stale, and shattered fabrications are raked up and used anew." They were "utterly false and without foundation."

As for plural marriage and political domination, the statement said flatly that polygamy had ended with the Manifesto of 1890, and that church authorities "never assumed to dictate to members politically." Those accusing the church of political domination were generally "those who have sought for that influence in their own behalf and are enraged because they could not obtain it."

This official statement was effective in buttressing the faith of the Utah Saints, but of negligible influence in the outside world. The muckraking campaign seriously damaged the church image, not only in America but in the missions throughout the world. In England, where in an earlier day Wilford Woodruff had personally converted thousands, the entire mission baptized only 363 new members in 1912, when "Anti-Mormon rallies turned to violence." Mobs stoned LDS chapels, tarred and feathered a missionary and ran others out of town. On the continent, Germany expelled Mormon elders.[14]

---

13. These charges were an updated reprise of those made by Senator Kearns in his only speech to the Senate, indicating both were written by the same person. Roberts said the Kearns speech "was not his in fact, either in its conception or in its polished composition," of which Kearns "was utterly incapable" (CHC, 6:408).

14. James A. Allen and Glen M. Leonard, *The Story of the Latter-day Saints* (Salt Lake: Deseret, 1976).

Fortunately, during this hectic period B. H. Roberts was performing a most effective service for the church image by telling the Mormon story in a national magazine, *Americana.* When the monthly had published an attack on the Book of Mormon, Roberts had requested space for reply, and did it so well that the periodical invited him to write a short history of the church. Except for Bancroft's *History of Utah,* no sympathetic story of the Mormons existed in the outside world; this account appeared some two decades previously—and Bancroft had been a Gentile. After Roberts explained the scope of the project to the editors, his "short history" ran for six years in the *Americana,* 1909–15, averaging more than forty pages an issue.[15]

During the muckraking campaign the Tabernacle Choir played an effective role as goodwill ambassador by accepting an invitation to sing at the American Land and Irrigation Exposition at New York City in 1911. The trip grew into a tour of twenty-five cities during which some four dozen concerts merited good notices which "helped remold the popular image of the Latter-day Saints." The choir sang for ten days at Madison Square Garden and in Washington gave a concert for President William Howard Taft and guests.[16]

Friendship is a two-way street. If the "world" began to understand the Mormons, by the same token the attitude of the Saints was changing toward the Gentiles. The United States government no longer was considered the arch-enemy of the church, and by the time of the Great War—the war to end wars—there was a surge of patriotism as Utah troops joined in the fight to "make the world safe for democracy." The Armistice brought not only peace between Germany and the Allies, but ushered in an era of good will between Utah and the outside world.

The broadening outlook is underlined by the fact that at the time of the Armistice Utah's governor was a Jew, Simon Bamberger, in a state whose voters were 75 percent Mormon. Moreover, it had been none other than B. H. Roberts who had nominated him at the state Democratic convention.

15. Roberts subsequently revised and updated the material, which was issued in six volumes as the *Comprehensive History of the Church* in 1930, the church's Centennial year.
16. Allen and Leonard.

This time also saw the turning point in the climate between the Salt Lake *Tribune* and the Saints.[17] In 1918 death took the leaders of the antagonists, Thomas Kearns of the *Tribune* and Joseph F. Smith of the church. The change of attitude was indicated by the respectful obituary of Smith in the *Trib* and of Kearns in the *Deseret News*.

However, the *Tribune* remained the watchdog, the voice of dissent to such church-sponsored legislation as the law of 1921 prohibiting the sale of cigarettes in Utah and the smoking of them in public places. The *Tribune* called this legal imposition of Mormon morality on the entire populace a "monumental mistake," and feared that it was the camel's nose under the tent: "It is even hinted that in the near future an attempt will be made to prohibit all forms of amusement on Sunday," it warned on March 13. During the next two years the *Trib* continued to ridicule the attempt to legislate citizens into heaven. Overzealous enforcement, which saw prominent citizens arrested for bootlegging cigarettes or smoking in public aroused grass-roots resentment within the state and caused the national press to deride Utah's blue laws. As a result, the *Tribune*'s campaign saw the law modified in 1923, despite church opposition.

But like the apostle Paul, the *Tribune* was on the road to Damascus, and of those who blazed the trail none did more than Flash Wilson and Earl J. Glade.

On November 22, 1920 the *Deseret News* began a program of wireless news flashes, using homemade broadcasting apparatus cobbled together by Herman C. Wilson, International News Service man at the paper. His audience was the Wireless Club, a hundred or so hams scattered from Washington to New Mexico, who were to transcribe the messages and post news bulletins for the public. Wilson, who inevitably became "Flash," was proud of his station, whose power was one kilowatt. It was a cloud no bigger than a man's hand in the sky of the newspaper world—instant news, which didn't need presses, paper, or ink, and which came free. Ironically, the newspapers themselves fostered this fox in their bosoms.

The *Deseret News* entered the field of regular radio broadcast-

17. "If one year were to be singled out as the most eventful and significant in the 100-year history of the Salt Lake *Tribune*," O. N. Malmquist stated, "1918 would be a formidable contender." See *The First 100 Years. A History of the Salt Lake Tribune, 1871–1971* (Salt Lake: Utah State Historical Society, 1971).

ing two years later with a 500-watt station, KZN. This was just five months after the first commercial broadcasting station of the west, KQL of Los Angeles, began operations.

Flash Wilson himself opened the new era of news transmission from a tin shack atop the *Deseret News* building, with equipment resembling a soap box festooned with tin cans. "Hello. Hello. Hello," he said into the mike. "This is KZN. KZN, the *Deseret News,* Salt Lake City, calling. Greetings! The *Deseret News* sends greetings to all of you far and wide!" Such were the first historic words over the air to the Intermountain West. The subsequent torrent have, mercifully, largely vanished like snow upon the desert's dusty face.

At first the station broadcast thirty minutes a day, which increased with demand to an hour and a half. Programs consisted of talks by prominent people, sports results, weather reports, and amateur entertainment. The commercial hadn't been invented. Nobody got paid for being on the radio; it was just a hobby for those involved, and the *News* maintained the station as a public service. When the paper acquired a new manager, B. F. Grant, in 1924, he decided that the station was an unnecessary expense and sold KZN to John N. Cope and his father.

The Copes had some crazy ideas about radio. They believed broadcasting would become big business, that people actually would pay money for advertising on the air, that, instead of a novelty, radio would become an important medium of information and entertainment. When they ranted in this manner, smart businessmen just smiled politely.

One man who took it seriously was Earl J. Glade, assistant professor of business administration at the University of Utah and on the staff of the Gillham Advertising Agency. Glade put his money where his mouth was, taking the part-time job of station manager and for eighteen months preaching the gospel of radio while contributing his monthly pay check from the university to the cause. His wife and four children didn't starve, though Glade often walked home at night, after sweeping out the station, because he didn't have streetcar fare. For two years his wife played the piano at the studio, as "Beverly Snow," at no salary.

Glade took his pay in air time. With his "Old Town Crier" he was literally singing for his supper. But there were few buyers.

Merchants considered Glade a wide-eyed visionary when he tried to convince them that a few words spoken on the breeze and then gone forever, would sell merchandise. And the field was crowded. Stations were springing up like weeds, withering, dying. In 1924 there were more than eleven hundred stations competing; much more money was being lost than made in radio. It was a game for promoters and gamblers, while hard-headed businessmen shied away.

The first company ever to buy time on the air in the Intermountain West was the Salt Lake Knitting Company, church-owned. It laid sixty whole dollars on the line for an hour's show, which paid for not only air time but talent. The second company to take the gamble was the J. G. McDonald Chocolate Company; the third was another church enterprise, the Utah Woolen Mills. As the word spread with agonizing slowness, Glade found the going tough.

The station could afford just two microphones, one at the studio and the other on location for outside events. There really was need for a third one, because rushing the field mike from one event to another presented problems. There was the night when Utah's governor, Charles R. Mabey, was broadcasting from the Salt Lake Theater as the time approached for another program. Politicians were not, as yet, accustomed to radio's tyranny of the clock. Mabey was in high gear, the theater audience in the palm of his hand, when time ran out. The immediate problem for John Cope, waiting in the wings, was to get that microphone for the other program. Mabey completed an anecdote and paused as the theater burst into applause. As the governor began pouring a glass of water, Cope hurried onstage, grabbed the mike from the lectern, and ran off with it.

It is impossible to ascertain if this incident was a factor in Mabey's subsequent defeat at the polls.

Glade needed money for better equipment and studio facilities. Flash Wilson's homemade transmitter was no more adequate than was the 20-by-20 tin box atop the *News* building. Glade set out to raise capital to put the station on a sound commercial basis. He laid the proposition before the presiding bishopric of the church, which normally would handle temporal affairs. Bishop Sylvester

Q. Cannon was impressed with the potential of radio, but not to the extent of laying cash on the line. Glade went elsewhere.

The first businessman to invest was an early advertiser, Briant S. Stringham, president of the Utah Woolen Mills. He knew that radio sold his product and wanted in on the ground floor. He helped Glade to interest other businessmen. Then came the day when Glade came out of the Kearns building walking on air and clutching a check for $25,000 from John F. Fitzpatrick, publisher of the Salt Lake *Tribune*.

With this investment the station turned the corner. When the church learned that its old enemy was backing radio, the brethren sat up and took notice. The church came in with money and found itself in joint partnership.

It is hardly a coincidence that from that day, the *Tribune* ceased lambasting the church. This business association was the road to Damascus for the *Trib*. It marked, some said, the paper's "baptism."

Subsequently, KZN became KSL, a 50,000-watt station on a cleared national channel, fifty times more powerful than any competitor in the Intermountain territory, and so solidly a success that merchants who had fobbed off Glade in his time of want now were queued up begging for time, with none available. The KSL signal was so powerful that a wire fence in Kansas picked up its signal, Glade stated in a broadcast, while a cookstove also became a receiver. A Canadian postmaster made affidavit that the Tabernacle Choir sang at a spot deep in the forest, evidently due to a mineral deposit. Glade himself became so popular that he left KSL to serve twelve years as mayor of Salt Lake City, then subsequently returned to the station.

With radio competition, the number of metropolitan dailies began to shrink. During the 1940s people began seriously questioning whether it was possible for Salt Lake to support two papers. Other cities of comparable size, or even larger, had only one. Would it be the *News* or the *Trib* to go under? During the period after World War II the Main Street scoop was that the *News* would be scuttled; both circulation and advertising had steadily dwindled. The *Trib* now was dominant. Radio had changed the previous advantage of an afternoon paper, particularly in the West, where news from New York, Washington, and Europe happened hours before the sun reached the same point in the western sky. But with radio furnishing spot news, the public favored the morning *Tribune* for its perspective and overall summary. The *News,* said the Main Street experts, was doomed.

Then in 1947, the centennial year of the pioneers' arrival in the Salt Lake valley, the church made a high-level decision and things began to happen. The *News* made a deal with the Los Angeles *Times* to buy an Oregon paper mill. Assured of an adequate supply of newsprint, still short following the war, the *News* launched an aggressive expansion campaign, adding new features and a big midweek edition, improving coverage, and printing a Sunday edition for the first time since shortly after the Civil War.

Commenting on gains in advertising and circulation, "How can they help it?" a reporter for the Provo *Herald* said to Joe Budro at the height of the campaign. "They're giving away a house and lot with a six-month subscription."

As the *Deseret News* entered 1950, its centennial year, it employed 550 workers and consumed 50 gallons of ink a day. Its job press had printed and bound 150,000 hard-cover books and 1 million paperbacks during the previous year, together with 3 million magazines. Things looked rosy.

At this time it became apparent that as the *News* expanded the *Trib* shrank. In an all-out circulation war, one of the two would have to close up shop. With the resources of the church behind it, the loser certainly wouldn't be the *Deseret News.*

In appreciation of this factor, the church decided that it wouldn't be good policy to have only one paper in Salt Lake, whether it be Mormon or Gentile. Utah needed an independent viewpoint just as the Mormons needed the voice of the church. And so out of this situation came one of the strangest alliances of record. The rival papers combined printing operations, circulation departments, and advertising staff. Only the editorial personnel were separate. As part of the deal, the *News* scuttled its Sunday edition.

Back in the days when the *Tribune* and the *Deseret News* were hurling thunderbolts at each other, no one in his wildest dreams could have envisioned that they would end up married, or, at least, be sleeping together.

Yet lest it be supposed that the church henceforth was without gadflies, be it said that the void left by the baptism of the *Trib* was quickly filled by the busy underground press of the Salt Lake *samizdat*, whose output is rivaled only by that of Russia.

9

Centennial

FOR THOSE of his generation, the day had to bring memories. On this bright Sunday morning, April 6, 1930, the church was one hundred years old. During the past year the Centennial Celebration Committee had been making plans to observe the historic date in an appropriate and memorable manner. Tens of thousands had gathered at Salt Lake for the Centennial conference. Eight thousand of them had had sufficient rank or connections to secure tickets and now had filled the tabernacle to capacity. And many more stood shoulder to shoulder within the walls of Temple Square to hear the services over the loudspeakers. Throughout the city visitors sat by radios in the living rooms of friends; it was traditional not to pay a hotel bill at conference time.

Matthias F. Cowley sat alone, with his memories. The phone was silent. He had no visitors. None wished to remind him that, except for circumstance, he would be sitting in the tabernacle among the dignitaries on the front row of the rostrum.

The previous evening he had walked to Temple Square, unrecognized in the darkness, to join the crowd awaiting the floodlighting of the temple, which would commemorate this week. The

Westinghouse Company had presented the church with a 10,000-watt bulb which, with other lights, would drench the historic edifice with 52,000 candlepower of illumination.

The chatter of the crowd ceased as the lights came on. Then after a moment of silence there was a gasp of awe and wonder. For Cowley, the experience was particularly poignant. He hadn't been inside the temple since his trial there, nineteen years ago.

The Centennial conference would continue for four days. At the opening session, the lower floor of the tabernacle was filled with representatives of the various priesthood quorums, seated in order of rank. Their wives and families filled the gallery. The general authorities sat upon a temporary stage, which covered the permanent rostrum and which had been constructed for the performance of a pageant, "Message of the Ages," to be given each evening of the conference and for as long as public interest required.[1]

A feature of the conference would be the announcement by B. H. Roberts of the publication of his monumental *Comprehensive History of the Church*. Five volumes were completed, and the final one would be ready before the end of the Centennial year.

The first session would open with "A Message from the First Presidency," broadcast to the Saints and to the world. As a climax to this session, the congregation would join in the sacred "Hosanna" shout of joy, accompanied by the waving of white handkerchiefs.

No one was alive who had witnessed the organization of the church, with six members, in the home of Peter Whitmer at Fayette, New York. But Cowley was among the graying generation who recalled the great Jubilee conference of 1880 in celebration of the church's fiftieth birthday. At that time the Saints were uplifted by its theme of generosity, brotherhood, repentance, the canceling of old scores, and forgiveness of debts.

The situation in 1880 was curiously parallel to that of 1930: hard times. The Jubilee conference was attended by people whose crops had failed the previous summer and whose livestock had turned tail to the blizzards of the succeeding winter and perished. The Saints then were ridden by misfortune and unable to pay debts. The Centennial conference was being held amid the creeping paralysis of fear following the stock market crash the previous fall. It wasn't a panic, the White House had tried to reassure the nation,

1. Its popularity kept the show running a month.

merely a depression; and that word had come to mean something far worse. Credit had been easy. People were rich with paper profits when the crash blew the paper away and left the hard rock of debt. Money was tight. Skilled labor walked the streets and stood in breadlines as wheels stopped turning. Every freight train carried hundreds of men looking for something that couldn't be found. In Utah men were glad to find work on farms for 50¢ a day and keep.

Sitting by the radio, Cowley wondered what the church would do to relieve distress, bolster morale, and rally the Saints, as President John Taylor had done in 1880.

"On the fiftieth year in former times, among the ancients," John Taylor said, "they had what was termed a year of jubilee. Slaves were liberated. People who were in debt were forgiven their indebtedness—that is, the poor, the needy and the distressed." And this, he said, would be the theme of the Jubilee conference.

It was 10 A.M. Cowley's radio brought into his living room the hymn, "We Thank Thee, O God, for a Prophet," sung by congregation and choir. The Centennial conference had begun. After prayer by the presiding patriarch, Hyrum G. Smith, and another hymn, the high-pitched but resonant voice of President Heber J. Grant read the Centennial Message. With the first vision of Joseph Smith, "the greatest gospel dispensation of all time was ushered in," Grant said, which, "illuminating the minds of men, increasing intelligence and knowledge," had culminated in "the Miracle Century of the ages."

The increase of scientific knowledge, invention, industrial development; the harnessing of the forces of the universe and adapting them to the comfort and convenience of man, have reached a degree of perfection not dreamed of by people who lived when the past century was ushered in.

In 1880 John Taylor had talked of the Perpetual Emigrating Fund, which furnished passage to converts in foreign lands to gather in Zion, an obligation they were expected to repay subsequently.

It occurred to me that we ought to do something, as they did in former times, to relieve those that are oppressed with debt, to assist those that are needy, to break the yoke off those that may feel themselves crowded upon, and to make it a time of general rejoicing.

Total debt to the P. E. Fund was $1,604,000. Taylor offered to cancel half this sum, to wipe the slate clean for "those who are poor and that are struggling with difficulties in life." The remaining half would still be due and payable by those financially secure. "For in former times they did not release the rich, it was the poor," he said. "The rich can always take care of themselves." Then he added: "That is, so far as this world is concerned. I do not know how it will be about the next." The congregation burst into laughter.

"In 1830 Abraham Lincoln attained his majority," Heber J. Grant said over the radio. "He was still pursuing his studies by the light of a tallow dip."

Since that time our system of education has undergone a miraculous change. The log or little brick schoolhouse of a century ago has been supplanted by temples of learning, in which our children enjoy conveniences and comforts that the wealth of kingdoms could not, at that time, have provided. They have maps of the world before them, books treating all known subjects, teachers better informed upon the subjects taught, heat provided; and when they require light they touch a button and the electric current does the rest.

A century ago, men harvested with a scythe, women carded and spun the wool, then wove the fabric for the family's clothing. To-day machines did the work. The cards, spinning wheel, and loom "are now to be seen only as heirlooms or sacredly cherished souvenirs."

At the Jubilee conference, John Taylor reported that $151,798 was owed the church on the tithing account. As with the P. E. Fund, half of this debt would be canceled by wiping the slate clean for the poor.

"Another thing," Taylor said, "we have had a great scarcity of water the last year and consequently short crops." Then with the severe winter, "some people have lost, perhaps, their last cow."

Now, we propose to raise one thousand head of cows—not old cows that do not give any milk; nor any one-teated cows—but good milk cows, and have them distributed among those who may be destitute.

There also would be five thousand head of "healthy sheep" appropriated "for the relief of the deserving poor."

"Looking backward to the organization of the Church," Heber

J. Grant said from the viewpoint of 1930, "and following its history through persecution, poverty, and distress, can it be denied that a great and marvelous work has been accomplished, that the promises of the Lord have been fulfilled, and His power to accomplish that to which He sets His hand to do, manifested?"

In addition to church measures to relieve want in 1880, John Taylor called upon commercial businesses to embrace the spirit of the Jubilee.

We invite Zion's Co-operative Mercantile Institution as the parent; and all other co-operative institutions as the children; and our brethren who are engaged in profitable railroad, banking, mercantile, manufacturing or other remunerative enterprises, to extend a helping hand. Free the worthy debt-bound brother if you can. Let there be no rich among us from whose tables fall only crumbs to feed a wounded Lazarus.

Heber J. Grant said, "The mountain of the Lord's house has been established in the top of the mountains, and people from all nations have flown unto it."

Through the blessings of the Lord upon their labors the desert has been subdued and made to blossom as the rose. . . . Many thousands have been brought from the poverty and distress of the old world to this blessed land of Joseph, to become wealthy and be happy as they have participated in the blessings which the Lord our God has pronounced upon it.

At the Jubilee conference, John Taylor reported that through the efforts of the women in the Relief Society, a total of 34,761 bushels of wheat had been stored for a time of want.

I spoke to Sister Eliza R. Snow, who is president of the Relief Society, and asked her what her feelings would be, and that of her sisters, in relation to the distribution of their wheat, for those who are in need of seed, letting the people have it as a loan, for which the bishops should become responsible and see that it is returned after harvest. She replied that it would meet her entire approbation.

When someone in the audience asked, "Is it to be loaned without interest?" Taylor replied, "Why, of course it is. We do not want any nonsense of that kind. It is a time of Jubilee."

In 1930 "Possibly no other human agency has greater influence upon civilization and the development of the people of the world than that which provides quick and easy transportation," Heber J. Grant said.

By it individuals, communities, and nations come to know each other better, exchange of commodities is made possible, and the commerce of the world is maintained.

John Taylor had taken an entirely different viewpoint of civilization in 1880. In outlying Mormon colonies, where the Saints were trying "to come as near to the United Order as they could—that is, to be united," Taylor said, a visitor "did not see a man drunk, he did not hear a man swear, neither did he see any person use tea or coffee." In contrast was the "licentious course exhibited around us here," in the very heart of Zion; and, he thundered, "It is this damned infernal 'civilization' that has introduced these infamies into our midst. Let us purge ourselves from them, and not mix up with their ungodly doings."

Excuse me for the remarks, but they are . . . both damned and infernal. . . . I do not care who sustains them, whether governors, judges, priests, or whatever they may be. . . . These crimes are not original with us; they are brought here to try to corrupt and enslave and debase and pollute us.

Progress and achievement was the theme of the message to the people at the Centennial conference. "For silver," Heber J. Grant said, "the Lord has given us gold, which has become the basis of exchange throughout the civilized world; while iron takes the place of wood and stone in construction."

By the application of scientific methods, which have been revealed during the past century, the profession of medicine and surgery has brought to the people of the world relief from the most dreaded diseases, which devastated communities and at times threatened the very existence of mankind.

At the Jubilee conference, John Taylor stressed brotherhood and the Golden Rule.

It is no more harm for private people to forgive one another than for public ones. If you find people owing you who are distressed, [and] if you will go to work and try to relieve them . . . God will relieve you when you get into difficulties. I will tell you that in the name of the Lord.

Let us act on a kind, generous, brotherly principle, doing good one to another and carrying out the principles of the everlasting gospel in our lives.

Heber J. Grant pointed to the accomplishments during the century. "In His sermon on the Mount, the Master declares that a tree is known by the fruit which it produces," he said.

We do not gather grapes from thorns nor figs from thistles. A bitter fountain cannot bring forth good water, nor does a good fountain bring forth bitter water. By this unchangeable law we ask the world to judge the accomplishments of the Church during the past century. . . .

With the present momentum with which the people of the world are moving forward in the determination of truth in every field of human endeavor, the outlook for the future passes beyond the vision of human comprehension.

At the Jubilee conference, John Taylor reminded the people to "reflect upon our weaknesses, our infirmities, our follies and our foibles."

We want among ourselves to learn strictly the principles of honesty, to have and maintain honest dealings one with another and be true to our word, and let our word be our bond. And never mind so much about litigation. I do not know that I ever sued a man in my life, and I do not think that I ever shall. I am not fond enough of law, or money either, to do it. . . .

The Lord has given unto us our various courts—Bishops' Courts, High Councils, etc.—and it is expected that the Saints will adjust any matters of difficulty or dispute that may arise among them before these courts, and that they do not go to law before the ungodly. And if any do so, I will promise them, in the name of the Lord God of Israel, that they will be destroyed by the ungodly.

"Undoubtedly the greatest miracle of the century," Heber J. Grant said, "is the accomplishment by which the human voice, with the personality of the speaker, may be indefinitely preserved and reproduced."

128

Whether uttered in the frozen arctics, or from the jungles of the tropics, without visible means of conduct the human voice instantly circles the earth, thus overcoming the hitherto insurmountable barrier of both time and space.

Contemplating these accomplishments of the past century . . . we are led to exclaim:

Great and marvelous are thy ways, O Lord!
From eternity to eternity Thou art the same!
Thy purposes fail not, neither are there any who can stay Thy hand!

John Taylor saw the hope of mankind in the human heart. "If we take care of one another," he said, "God will take care of us."

And he will deliver us and stretch out his hand in our behalf, and we will be his people, and he shall be our God. And we will treat one another as we wish to be treated by one another, and then we are prepared to receive blessings from his hands.

In closing, Heber J. Grant quoted Scripture regarding the millennial reign, and exhorted the Saints "to put their houses in order, that they may be prepared for that which is to come."

Refrain from evil; do that which is good. Visit the sick, comfort those who are in sorrow, clothe the naked, feed the hungry, care for the widow and the fatherless. Observe the laws of health which the Lord has revealed. Pay your tithes and offerings, and the Lord will open the windows of heaven and pour out blessings until there shall not be room to contain them.

Matthias F. Cowley leaned forward in his chair and snapped off the radio, then sat awhile with his thoughts. The contrast between the pioneer and the modern attitudes was more than merely a nostalgic memory for him. As the door swung shut on principles of an earlier day, he and his fellow apostle, John W. Taylor, were caught in the hinge. They had stepped down from the Quorum of the Twelve in order that Reed Smoot should retain his seat in the United States Senate.

That was in 1905. By 1911 the old order was so firmly rejected that John W. Taylor was unchurched for taking a plural wife. A month later Cowley received a summons to appear before the

Council of the Twelve "to answer complaints against you of marrying wives yourself and of giving plural wives to others."[2]

At the hearing, the quorum president, Francis M. Lyman, charged that "Brother Cowley is more responsible" for the underground persistence of polygamy "than any other man in the church," and that "no man did more toward getting Presidents of Stakes and Presidents of Missions to enter polygamous marriages."

"The report is that he said you should not talk with Brother Lyman or with Brother Joseph F. Smith," Lyman said, "as I was opposed to [it,] and President Smith did not want to know anything about it." Lyman was convinced that from Canada to Mexico Cowley "has been effecting plural marriages among the people and has done a great deal of harm in this respect." In particular, Lyman wanted to know "every case that he has been connected with, and if he had authority, where he got that authority."

Cowley testified that the first plural ceremony he performed after the 1890 Manifesto was in 1898, the couple being "sent to me by President Cannon; and all the authority I exercised on that occasion came from President George Q. Cannon," counselor in the First Presidency. "President Cannon told me he had the authority from President Woodruff, and Brother Joseph F. Smith told me on two occasions that Brother Cannon had the authority and [that] Brother Woodruff didn't want to be known in it."[3]

Marriages he had subsequently performed, Cowley said, had been by this same authority.

Cowley testified that he had recently had two conversations with President Joseph F. Smith,[4] "and he said if you are free of these later offences, that is all we want to know." This had reference to plural marriages after the second manifesto, of 1904.

As to this, Cowley said, "I have done nothing since 1906, nor taken a plural wife myself. I married my last wife in Canada in the summer of 1905."

The quorum members quite obviously were skeptical. When they asked who performed the marriage ceremony, Cowley said he was "under solemn covenant binding me not to tell." He was

2. From minutes of meeting. Typescript. See also pamphlet, "Trials for the Membership of John W. Taylor and Matthias F. Cowley" (Salt Lake: Fred C. Collier and Robert R. Black, 1976).

3. Smith was second counselor in the First Presidency.

4. At the time of Cowley's trial in 1911, Smith was president of the church.

then asked if he would lie to protect others. He said that he had always been true to the work, the brethren, and himself. However, "We have always been taught that when the brethren are in a tight place that it would not be amiss to lie to help them out."[5]

He then was asked another searching question, whether it was considered permissible with late marriages "to date these things back before the manifesto?" Yes, Cowley admitted, "I believed it was."

Thus, the official records of plural marriages were suspect.

"I want you to know that I am not rebellious and never have been; and if I have erred it has been because of these circumstances and the example of my brethren," Cowley said in conclusion. "I would rather die than be cut off from the church."

The following day the Council of the Twelve voted to disfellowship Matthias F. Cowley, "for insubordination to the government and discipline of the Church."

That hearing had been nineteen years ago; but it seemed as yesterday. Cowley arose from his chair beside the radio, put on coat and hat, and went outside. The streets of Salt Lake were almost deserted. Stores were closed, virtually everyone either attending conference or listening to the Centennial services on the radio. He enjoyed the solitude; he'd never become inured to a gaze shifting to avoid recognition; it still hurt to be pointed out, with the whisper, "he was handled."

It was 1936, six years later, when the church began its Welfare Plan; and on April 3 of that year Matthias F. Cowley signed a public statement, confessing he had "been deceived"; and now, "humbled and with a contrite spirit," he asked forgiveness.

"We rejoice in the spirit of humble confession and repentance," the First Presidency replied. "We welcome you into full membership and fellowship in the Church."

Once more he stood before congregations. Once more people were eager to shake his hand and greet him on the street.

It had been a long road.

---

5. This, perhaps, explains his denial of having performed the marriage ceremony for John W. Taylor and Ellen Sandberg. "This is new to me," he told the quorum members. "I don't know anything about the Sandberg girl."

During the 1880's the Mormon Church was stripped of almost all of its property in its conflict with the Federal Government over polygamy. The decision seems to have been made by the Church, perhaps subconsciously, that money talks in this country. . . .

—WILLIAM J. WHALEN, "The Latter-day
Saints In the Modern Day World"

In Boise, Idaho, a responsible citizen told me: "The Mormons aren't a church any more; they're a business."

—NEIL MORGAN, "Utah: How Much
Money Hath the Mormon Church,"
ESQUIRE, August 1962

There has never been an accounting of modern church income or wealth.

—"Mormon Money and How It's Made,"
UTAH HOLIDAY, March 22, 1976

10

Latter-day Profits

THE TESTIMONY of Joseph F. Smith at the Smoot investigation regarding church business enterprises had a significance that the national press overlooked. Within Utah, and particularly among old-timers, Smith's testimony revealed that a profound change had taken place in basic pioneer values. There had been an alteration of concept and practice as definite, and as far-reaching, as the wrenching reversal of attitude toward plural marriage. Yet amid the hue and cry of the muckrakers' purple prose anent the "Mormon menace," the only one among them who realized the real significance was Frank J. Cannon, who had an insider's viewpoint.

It was not church involvement in business affairs that was new, strange, or different. This had characterized the faith from earliest days. The infant church was involved in real estate speculation, commerce, manufacturing, banking, publishing, farming, building, and in fact in all aspects of temporal life of the times. The founder and prophet, Joseph Smith, had been reputed by critics at Nauvoo to be a millionaire. The estate of his successor, Brigham Young, was estimated at $2.5 million until a lawsuit by disgruntled heirs disclosed that Brigham had been so involved in church temporal activities that he actually had lost track of what was his personal business and what was church enterprise. He had bequeathed various church assets to his heirs, and it was necessary for the next president, John Taylor, to take back $1 million of the estate's assets in straightening out accounts.[1]

Brigham's wealth was not the issue. The significant factor was the twilight zone between church and private enterprise. The first law of the gospel in the early church was the United Order, a type of communal ownership in which each member donated his worldly wealth to the church and drew according to need. While in practice this Utopian ideal foundered time after time upon the rocks of human nature, Brigham's temporal enterprises were directed to mutual welfare through cooperative effort. He believed implicitly in the United Order, and in 1874, three years before his death, organized such cooperatives in towns throughout Mormon country, which, as in previous attempts, failed because of human imperfection.

"During the early years of the church, the priesthood not only had an interest in temporal affairs, but claimed the right to command in temporal affairs," Leonard J. Arrington said.[2] While some men were called as missionaries to preach the gospel, "others were called, in the same spirit, to mine gold, manufacture iron, raise silk, settle a difficult country, and teach Indians the arts of agriculture."

In fact, "the construction of water ditches was as much a part of the Mormon religion as water baptism," he commented. "The redemption of man's hope (the earth) was considered to be as important as the redemption of his soul."

Cannon perceived that the Smoot investigation proved beyond a shadow of doubt that the United Order had as little chance of being revived as did polygamy. The basic goal of the first principle of the gospel had been abandoned, along with the doctrine that

1. For details, see the author's *The Kingdom or Nothing* (New York: Macmillan, 1976). Also Leonard J. Arrington, "The Settlement of the Brigham Young Estate," *Pacific Historical Review*, February 1952.
2. *Great Basin Kingdom. An Economic History of the Latter-day Saints, 1830–1900* (Cambridge: Harvard University Press, 1958).

plural marriage was essential to the celestial glory of the hereafter. Cannon pointed out that church temporal enterprise no longer involved the welfare of the people as a whole, but was for the benefit of a select coterie of stockholders. With this change of economic policy, he said, "One of the most promising modern experiments in communism has been frustrated and brought to ruin."

In an *Improvement Era* article, "You have probably heard it said that 'commercialism' is rampant in the church," Joseph F. Smith wrote in answer to the muckraking crusade, "to such an extent that it has lost its spiritual force and mission." Such accusations of having sold out to Mammon, were "falsely uttered and industriously circulated," but "Nothing could be farther from the truth."[3]

Regarding ZCMI department stores, sugar factories, banking, and other ventures, "This is not commercialism—barter and trade for profit—it is common sense help" extended to the Saints for their temporal as well as spiritual advancement.

"There are those who object to the authorities of the church being directors in these institutions," he wrote. But when the enterprises prospered under such management, "I can see no wrong in having them serve in this capacity." When business thrived, the people prospered. "Spiritual salvation alone is not all that people need in this life," he pointed out. The dual mission of the church was to bring both spiritual and temporal salvation.

Brigham Young's motto, "Mind Your Own Business," is one pioneer concept that has remained unchanged. Privacy regarding church income, outgo, and total wealth has caused lively speculation from the very beginning. The modern church continues to mind its own business, while the Salt Lake *samizdat* remains busy with reports. Periodically the national press picks up the story of Mormon wealth.

A recurring *samizdat* subject concerns the special underwear worn by faithful adult Saints. Cannon noted that Joseph F. Smith was president of the Salt Lake Knitting Co., which had a monopoly on garment manufacture, and no garment was approved for wear without the official label. "By which ingenious bit of religious commercialism," Frank remarked, "the sacred marks on the garments (accepted as a sort of passport into Heaven) have been increased

3. April 1912.

by the sacred Smith trademark that admits the wearer to the Smith Heaven."

In pioneer times, Utah wives used to make the garments from muslin or any other material available, from flour sacks to bed ticking. Because of the scarcity of buttons, they were fastened by strings. When the church took over the manufacture, strings remained, but the fabric was knit. This caused the first cry of outrage from the devout, which has followed every change of detail or pattern since. Over the years, buttons replaced strings; arms and legs were shortened to adapt to modern style trends.

Following the excommunication of Apostle John W. Taylor for post-Manifesto polygamy, one of his brothers in fury announced that he was taking off his garments. This, in the Mormon society, is comparable to public burning of the United States flag. When a Saint is on trial for church membership, a most serious charge is that he doesn't wear the garments.

The air-tight monopoly by the church of the LDS underwear market had long been a thorn in the New York clothing industry, which yearned for a piece of the action but couldn't muscle in. Even though New York could offer the identical pattern and equal quality at one third the price, Mormons refused to wear anything without the approved label. However, New York noted that with the trademark due to expire, the church hadn't applied for its renewal. The day after the trademark was in the public domain, bales of garments from New York appeared in the Utah market, bearing the approved label. For awhile there was consternation in Salt Lake. Then came the inspired solution: a new trademark, this one with purple printing. As the Saints rejected anything without the purple label, New York retired in confusion.

As church wealth and power increased, an anonymous *samizdat* book, *Gospel Problems,* appeared in 1920, calling the Saints to repentance. "When were the people of God prouder of their fine houses, costly autos, broad acres, flocks and herds, and big bank accounts? Are we free from the pride and vanity of the world?" the author asked. "Can there be any true affinity between the Kingdom of God and the kingdoms of this world, between God and Mammon," he cried as a prophet in the wilderness of smugness and complacency.

Church authorities pointed with pride at the success "of our

Zion's Savings Bank, Beneficial Life Insurance Co., Utah-Idaho Sugar Co.," and other ventures. "But are big dividends and big salaries all that is to be considered?" Zion's Savings Bank "pays 4 percent to the poor depositors, and 30 to 40 percent to the well-to-do stockholders," while increasing the value of the stock some 600 percent.

With Reed Smoot called the "sugar-coated senator" for his valiant support of the price of beet sugar, the author charged that the church sugar company "has made millions by pinching the beet growers on the one hand, and the sugar consumers on the other." While Utah exported sugar, it retailed there at "the highest price in the world."

"We believe the present financial institutions of Zion tend not to the building up of Zion, but the amassing of private fortunes," the author said. "They do not help the unfortunate, but only the rich and prosperous." And in conclusion he thundered, "they are all of Babylon, and must fail."

Heber Bennion, formerly bishop at Taylorsville for many years, had been a member of the state legislature and a prominent farmer and stockman before being incapacitated by an accident. Bennion attended the Alpine Stake conference April 28, 1920, where "Apostle James E. Talmage lashed out at the publication and its author." In reply, "he wrote an 'Open Letter' to the learned Dr. Talmage."[4]

"You especially warned the Saints against these anonymous effusions of a crazed mind," Bennion wrote, and "of this anonymous author not paying his tithing." How did he know the "nameless author" and, without examining his financial status, judge his tithing record?

It was precisely from a desire to avoid the *ad hominem* device of attacking the author instead of meeting his arguments, Bennion explained, that he had withheld his name. Now that his identity was known, "The author has paid thousands of dollars in tithing and liberal donations in the days of his prosperity," he said, "and in the late years of his adversity he has probably done about as well as Job did in his adversity."

Talmage had explained that no action had been taken against the author because "We do not cut crazy people off the church."

4. See "Introduction" to 1976 reprint of *Gospel Problems*. Dugway, Utah: Pioneer Press.

"Now perhaps I should not complain of being called crazy," Bennion concluded, "especially if it excuses me from responsibility and possible excommunication."

The income and wealth of the church is known by very few people, and they want nothing said about it. Perhaps because of this very challenge, there have been persistent attempts over the years to assemble data. In 1925 Hamilton Gardner wrote an excellent book, *Economic Activities of the Mormons.* Whether or not official displeasure had anything to do with it, Gardner couldn't find a publisher.[5] Estimates of church income grew as the church waxed wealthy. Frank J. Cannon estimated it as "several millions a year" in 1911; by 1962 church income was reputed to be $1 million a day, and *Newsweek* called the church "The biggest commercial enterprise in the West, excepting only the massive Bank of America."[6]

Income pours in from the church's vast collection of business and real-estate investments. . . . All told, the cash flow reaches an estimated $1-million a day—enough to finance the Mormons' schools, missionary work, temple-building, and other church expenses, and still leave millions to plow back into other worthy commercial investments.

Neil Morgan repeated this figure of daily income in an article for *Esquire,* "Utah: How Much Money Hath the Mormon Church."[7] His source, Mayor J. Bracken Lee of Salt Lake, a Gentile, denied having furnished the information, though it remained on Morgan's tape recorder.[8] "The reticence of the Mormon church to discuss its wealth is understandable," Morgan concluded:

A poor Mormon farmer near the hamlets of Moroni, Ephraim or Manti . . . might occasionally bristle at some family sacrifice necessary to meet the tithe if the extent of church wealth was known to him. . . .

The church has attained—through faithful tithes and shrewd investments and business operations—a spectacular wealth. It is becoming, if it is not already, the richest church of its size in the world. Unques-

5. Manuscript copy at Utah Historical Society.
6. January 22.
7. February 1962.
8. Lee subsequently confirmed his statement, naming Henry D. Moyle of the First Presidency as his source of the information. See "Mormon Money & How It's Made," *Utah Holiday,* March 22, 1976.

tionably it controls the greatest aggregation of capital in the states of the Rocky Mountain area.

Because of "a policy of secrecy on financial matters," Wallace Turner stated in *The Mormon Establishment*,[9] "it is difficult to discuss the financial status of the LDS church. Precise information is lacking." However, after assessing church real estate, media holdings, commercial enterprises, and business interests, it was clear that "the church each year amasses its millions and millions. What happens to all this money? No one outside the top administrative levels of the church can say in detail."

Just one church property, Deseret Farms of Florida, is indicative of the scope of various projects—300,000 acres, with 50,000 head of beef cattle, 2,400 acres of citrus groves, and 150,000 acres of timber land.

The ranch is divided into various sections, each with its own crew and supervisor. There are fifteen units in the cattle operation, each equipped and run like an individual ranch.

Chief ramrod over the entire spread, according to the *Church News*, June 18, 1977, was Harvey A. Dahl, who had been general manager since 1970. Dahl had served as special assistant to Ezra Taft Benson of the Quorum of the Twelve, when Benson was secretary of agriculture during the Eisenhower administration. Dahl was a practical rancher, who owned a 14,000-acre spread of his own in Nevada.

Though Deseret Farms is a commercial undertaking, not a welfare project, Dahl's appointment as manager was in the nature of a church calling. He previously had served as bishop, stake president, and mission president, and currently was a patriarch.

How much is it worth? When the church was negotiating to sell Deseret Farms, the asking price was $100 million.[10]

In speaking of the banking business, church ownership "definitely gives them an edge on competition," said Willard L. Eccles of Salt Lake's First Security Bank. "They've got five apostles on their board. We've only got two."[11]

9. Boston: Houghton Mifflin, 1966.
10. *Church News*, January 4, 1969. The deal fell through.
11. *Business Week*, March 14, 1970. Subsequently, the church went out of the banking business, retaining an interest as stockholder.

Members of the top echelons of the church hierarchy hold positions on the boards of directors of the multitudinous business enterprises owned or controlled by the church. For example, Beneficial Life Insurance Company listed the salaries of four board members for 1969: Church President David O. McKay, $13,400; counselors Hugh B. Brown, $9,200; Nathan Tanner, $9,200; and Joseph Fielding Smith $6,200. Considering the number of church enterprises in which they would be officers, and that "they hold those positions solely because they are church officials," Jerald and Sandra Tanner stated,

would it be presumptuous on our part to conclude that we in the LDS church have the dubious distinction of having the highest paid ministry on the face of the earth?[12]

In his dissertation, *The Mormon Hierarchy, 1832–1932: An American Elite,*[13] Dennis Michael Quinn analyzed the wealth of church general authorities from probate records of their estates. Despite the fact that with advancing age various officials prudently put their assets into family corporations or assigned property to family members, to minimize inheritance taxes, Quinn found that during the period 1905–38,

Every member of the First Presidency and Presiding Bishopric whose will was probated in Salt Lake County was within the top nine percent of wealth, and forty percent of the Quorum of the Twelve was likewise within this level of affluence.

Quinn found that economic opportunities "corresponded roughly to the ecclesiastical status of the echelons of the hierarchy," and he concluded that "it is evident that extreme wealth for Presidents of the Church was almost axiomatic."

Aside from corporate positions accruing to office, church authorities have a lucrative source of income in producing books, published by the church press and retailed through church outlets. Every ward chapel has its bookcase with offerings by the brethren.[14]

12. *Mormonism, Shadow or Reality* (Salt Lake: Modern Microfilm Co., 1972).
13. Ph.D., Yale, 1976.
14. In May 1976, home teachers distributed a brochure to Mormon families throughout the United States containing the notation: "These lessons were adapted from Elder Mark E. Petersen's book, *The Great Prologue* (Salt Lake City: Des-

In the smaller towns of Utah no other books are available, except for a rack of paperbacks in the local drugstore. When President Joseph Fielding Smith (Joseph F.'s son) died in 1972, "his uncollected royalties (apparently for a six-month period) were $9,636.48"; and he left an estate in liquid assets of $509,030.

"The structure of Mormonism itself inevitably made the Mormon hierarchy an economic institution," Quinn decided.

The combination of economic communitarianism, religious faith, and a rigid authority system gave the Mormon hierarchy not only the opportunity but the responsibility for economic management; . . . and the men who served in the hierarchy's echelons of power constituted an economic elite within their own community.

Certainly one thing can be said for sure: the vow of poverty is utterly incomprehensible in the Mormon culture.

In 1975 Bill Beecham and David Briscoe, on assignment by the Associated Press, spent six weeks researching church wealth. They produced a three-part story that was featured by newspapers nationally and won an award from the Society of Professional Journalists as the best single piece of print journalism in Utah for the year. However, "the story was never carried in Utah newspapers," *Utah Holiday* magazine reported, in publishing a story prepared by the authors with additional material, "Mormon Money & How It's Made."[15]

"Today, the LDS church is a religious and financial empire," the authors stated, with "assets in the billions of dollars and an income in contributions and sales by church-controlled corporations estimated at more than $3 million a day."

This amounts to $1.095 billion a year, which, as the man on Main Street would say, ain't hay.

Its holdings would rank it among the nation's top 50 corporations in total assets. Top officials of the worldwide church are businessmen as well as spiritual leaders.

---

eret Book Co., 1975). It is recommended that a copy of this book be in every Latter-day Saint home in the United States of America. You are also urged to share a paperback copy of this book with a nonmember family. . . ."

15. March 22, 1976. For details of the suppression, see "Sacred Cows and the Utah News Media. . . . The Story They Wouldn't Touch," by Gary M. Smith, Logan *Herald Journal,* February 27, 1976.

The AP reporters estimated that $550 million of the yearly income came from tax-exempt tithes and other contributions, major items being: $360 million in tithes; $15 million for building funds (the church was constructing 500 structures a year); $80 million for building maintenance; and $43 million contributed by parents of 23,000 full-time missionaries for their support in the Lord's vineyard.

Gross business income, "exceeding $450 million," included:

—$237 million in sales by Utah-Idaho, Inc., in which the church holds an approximate 50 percent and controlling interest. Formerly called Utah-Idaho Sugar Co., the firm has controlling interest in Gourmet Food Products, Inc. . . . and also has irrigated farmland in southeastern Idaho and southern Washington.

—$57 million in sales by five ZCMI department stores, in which the church holds a controlling interest (about 30 percent) . . . .

—$79 million in premium and interest income to three insurance companies wholly owned by the church—Beneficial Life . . . Utah Home Fire . . . and Deseret Mutual. . . .

—$16 million in estimated income to the *Deseret News*. . . .

—$4 million estimated revenue for KSL Television. . . . Added to this, would be millions more in sales by the church's other television station, KIRO in Seattle, and 11 radio stations in Salt Lake City, New York, Los Angeles, Seattle, Kansas City, Chicago, and San Francisco. All are owned by Bonneville International Corp., which also has other media-related interests.

—$10 million in estimated sales by Deseret Press. . . .

—$10 million in sales by Deseret Book, which has seven stores in Utah and Southern California. . . .

—$6 million from Utah Hotel Co., which owns the 406-room Hotel Utah, 186-room Temple Square Hotel and 160-room Utah Motor Lodge. . . .

—$4 million in sales by the non-profit Deseret Industries. . . .

Other church holdings included the Beehive Clothing Mills, which manufactured temple clothing and the garments worn by the faithful; the 300,000-acre cattle ranch in Florida; the ZCMI Center in Salt Lake, a large mall entirely church-owned; a thirty-six-story apartment building in New York City, part of which was used for religious services; a computer firm; dozens of commercial buildings in Salt Lake City, including the Kennecott, Union Pacific, J. C. Penney, Utah Power & Light, Constitution, Medical Arts, and Beneficial Life buildings; a ten-story parking garage; and $18.3 millions in stock of the Times-Mirror Corp., which published the Los Angeles *Times*.

The total income figures for the church and its corporations reach $1 billion without considering rental of commercial buildings and apartments, real estate transactions, interest and dividends from investments not made public, large individual donations, or royalties to the Tabernacle Choir for its record albums.

Unmentioned in the article were the vast acquisitions of welfare holdings, which represented an enormous capital investment. Every stake is urged to have its welfare project. In Joe Budro's area, the San Francisco Stake ran a pants factory. His own stake built and operated a cannery at Redwood City, the fruit supplied by another stake in San Jose. With changing stake boundaries resulting from church growth in the area, his stake relinquished the cannery to another stake, then purchased a truck farm at Half Moon Bay. After still another change, his stake joined others of the area in ownership of a big ranch in the Sacramento valley.

The extent of tax-exempt property reached the point in Utah where it constituted a definite burden on the taxpayer, claimed Earl M. Baker, assessor for Salt Lake County. He estimated that in 1971 the Mormon Church owned 80 percent of privately owned tax-exempt property in the county, with a value of from $1 to $1.5 billion. One example was the new Church Administration building of twenty-eight stories and costing $33 million in construction costs (the church owned the land), which was tax-free although not used for religious services and though it housed the offices directing church temporal affairs.

Baker estimated that if all exempt property were taxed, county taxes could be reduced 25 percent, whereupon, for starters, he mailed tax bills to the church totaling $87,616 for welfare property —farms, storehouses, and Deseret Industries retail outlets.

The church promptly issued the first financial report on the welfare program in the thirty-six years since it began in 1936. "Responding to criticism that it is not carrying a fair share of the tax burden, the Mormon Church said yesterday it has spent $17.7

million aiding the poor, the needy and the sick during the past 12 months under its own welfare program," an Associated Press release stated September 24, 1972.

The report listed 478 welfare projects throughout the United States, "where members produce and process 126 items ranging from meat to shoe polish."

In Salt Lake County during 1971 "Our church welfare program assisted 19,756 persons," announced managing director Junior Wright Child. The total, in cash payments, commodities and hospital care, came to $2,098,514.71. "The figures tell the story. The savings to the county and other government agencies through our welfare assistance far exceed what the tax would be."

The County Board of Equalization overruled the assessor, and two years later Baker blamed his election defeat on the attempt to tax welfare property in a county 66 percent Mormon.

In Idaho, the State Board of Tax Appeals upheld action by the boards of equalization in Bannock and Bingham counties, which had refused to grant tax exemptions for four LDS church-owned welfare farms in Bannock and six in Bingham County.

"Very little of the commodities produced on the farms," the board ruled, "went to needy persons." Instead, most were marketed, the proceeds used for investment and going into the general welfare funds of the church. "Here the land was used for commercial purposes."

The Salt Lake *Tribune* reported October 1, 1971 that a similar stance was taken in Pierce County, Washington, where all LDS property was placed on the tax rolls because both local and Salt Lake church officials refused to disclose "any information regarding tithing and welfare offerings," although "all other denominations represented in the county" had done so.

The church also had tax troubles in England, when the London Temple was assessed because its requirements for admission disqualified it as a place of public worship.

The church certainly can afford the added taxes. William J. Whalen, in his book *The Latter-day Saints in the Modern Day World,* said "the Mormon Church is the dominant financial institution in the Rocky Mountain area, and the wealthiest church per capita in the world." He claimed that

Church investment in real estate is so extensive that some have said there is no such thing as a two-way property transaction in Salt Lake City. The Mormon Church is a third party to every large transaction.

When the Associated Press reporters in researching their story asked N. Eldon Tanner of the First Presidency, who was in charge of church financial interests, why there had never been a disclosure of church income or wealth, he replied, "I don't think the public needs to have that information." Wendel Ashton, church communications director, checked the AP story for accuracy, "but declined to either confirm or deny estimates of church wealth," Beecham and Briscoe stated.

Which leaves it up to the *samizdat*.

However, "Faithful Mormons rarely show an interest in the business side of the church," the AP team reported, "generally relying on their leaders to direct expenditures with the same inspiration they direct its spiritual affairs."

Whalen concurs, summing up thusly:

"The average Mormon seems content to believe that this wealth is used only to aid needy Mormons and that there is nothing incompatible between spiritual values and success in the business world. He glories in the temples being built around the world and takes satisfaction in the reports of record conversions. Perhaps this feeling is well worth the tithe he has paid all his life and expects to pay until he is clothed in his LDS Approved Garments and laid to rest from the Deseret Mortuary."

BOOK TWO

Happy Valley

We believe the Bible to be the word of God so far as it is translated correctly; we also believe the Book of Mormon to be the word of God.

—"ARTICLES OF FAITH"

What about the Book of Mormon? Was that supposedly sacred record to be accepted on faith alone? Or could sufficient evidences be discovered and assembled to demonstrate the truth? . . . If the "Mormon Bible" actually does give an accurate record of past civilizations on the American continents, those civilizations must have left definite and discoverable evidences. . . . Why not do something about it? Would it not be commendable even though difficult for the Brigham Young Academy?[1]

11

Benjamin Cluff's Magnificent Dream, and Professor Wolfe in Sheep's Clothing

THE TREMOR felt on the morning of January 9, 1977 was not an earthquake, but derisive laughter from the graves of Benjamin Cluff and his travel companions at a story in the San Francisco *Chronicle*. Bill Barriere was in town promoting his Inter-American Expedition from Point Barrow, Alaska, to Puenta Arenas, Chile, a scheme he had worked on for two years. Barriere had advertised for eight tough men to accompany the proposed fifteen-vehicle caravan, preferably "war-hardened mercenaries or rugged explorers able to handle poisonous snakes and man-eating natives." He hoped to sell 300,000 expedition T-shirts to help

---

1. Eugene L. Roberts and Mrs. Eldon Reed Cluff, "Benjamin Cluff, Jr., Scholar, Educational Administrator, and Explorer"; typescript, Provo, July 24, 1947. Brigham Young University, Special Collections. Hereafter, "Cluff."

finance the "magnificent, historic, breathtaking" trek; but as yet had "13,000 Miles and $1-Million Still to Go," the *Chronicle* reported.

This fifteen-vehicle expedition would be an armchair luxury tour, compared to the Brigham Young Academy South American Exploring Expedition of 1900, which went by mule and horseback. Instead of war-hardened mercenaries, the first party to cross by land from North to South America was composed of college students and faculty members of the Brigham Young Academy, of which Benjamin Cluff was president.[2]

The route of the expedition was to go south through Utah and Arizona to Mexico, continuing on through the mountains and jungles of Guatemala, Salvador, Honduras, Nicaragua, Costa Rica, and Panama, crossing the fetid Darien of the Isthmus into South America and to the Magdalena River in Colombia. Here, they expected to find the ruins of Zarahemla, capital of the Nephites, a Book of Mormon people.[3] From there they would continue south to Valparaiso in Chile. Such was the dream. An amazing part of it came true.

While the prime purpose was to authenticate the Book of Mormon by the discovery of Zarahemla, Cluff visualized the expedition as a prestigious scientific expedition for the Brigham Young Academy. Other universities sponsored field trips "to gather scientific data regarding geology, archeology, paleontology, . . . and other subjects suitable for scholarly research. Why not have Brigham Young Academy join with its sister institutions in pushing back the limits of the unknown?"[4]

Cluff dreamed of the trip for three years before presenting it to Salt Lake. After having received the official approval and blessing, he picked twenty-four men to accompany him, most of them acad-

---

2. The second expedition known to have accomplished this feat was a one-man adventure. In 1925, A. F. Tschiffely rode horseback from Buenos Aires to Washington, D.C., a trip taking two and a half years. See *Tschiffely's Ride* (New York: Grosset and Dunlap, 1933); also, *National Geographic,* "Buenos Aires to Washington by Horse," February 1929.

3. George Reynolds of the First Council of Seventy had written a 7-volume commentary on the Book of Mormon, in which he oriented the location of Zarahemla on the Magdalena River. The Nephites were a Hebraic people who had emigrated from the Old World. They recorded their history on golden plates, which Joseph Smith translated into English as the Book of Mormon.

4. Cluff.

emy students.[5] In at least one instance Cluff made an unfortunate choice that was to haunt him. He selected Professor Walter M. Wolfe, a personal friend, as his first counselor in the enterprise. He didn't suspect that Wolfe held a deep resentment, born of envy, because of Cluff's commanding appearance and mantle of authority. Wolfe was small and scrawny, with weak eyes, introverted, one to harbor grudges. By contrast, Cluff was tall and strikingly handsome, with dark hair, sideburns, and trim moustache, a leader with outgoing personality. Despite himself, Wolfe couldn't like him.

Wolfe tried to avoid the assignment with a dozen excuses. He wasn't qualified for the role of biologist, historian, and counselor, he protested; besides, he couldn't afford the trip. To the regret of both, he was persuaded.

Preparations for the expedition were rather wonderfully quaint. Financial backing by the academy for an exploratory trip through two continents was $100 a man, a total of $2,500. In addition, each member was required to have $125 plus his outfit—saddle horse, pack horse, gun, cartridge belt, bowie knife, and camping equipment. Two baggage wagons accompanied the riders. The wagons held tents and provisions, with equipment for photography, surveying, painting, excavation of ruins, preservation of specimens —everything deemed necessary for a scientific exploration.

Young George Q. Cannon, just nineteen years old and known as "Q," was called to the mission, and in January 1900, enrolled at the Brigham Young Academy (BYA) for a three-month study of language and science in preparation for the trip. He attended conferences of Book of Mormon authorities, listening to discussions of the parts of Central and South America which most likely were sites of the Nephite civilization, together with receiving instructions regarding the objectives the explorers must keep in mind. Q Cannon was inspired with zeal at the magnitude of his mission, to verify the word of God.

After being ordained an elder, he went through the Salt Lake Temple on April 7 with the others of the expedition, where they

5. Eugene L. Roberts, who subsequently wrote the story of the expedition, was a member of it, as was George Q. Cannon, namesake and grandson of the counselor in the First Presidency. Joe Budro interviewed Cannon on the subject in 1960, at which time Cannon was the last surviving member of the expedition.

were blessed and set apart for the mission by apostles Francis M. Lyman and John W. Taylor.

Q Cannon found himself lionized as excitement mounted with approach of the departure date, April 17. On the eve of departure, "A grand farewell party was given at the Academy Building."[6] The assembly hall was packed. From outside came a bugle call; then as the expedition force marched in, wearing travel attire—leggings, gauntlets, sombreros—and with their color bearer leading the procession, the crowd cheered. After a grand march, Q Cannon enjoyed dancing and feasting until 2 A.M.

A bugle roused him at seven next morning; at ten he listened to final counsel from church authorities for two hours; then at noon sat down to a lunch for five hundred people. "After many toasts and accolades," he saddled up. "As the procession rode down Academy Avenue, the street was lined with well-wishers" cheering the "heroic journey to the land of the Nephites."[7]

Travel the first day was 6 miles, to Springville, where a program featuring four hundred school children greeted the expedition. There was another dance and banquet, and a departing gift of $16. Next day the company went five miles, to Spanish Fork, where a brass band escorted them into town for another shindig lasting into the early hours.

The route was zigzag, progress slow, as the citizens of every Mormon town between Provo and the Arizona border insisted on feting the heroes. After sixty years, Q Cannon remembered fondly the hospitality and wonderful food. "They didn't just give you a piece of pie. They stacked up pies four deep, and cut them like layer cakes."

There was intense rivalry between the towns of Paragona and Parawon. Both insisted on serving a banquet, yet they were only 3 miles apart. The men feasted at Paragona at 6 P.M., then went on to another banquet at Parawon, which, fortunately, wasn't served until 10 P.M.

After seventeen days the expedition reached Kanab, 264 miles from Provo. This was the jumping-off place. Beyond stretched the broken desert of the Arizona Strip, the Buckskin Mountains and

6. Ernest L. Wilkinson and W. Cleon Skousen, *Brigham Young University, A School of Destiny* (Provo: BYU Press, 1976). Hereafter, "BYU."
7. BYU; quotations from Chester Van Buren diary.

the Kaibab forest, Houserock valley, Lee's Ferry over the Colorado River, then the Painted Desert south through The Gap to Cameron on the Little Colorado. This leg of the trip would be 200 miles of rock and sand.

Cluff called a halt for two days at Kanab to provision the expedition and organize the men into squads of four, each with its designated cook, dishwasher, horse wrangler, and a supervisor who would report to Cluff each evening. While the reorganization was ostensibly in preparation for desert travel, there was another reason —dissension, griping, resentment at Cluff's strict leadership. When "Cluff paired off the boys, regardless of personal friendship and of what financial dealings they had made among themselves," Walter M. Wolfe complained, "this resulted in much hard feelings; but he claimed priestly authority for his action." Though Wolfe and Gordon S. Beckstead "left Provo as counselors to President Cluff," Wolfe said, "not once were we consulted."[8]

With expedition affairs, Cluff "claimed the authority of an apostle," and told members that "in differing from him they were questioning divine authority," Wolfe said. "He forbade laughing or jesting among the line of march and even singing, unless it was Latter-day Saint hymns."

Despite Cluff's puritanical strictness, he forced the company to travel on Sundays, contrary to "special instructions concerning observance of the Sabbath." The first Sunday found them at Richfield, where despite bad weather and pressing invitations to stay and rest up, Cluff ordered travel, "A long, cold ride (several snow squalls) over the ridge to Kanosh." There was the usual banquet and dance, then, after midnight, "Cluff ordered us to saddle our horses and proceed to Beaver." They rode all night "through storm and cold," reaching Beaver in the late afternoon after "thirty-six hours of unnecessary travel without rest." Cluff explained that the forced march was "that we might be inured to the hardships of the journey."

Cluff was away the second Sunday, when Wolfe and Beckstead gave the boys a day of rest at Panguitch. "For this we were reprimanded by President Cluff on his arrival at Panguitch." The third Saturday, "it seemed that President Cluff was determined to show his priestly authority" by not only ordering travel next morning in-

8. For his viewpoint, see "Testimony of Walter M. Wolfe," SI 4:4–68.

volving eighteen miles to Kanab, but by proclaiming that every Sunday would be a fast day.

When B. T. Higgs accidently grazed the leg of Heber Magelby with a pitchfork while feeding the horses, "Higgs received a stinging rebuke"; then a few days later Cluff upbraided the company because someone had written home of the incident. "Cluff said that no one had a right to send home any such news from the expedition."

Such were the tensions as the party headed from Kanab into the wild Arizona Strip. At Houserock valley they camped at the old stone house, behind which was a solitary grave near the brilliant Vermillion Cliffs. It was three hard days across sand and slickrock from there to Lee's Ferry.

Two camps were made where there was no feed for the horses, no water for man or animals, and scant wood for cooking. This was an excellent conditioner to prepare the men for anticipated hardships in the future.[9]

The future arrived quickly. The last good water was near Lee's Ferry at Navajo Spring; then for five days the expedition fought the desert under a brass sun, making dry camp or stopping at water "unfit for human consumption." The very worst water they found was just before a group of Mormons from Tuba City drove into view through the shimmering heat waves, bringing wagons loaded with "all delectable foodstuffs" excepting the one thing desperately needed, water.

After reaching the Little Colorado the expedition was again in Mormon country. At Joseph City, Holbrook, Woodruff, Snowflake, and Taylor, each town went all out to provide the best banquet, dance, and hospitality. The expedition then headed south across the Apache reservation to the Gila valley, where trouble came to a head at Thatcher.

Here, Cluff said he would go ahead and make arrangements for entering Mexico. While awaiting his return, the men would be missionaries, "visiting, teaching, and preaching among the Mormon people." This situation "was received with scant enthusiasm," the

9. Cluff.

Roberts-Cluff account admits, "because everybody desired to get on with the trip." But, having issued orders, Cluff disappeared over the southern horizon.

"Mr. Cluff was absent from the expedition for about two months," Wolfe testified, "and the rumor came that he was in Mexico with Florence Reynolds," his plural bride of ten months. Wolfe identified her as a recent student of Cluff's at the BYA. In August of the previous year she left Utah, and "it was common rumor that she had gone to Mexico with Benjamin Cluff, Jr."[10]

While waiting at Thatcher, the expedition wore out its welcome. Cluff had assigned the members to missionary work in the absence of the stake president, Andrew Kimball.

During twenty-four days of waiting at Thatcher, temperatures reached 117 degrees. "This delay was disastrous to the morale of the company," the BYU account states. "The heat, idleness, and frustration finally brought the griping and grumbling in the camp to a boil, and there was a series of rather serious infractions of camp rules."

Such was the situation when Stake President Kimball returned, in company with Apostle Heber J. Grant. Both men were angry that the boys had been sent out preaching, and Kimball declared the company was a burden on the community. "This expedition had run into deep trouble before it had negotiated its first crossing into a foreign country."

On returning to Salt Lake, Grant "freely and frankly" told the brethren "that the expedition ought to be abandoned." The First Presidency notified Joseph F. Smith, who was en route to Mexico, to evaluate the situation.

The expedition headed south again in response to a telegram from Cluff to meet him in Mexico at Nogales. On reaching the border eleven days later, however, the way was blocked by a demand by Mexican custom officials for a cash bond of $2,367. The officials refused the offer of Mormon colonists in Mexico to guarantee the bond. Cluff finally got permission for the expedition to camp near Nogales under guard while he raised the cash.

10. Florence Reynolds is listed as the third wife of Cluff in *The Sons of Brigham,* by T. Earl Pardoe (Provo: Brigham Young University Alumni Association, 1969). She is also acknowledged as such in BYU. The Roberts-Cluff manuscript makes no mention of this aspect.

The next day, Wolfe stated, "it was Sunday and we had a memorable meeting" at which the festering discontent came into the open. To quell the bickering, Cluff "had the members of the expedition hold up their right hand and swear without mental reservation to obey implicitly whatever he wanted to be done." This didn't set well. "There had been a great deal of murmuring, . . . and now it approached almost an actual rebellion."

For a period of twenty-nine more days the restless men camped at Nogales while Cluff again was gone. Food ran low. The men got hungry, and so did their Mexican guards, who unsealed the Mormon guns and let the men forage for food. "I remember we got a bear and some deer," Q Cannon recalled, "but it was pretty slim pickings."

There were breaks in the monotony. One night the camp was overrun by a horde of giant tarantulas. On another night they scrambled to high ground in the nick of time as a flash flood filled the ravine where they camped. Q Cannon lost his collection of specimens in the flood. Next morning he joined in climbing trees to retrieve tents and articles of clothing snagged high in the branches.

On August 10 a rumor spread through the company

that all the young men were to be sent on missions, . . . and a few of the older men including the teachers and more experienced travelers were to continue the trip. . . . Each of the men felt himself definitely disgraced. . . .

The Brigham Young Academy South American Expedition had marched out of Provo, Utah, amid the cheers of hundreds of its citizens. The party had been received, feted, and entertained by Mormon towns and villages all along the route. The men had been glorified and heroized by admiring crowds everywhere, because they had been chosen to perform a great service at tremendous risk. What an embarrassing awakening from a wonderful dream![11]

Two days later, Joseph F. Smith of the First Presidency arrived with several brethren from the Mormon colonies in Mexico to confirm the rumor. He read a wire from Salt Lake:

LETTER RECEIVED. UNANIMOUS MIND OF THE COUNCIL OF FIRST PRESIDENCY AND APOSTLES TODAY IS THAT THE EXPEDITION DISBAND

11. Cluff. When Joe Budro interviewed Q Cannon sixty years later, the last survivor still felt humiliation, and was reluctant to talk about the expedition.

AND RETURN HOME. . . . [IF] BROTHER CLUFF AND OTHERS PROCEED, THEY MUST ASSUME ALL RESPONSIBILITY.[12]

Cancellation of the project was a tremendous blow to Cluff's pride.

It was indeed a moment of crisis, undoubtedly the greatest in his life, and the beginning of a turning point which should determine the direction of his forty-four years of living afterwards.[13]

Declaring, "Because that which is sweeter than life itself depends upon it," Cluff decided to continue on his own hook, without BYA or church support. He chose eight of the older and more experienced men, including Wolfe, the others being Asa Kienke, Chester Van Buren, John B. Fairbanks, Joseph Adams, Paul Henning, Heber Magelby, and Walter Tolton.

As the expedition ate the last meal together before separating, gripes and friction were forgotten. Despite the personality clashes, the group had been welded together by the magnificent dream, and as they ate they remembered the good things, the funny incidents, the spiritual exaltation of their mission, and the marvelous faith of the people who had feted and feasted and sustained them. Asa Kienke recorded:

Eyes were wet and sobs were heard; then we lined up, those who were going on South on one side, and those who were going home on the other; then we passed them by and shook hands, bidding them goodbye. I wept like a child and so did the others.[14]

Most of the young men released from the expedition went on missions. Q Cannon was given the job of disposing of the horses and equipment. A year later he had sold everything and forwarded payments to missionaries throughout the world; then he went home. Embarrassed by the failure, he didn't discuss the expedition until sixty years later.

Cluff again went ahead to the colonies. Wolfe, following with

12. Joseph Fielding Smith, *Life of Joseph F. Smith* (Salt Lake: Deseret Book Co., 1969). The determining factor, BYU adds, was "reports that had reached the Presidency that during these times, with polygamy still a sensitive issue, President Cluff was spending part of his time in [Colonia] Juarez visiting Florence Reynolds."
13. Cluff.
14. BYU.

the seven men of the reduced party, found the leader at Colonia Oaxaca.

He took me for a little walk in the grove, and he said, "Brother Wolfe, I have Florence here with me. I know you have suspected for a long time that I have been married to her; . . . and I beg of you not to tell anybody this."

The bride traveled several days with the party, leaving it at Colonia Juarez.

To avoid paying duty the men had sold their horses on the American side, and bought mules in Mexico. As they traveled south they were in lush country, a veritable Garden of Eden, with game plentiful, streams of water, high grass for the mules. The ranch owners were hospitable, and the peons entertained the travelers at night with songs and music. But evidently there were serpents in Eden, for one of them bit Paul Henning while he slept. Wolfe injected him with morphine to relieve the pain, and others administered by the laying on of hands. After a day's rest, Henning kept on.

Then followed three weeks ascending the rugged Sierra Madre Mountains, the going so rough that Joseph Adams' mule lost footing at a steep ravine. Animal and rider went over and over to the bottom, fortunately suffering nothing but bad bruises.

When they reached the highest point on their trail, 9,000 feet above sea level, they held a fast meeting, prayed, and bore their testimonies before beginning the descent, which fell away 7,000 feet in three miles.[15]

Now they pushed through country where game was scarce. Food dwindled. Van Buren, the cook, spent hours picking weevils from the flour before making sourdough. "We eat bread but once a day and do not afford baking powder," Cluff wrote Brimhall at BYA. "In every way possible we cut down expense." Mail from home was irregular and scant, and now it rarely contained funds. As a mission it would have received support from the home front. As a private enterprise, and under a cloud, it was root, hog, or die. Cluff authorized Brimhall to dispose of his valuable library, but it brought little at a forced sale. The expedition kept on with short rations.

15. Cluff.

The men were forced to live off the land and purchase what little they could afford from the Mexicans. Many nights they had only cornmeal or beans mixed with water for supper. Hunger became a daily companion. Even so, the men remained optimistic. Van Buren wrote, "What we have endured, what trials of mind, and weariness of body, what anxiety, what joy and pleasure, are now given to the past. The present is ours and all is well.[16]

Accidents and sickness added to the hardships of the trail. Tolton "suffered terribly for 24 hours" when a poison insect flew into his eye. At one camp he was stricken seriously ill, a scorpion bit Cluff, and Wolfe severely wrenched his knee in falling into a ditch. They christened the place "Camp Accident." Such incidents became so common they merited but brief mention. Tolton wrote:

October 16, warm Doctor Camp, 20 miles. Left at 7:30, passed over a very steep mountain into a divide for dinner. As I was saddling "Kitchen" mule, she kicked me in the face. Journeyed on and camped at a Mexican ranch. A woman was sick. Brother Cluff doctored her and she paid him two jugs of milk.

And no more is said about being kicked in the face by a mule.

As they neared the west coast, Cluff divided the party, sending Wolfe, Adams, and Van Buren south to Mazatlán, while he took the others west on a trip of eleven days through wild mountain country and into the land of the fierce Yaquis to Navojoa on the Rio Mayo near the Gulf of California.

Navojoa was one of the villages of the "white Indians." These were, according to Mormon theory, direct descendants of the Nephites mentioned in the Book of Mormon. The Indians were blond with blue eyes and light hair, and so different from the native tribes surrounding them that it was easy for the Mormon visitors to conclude that the forefathers of these whites were indeed Nephites.[17]

Whatever their ancestry, the present Navojoans were all devout Catholics, and Cluff failed to find any Nephite archeological evidence. He pushed on down the coast, through Los Mochis and

16. BYU.
17. Cluff.

Culiacan, joining the others at Mazatlán. Here the company shipped off to the BYA a collection of specimens gathered en route.

Meanwhile, Wolfe continued his role as gadfly. He took sick, and as his strength ebbed his choler swelled. From Tepic, as the party headed toward Mexico City, Wolfe, "sorely tried and tempted," fired off a letter on December 9 to J. B. Keeler, a fellow faculty member at BYA and Wolfe's bishop at the Provo Fourth Ward.

Dear Brother Keeler: Though I ought to be in bed resting, I feel it a duty to write to you tonight a confidential letter as my bishop. . . .

You know how I felt about coming. I did not seek a place in the expedition. I was forced into it; had to borrow money to equip with, and then started out in an almost penniless condition. . . .

I wanted to return home at Nogales, but I did not think that it would be right to desert President Cluff under such trying circumstances. . . . So I kept on, day after day, week after week, month after month. My animals gave out and I had no money with which to purchase others, so for over 200 miles I walked under the tropical sun, clothing almost worn out, and soleless shoes. Little by little my strength gave out. The boys all noticed my condition and are very kind to me. I can no longer lift my packs, and when the day's journey is done I go directly to bed and get up at the 5 A.M. call, feeling even weaker and more miserable than I did the night before.

In subsequent testimony at the Smoot hearing, Wolfe complained about Sunday travel during this period, "that was done simply to show the authority of the president," and of Cluff's unchristianlike attitude. One night Wolfe fell behind, got lost, and arrived in camp late. He was sick, worn out, and didn't sleep. Next morning Cluff told him "we must go on," and if Wolfe stayed behind it would be alone. "Now, President Cluff would stop if one of the mules was lost, but not when a man was sick."

The other side of the coin is that Wolfe admittedly "drank like a fish." His attacks of illness were considered binges, and Cluff had scant sympathy for the hangovers. Cluff told how Wolfe reported that his mule had been stolen near Guatemala, but "this was questioned by other members of the expedition who were well acquainted with his periodic craving for alcoholic beverages" and suspected he had sold the mule to quench his thirst.

At Nogales the party had received a gift of $100. Wolfe took the check to town to buy supplies, "and with this money went on an extended three-day alcoholic spree while expedition members remained . . . without provisions."

"President Cluff realizes that my strength will not carry me much farther," Wolfe wrote to Bishop Keeler. After a discussion, Wolfe agreed to go as far as Guatemala, then return home, for "I could not go from there down to the fever-infested Isthmus or stand another summer's hardships." He was stunned during the discussion when Cluff "told me that in view of my failing health I could have my honorable release on condition of giving the expedition an order for $300 on my this year's salary." When Wolfe explained that he was destitute, returning in rags, "He told me that without a release I could not again teach in the Academy, and the expedition needed the money."

Wolfe felt he had served the Academy too long to have to "buy back my position there." He was too old to begin life over, for "I love Utah, my religion, the B.Y.A., and my friends," too much. "It is hard, though, to feel that I am selling my very life's blood," he wrote, "to gratify another man's ambition."

Wolfe wrote Keeler to sell his house "for enough to get me home" and ended with the plea, "Please write me at the City of Mexico and pray that my faith fail not."[18]

In justice to Cluff it should be noted that at a hearing before church and BYA officials, after Cluff's return, Wolfe withdrew a number of his charges. The disputed $300 evidently was a matter of misunderstanding. Cluff maintained that before the expedition started Wolfe agreed to contribute that amount from his salary for travel expenses. Wolfe denied that he had made such an agreement.

Cluff pushed on through mountain and jungle to the Zapotec ruins of Mitla on the Isthmus of Tehuantepec, from where he wrote George Brimhall at the BYA:

Geographically we entered Central America and Tehuantepec, and, we think, entered the land of the Book of Mormon at the same place. . . . Over the country we now travel lived many a happy Nephite family.

Cluff felt himself on the verge of great discoveries. "I only ask that you and Bro. Keeler do not waver, do not lose courage," he wrote.

18. SI.

There is a revolution in Colombia. It may or may not be over by the time we get there, but I ask that you see to it that no great scare is raised that will call us home.

With the mules in bad shape, he set out afoot with three men—Henning, Kienke, and Magelby—for a three-week back-pack trip from the lowland jungle to the high plains of Chiapas and the Mayan ruins of Palenque. On this trip Cluff narrowly escaped drowning when he tried to swim a swift river in his underwear. The drawers slipped from his hips and hobbled his legs.

I could not kick myself loose and was being carried to the rapids below. I made a surface dive and ripped the garment from my ankles just in time.

The men averaged 25 miles a day on the back-pack trip.

Most of the nights were spent under some kind of shelter. At one place we were allowed to sleep in the village jail. . . .

It was at this place that we had our first taste of monkey meat. The man of the house informed me secretly that he had [nothing else]. . . . Should he serve that meat before the travelers? I told him to do so, but be careful that no bones should be in sight. . . . However, our host was careless enough to leave on a side table one little arm and hand with the fingers all tightly flexed by the heat.

At sight of this, when leaving, "My companions lost their dinners," Cluff stated.

On returning from Palenque, Cluff rejoined the others at Comitan. On the seventeen-day trip from there to Guatemala City four men fell sick, Paul Henning so seriously that he stayed at Heuheutenango for treatment while the others went on. Joseph Adams went home; Wolfe left in a huff. Chester Van Buren decided to stay awhile in Guatemala to study other Mayan ruins. This left five survivors of the original nine who had continued from Nogales: Cluff, Kienke, Tolton, Magelby, and Fairbanks.

At Quirigua, the Cluff party met an archeologist named Gordon, who was exploring the ruins for Harvard University.

The Harvard scholar also served as guide to assist the men from the Brigham Young Academy in exploring the ruins. He was interested in the story of the Book of Mormon, but was cautious and diplomatic in expressing any opinion regarding the authenticity of the Nephite record.

The Roberts-Cluff narrative is remarkably frank in several places regarding the scientific aspect of the Cluff expedition.

"It is doubtful if there ever was as devout a group of 'archeologists' as was the Mormon expedition from Utah, as its members attempted to explore and explain what they were sure were remains of the cities built and inhabited by the Nephites. Little did they realize that they were amateurish and unscientific in their work, because they were unprepared to interpret their findings, and they were proceeding with minds closed to any other than their own preconceived assumption that the Book of Mormon is divine."

As for Cluff himself, he became convinced that the ruins of the Mayan period "were not of the Nephites." He did, however, confidently expect to find Nephite country in Colombia, where the Magdalena River had been the goal from the beginning. "Along the Magdalena," he wrote Brimhall, "we shall do our most important work."

On the way to Honduras, one mule gave out and three others died, as the tropical rains came in torrents. Time after time the mules mired in belly-deep mud and had to be dug out. With the humidity, the oppressive heat enervated man and animals. More mules neared exhaustion. When Fairbanks' saddle mule died, the middle-aged artist took turns riding other mules while the younger men walked, as the party pushed on through Honduras, Nicaragua, and into Costa Rica. Tolton wrote on June 14:

Again we find much rain and mud, mules mire to their knees, burros fall down in mud, have to lift them out. As Bro. Fairbanks and I were helping a burro out of water knee deep, Bro. Fairbanks fell over on his back in the water. I also fell in the water. It was comical, if it was wet. Walking in the mud pulled my shoes all to pieces. I have no others, and no money to buy any. Bro. Kienke loaned me a pair of moccasins. We are having great experiences. Talk about [the pioneers] crossing the plains and pushing hand-carts—nothing to it.

Chattering monkeys raced overhead in the rain forests; alligators slid into the streams; thousands of ducks enjoyed the wet weather of the swamps. On leaving the jungle, the men found the

region of Lake Managua in Nicaragua "indescribably beautiful."
Here was a garden region where "towns and cities were remarkably
clean and inviting. How could they be otherwise, . . . when they
were constantly washed with torrential showers."

At San José in Costa Rica, Fairbanks decided the rigors of the
trail were too much for an artist of middle age. He decided to take
ship to South America, and spend his time painting scenes of the
Nephite culture along the Magdalena River in Colombia. This left
four men remaining of the original party. Then the very next day
Heber Magelby took sick. Cluff left Tolton with him, with instructions to take train to Panama City when Magelby was well. Cluff
and Kienke then swung into the saddle, "determined to go all the
way to South America in the manner originally planned, regardless
of difficulties and unmindful of dangers from wild animals, Indians,
revolutionists, and tropical fevers."

With an Indian guide who agreed to lead them from San Marcos
to his native village of Boruca, but no farther (a distance as the
crow flies of about 75 miles but much longer by mule trail) they
"plunged immediately into a dense forest for what they had good
reason to believe would be the most difficult and trying part of
their entire journey."

Regarding this leg of the safari, Kienke reported:

The first day out was over a mountain trail and through a very dense
forest. . . . My mule plunged off a twelve-foot embankment. I succeeded
in getting her back on the trail. About an hour later her pack struck
a tree and threw her down the mountainside end over end six times.
Fortunately, no bones were broken and not much damage done. . . .

In some places the storms had washed away the trails, and in others
they had cut them so deep that the banks were twelve to fourteen feet
high. Trees had fallen across from bank to bank making veritable tunnels out of the trail. . . .

We discovered this trail to be a very old one leading southeast for
many days' travel. It may have been an old Nephite road unused for
hundreds of years. In some places the trail was steep, wet, and slick.
Our mules would start sliding and skid fifty feet or more with their legs
out before they could stop. We did the same thing and got a lot of
fun out of the adventure.

The Majaranco River "was wide and the current very swift." About 50 yards below the ford were rapids

where water was dashing up eight feet or more as it plunged over huge boulders. We rafted our things across and swam our mules. My mule got too close to the rapids and would have gone over them if I had not prayed to the Lord to give her strength to overcome the current.

On the fourth day they followed the Rio Savagra to the Pacific Ocean, and traveled along the beach when the tide was out to avoid the dense jungle at the shore line. While the men were making camp for the night the mules disappeared. Cluff went in search while Kienke cooked supper. Cluff returned with all the animals except Kienke's saddle mule.

This placed us in a very dangerous predicament. The tide was fast coming in and we had no time to lose. I threw a saddle on my other mule and dashed off for a race with the tide. It was almost in and licking up the sand within a rod of the shoreline. I found the mule, then looked back. There was only a narrow ribbon of sand left. . . . Applying spurs and whip I forced the animals into a run. During the last hundred yards or more the mules were splashing through two feet of water. It was to me the thrill of a lifetime. President Cluff laughingly declared me the winner of the race against tide and time.

After thirteen days they reached the Indian village of Boruca, situated on a beautiful plateau. The town "lay apparently at peace with itself and seemingly unaware of the existence of an outside world," Cluff said. However:

Evidence that the little Indian village was no peaceful Utopia, but just one of a million communities in this troubled world, was revealed by the fact that the community had just completed the construction of a jail, into which they had already moved instruments of torture. . . . We were granted the privilege of occupying the new building.

Though well fed and prosperous, the Indians refused to sell provisions to the travelers. Cluff and Kienke were discussing the situation while cooking what was almost the last of their food when a woman arrived at the jail in tears and bearing a gift of six eggs. Her little girl was sick with fever. Did the North Americans have medicine? Cluff dispensed quinine to the child and with Kienke administered faith healing by the laying on of hands. Next morning the little girl was playing about happily, while a queue was at the jail seeking treatment, the members bearing chickens, sweet potatoes, molasses, eggs, and other provisions.

Then dense jungle from Boruca along the Isthmus and across the border of Panama to David was too forbidding for any guide to undertake alone. No less than ten men would have to be hired, for mutual protection. Not being able to finance such a safari, the two Mormons asked directions and struck off by themselves.

This journey of less than 100 bee-line miles took thirteen difficult days. "Day after day we traveled through a dense forest," Cluff recalled, "expecting to come into contact with wild animals at any time."

While we frequently heard them at a distance, and often saw their tracks along the trail, we never actually did get to see anything more dangerous than monkeys and beautiful wild birds.

The Borucans had warned that the greatest hazard would be fording a river, where many had drowned.

Finally we reached the dreaded river, and took considerable time studying the currents before attempting to cross. While the information we had received from the good people of Boruca was helpful, I believe our past experience with rivers was most valuable. We were able to select the right course and landed on the other side without mishap. Our delight was unbounded, because we had been subconsciously fearing that dangerous stream ever since we left the little Indian village.

Soon afterwards we emerged from the dense forest and found ourselves entering the cultivated lands around the city of David, in northern Panama.

They found that here the roads were better but the hazards worse—a revolution was on. They continued, nevertheless, and after an arduous ten-day ride through rugged mountains reached Santiago, where an American rancher named Hill put them up. He and other citizens strongly advised against continuing the journey, predicting the Americans would be killed or at the very least have their mules and equipment confiscated. Cluff thanked them kindly and after a three-day rest pushed on.

As darkness was closing in on the third day out from Santiago, a detail of government troops stopped the two-man expedition and began taking possession of the equipment. When Cluff identified himself as a scientist from far-off Utah seeking evidence that these soldiers were descended from God's chosen people, the troops returned the equipment and rode away.

Again at Santa Maria they were strongly advised against continuing the trip.

But they did go on in the face of all advice to the contrary, and were soon riding through the stronghold of the revolutionists apparently unconcerned regarding the possible dangers that lay ahead. At least, they were confident that somehow they would be protected from serious harm, and would be permitted to continue their mission.

In short, they believed they were on the Lord's work, and that he would protect them in it. To Cluff's delight, "I learned that I could obtain written permission to see the head man of the revolution" and "get from him a free pass to travel through the country."

Cluff got the letter and "struck out immediately to get in touch with him."

We had traveled only a few miles before we met a company of soldiers, but we had no idea to what faction they belonged. If they were government soldiers I should show them my regular government pass. . . . If they were revolutionists I should show their commander my letter.

But fortunately, just as we were approaching close to the company, the road divided into two parallel highways, and we took one which would take us past the soldiers a little distance away. As we were passing them, their captain called out, "Have you got your passport?" I called back, "Yes." We moved on unhindered, and an hour or so later entered the little village where we were told we could contact the revolutionary leader.

With the mayor's permission they camped in an empty house. Presently a revolutionary officer arrived to question them. He took the letter and returned the next night. He took Cluff into a heavily guarded house and upstairs, where a man Cluff never saw examined the letter. Next day the two travelers were escorted to the camp of the rebel army, "and found ourselves well received." The revolt, they learned, was to overthrow the oppressive rule of a ruthless dictator.

After a visit of several days, Cluff and Kienke went on. Evidently their guide knew something they didn't, for at the noon camp he complained that the rocks were hurting his feet, and begged to be allowed to return.

We let him go, and . . . as we were sitting down to lunch a shot was fired from a clump of trees about three hundred yards away and a bullet lodged in the tree just above our heads. This was followed instantly by a second shot, then several more, all the bullets whizzing close to our heads.

I tied my handkerchief to a stick and stepped out, calling, . . . "We are friends! We are friends! Don't shoot!" Two more shots rang out. Then one of the rebels came out to meet me, and when within fifty yards dropped to one knee and took dead aim at me. It all happened so quickly and unexpectedly that I didn't have time to be frightened, but kept on walking toward him and shouting, "Amigos! Amigos!" He arose and came toward me while keeping his gun ready for instant use. . . . The rebel asked who we were and what we were doing here. I explained and he seemed satisfied. I requested to be taken to his camp and to be permitted to show our credentials to his commanding officer.

The men took the explorers to the rebel army camp, where they were assigned a place in the civilian area and told the captain would see them next day. That night, Cluff woke up to find a woman crawling toward his cot. She whispered, "Make no noise. They are preparing to kill you tonight," then crawled away. The two men lay with guns ready.

The remaining hours of the night seemed an eternity. When day broke and found us alive, . . . we thanked God for our deliverance.

Evidently it was a false alarm, for when they met the captain they were "treated with the utmost respect and courtesy."

After learning that we were explorers in search of scientific truth and that we represented one of the universities of the United States, our hosts were all gentlemanly to the extreme. We were furnished excellent food and a good place to sleep with no fear of mysterious nocturnal visitors. The next morning, after a sumptuous breakfast, . . . the captain furnished us a guide and away we went on our travels.

The guide took them through the rebel area, and "From there until we reached the Panama Creek the road was clear and in good condition." They pitched camp on the outskirts of Panama City, and Cluff took a train into town.

I found Brothers Van Buren, Tolton and Magelby waiting for us. We were overjoyed at seeing each other again, and had a most happy reunion. The next day, Sunday, September 15, 1901, all five of us found ourselves together again and in camp. On this long to be remembered Sabbath, we held a meeting, joined in song and prayer, and discussed future plans. We were determined to travel on into South America, and I was equally determined to cover every foot of the way by muleback if possible.

This Sunday was the highlight of the adventure. From that day, things went wrong.

When we tried to hire guides, we learned that the country over which we would be compelled to travel on the Isthmus of Panama was peopled by enemy [Choco] Indians who would allow no strangers to enter or pass through their territory. To attempt such a trip as we were planning would be not only to court disaster, it would be to commit suicide.

Before leaving Panama City, Cluff gave his six large journals of the trip to a local banker, Henry Ehrman, who had graciously offered to post them to the BYA. Then Cluff took train across the narrow neck of the Isthmus to Colón, and he was never to see the journals again, nor find a trace of the affable Henry Ehrman.

Cluff still hoped to continue by mule, for he had the men bring the outfit to Colón. They traveled along the route being excavated for a ship canal by the French, a project with an appalling toll of life. Men wrote their wills before leaving for "the hell-hole that is Panama"; some brought their coffins along. Malaria and "black vomit"—yellow fever—killed an estimated 20,000 on this ill-fated venture, while medical science tried vainly to find a cure. There were crackpots who claimed that both the ague and the black vomit were caused by mosquitoes; but this preposterous theory was firmly rejected, and men continued to die by thousands.

Perhaps the death toll at the canal was the final factor in dissuading Cluff from entering the forbidding Darien stretching along the Isthmus to Colombia. At Colón he learned that no guide would venture into the fetid swamps and dense jungles of the Darien. No roads existed. There were no towns except a few seaports. The jungle teemed with insects, snakes, crocodiles. Vampire bats would drain the blood of the mules at night, the animals becoming thinner each day until they died. But worst of all were the naked Choco Indians, who allowed none to enter their territory. The Chocoans would never be seen; their presence unsuspected until poisoned arrows and darts from blowguns brought death. No one in history had traveled by land from Colón to South America.[19]

Cluff sold the mules and equipment. The party boarded the steamship *France* for Colombia. At Barranquilla, at the mouth of the Magdalena River, they were at last near their goal, the Nephite civilization. Zarahemla had been built somewhere along the drainage basin. With great expectations they boarded the riverboat *Barranquilla,* and the wood-fired sternwheeler began churning upstream. As one day followed another, something happened to Cluff. The boat moved through muddy water of a stream that snaked through swampy jungle so dense that no roads led through it. Except for occasional clusters of thatched huts on the bank, towns were spaced a hundred miles apart. The Colombian civilization thrived in the temperate regions of the highland plateaus, not down in the steaming jungle of the river bottom.

Then why would the Nephites choose this as the site of Zarahemla? Cluff no longer had an answer.

At Magangue, some 250 miles upstream, Walter Tolton and Chester Van Buren landed to conduct scientific research of the river and its tributaries. The others continued upriver, and came across the artist, Fairbanks, just out of the hospital after several weeks of jungle fever. He was calling it quits. The Cluff party helped him

---

19. When A. F. Tschiffely made his horseback ride a quarter century later, he, also, though "bitterly disappointed," bypassed the Darien, taking ship from Cartagena to Colón. "These regions are vast swamps and virgin forests, many of which have never been trodden by human foot," he said. "No land, but only fluvial means of communication exist, and to attempt this crossing would be a foolhardy enterprise in which both horses and rider would perish. This opinion was confirmed by General Jaramillo, who had unsuccessfully attempted to take a Colombian army across these regions during the war with Panama."

As late as August 1970, the *National Geographic* noted that from Cartagena, "Panama City lay only 250 miles to our west, on the other side of a region as impassable today as when Pizarro worked down the Pacific Coast in 1526-7. The tangle of mountains, jungles, rivers, and swamps remains the only gap in the Pan American Highway System."

pack and saw him on a boat downriver, then went on to Honda and took train to the capital, Bogotá.

There, the American consul was their host for several days, during which time he dissuaded Cluff from continuing by mule "through Colombia, Ecuador, Peru and Chile to the destination point at Valparaiso which President Cluff had set for the expedition," the Roberts-Cluff story says.

Nevertheless, he offered to consult the Colombian government officials to see if they would favor such a trip and if they would furnish an escort for the journey through their country because of the revolution going on. This he did, and received a very definite and negative reply. The Colombian government could not guarantee their safety. Indeed, according to officials who were best informed, . . . the Americans would most likely have all their possessions confiscated by revolutionists before they had travelled far, and they would almost certainly be killed.

Cluff had encountered similar advice in Costa Rica, but had kept on. He'd gone through Panama during a revolution. Yet now at Bogotá he gave up and headed back. Why? A clue is found in the Roberts-Cluff manuscript:

All that the subject of this biography did throughout his educational life—his missionary labors, his teaching and leadership at the Brigham Young Academy, and his great venture on the expedition—all these things were outcomes of an *assumption,* a magnificent assumption unproved and perhaps unprovable but tremendously stimulating.

But the Magdalena basin had failed to corroborate this assumption. Cluff's own observations, and the research of others of the party, had unearthed no evidence of the Nephite culture here or at the ruins of Central America. The magnificent assumption was shattered. Disheartened, he turned back. The party returned to Provo, arriving on Cluff's forty-fourth birthday, February 7, 1902, some twenty-two months after the expedition embarked with such high expectations.

Despite the fact that Cluff had led the first safari across the land route from North to South America, and regardless of the genuine scientific value of data and specimens collected, Cluff found the homecoming definitely chilly. Disgruntled expedition members who had been called back from Nogales had blamed Cluff for their embarrassment, while "the bespectacled little Walter M. Wolfe," the Roberts-Cluff account states, "had completely discarded his sheep's clothing." Wolfe had bad-mouthed Cluff to everyone who would listen, including the eager snoop, Charles Mostyn Owen.

At the homecoming parade, the accolades were rather hollow. Provo even witnessed the unprecedented spectacle of public dissent by BYA students, traditionally known for conformity. A group who wanted the acting president, George H. Brimhall, to remain in office, paraded in noisy dissent, chanting, "We want Brimhall!"

Wolfe tried to capitalize on the disappointment "of the expedition boys by having them sign with him a list of complaints against President Cluff and have him tried by the Board of Trustees," the Roberts-Cluff story stated. When the boys backed off from making formal complaint, Wolfe and his former fellow counselor, Gordon Beckstead, filed charges with the Board of Trustees.[20]

Charges against the president . . . included numerous specified accusations which might be classified under the terms mismanagement, misrepresentation, misappropriation of funds, and immorality. The charge of immorality was confined to the accusation that Benjamin Cluff, Jr., had taken a young woman to wife while on the expedition, even though he was already married.[21]

At a hearing before a committee representing the Board of Trustees, Wolfe withdrew several charges. Expedition members defended Cluff, detailing Wolfe's alcoholic bouts, telling of his professions of love for Cluff while en route and his tearful farewell on leaving the expedition in Guatemala. When the board met for final action, Joseph F. Smith, now president of the church, made "significant remarks" in support of Cluff, as did influential board members John Henry Smith and Susa Young Gates.

Nevertheless, when the Board made its final decision whether or not to reappoint Benjamin Cluff, Jr., . . . he received a bare majority of one vote. . . . President Cluff was deeply unhappy over this situation, and it was undoubtedly a contributing factor in causing him to leave his beloved school one and one-half years later.

20. For text of complaint, see SI.
21. This is the only mention of the plural marriage in the entire Cluff manuscript.

The actual reason for Cluff's resignation was the Smoot investigation. In marrying a plural wife a decade after the Manifesto—at a time when the official posture of the church was that polygamy had entirely ceased—Cluff had only followed the example of many other men, as Charles Mostyn Owen had been busily proving. So it was not what Cluff had done, but the fact that it had become public knowledge. Every man entering the Principle during this period was fully aware that he did it on his own responsibility, and that if he was exposed he could expect no support from the church.

The protests against Apostle Reed Smoot retaining his Senate seat had been mounting for a full year when the Senate Committee on Privileges and Elections scheduled hearings to begin January 16, 1904. Federal marshals began delivering subpoenas in Mormon country to church officials and to alleged polygamists on Charles Mostyn Owen's list.

If Cluff testified under oath regarding his last marriage, it would involve men of high church position who had known of it. He resigned from the Brigham Young University December 23, 1903.[22] When hearings began in Washington three weeks later he was beyond reach of subpoenas, south of the border as superintendent of the Utah-Mexican Rubber Company.

Almost forty years later, Gene Roberts ran into Cluff, then in his eighties, running a small fruit stand on the highway near Redondo Beach, California. Cluff told him the story of his magnificent quest.

He had sought a greater prize than wealth, fame, or power: he had been touched with the divine fire in a search for evidence to verify the word of God. Though he hadn't found Zarahemla, what man ever reaches his ultimate goal?

Meanwhile in his later years he had had a change of mind regarding Nephite ruins. Although he hadn't discovered the capital of the Book of Mormon people, that didn't mean it didn't exist. It was there, somewhere, awaiting discovery. He had pioneered. Cluff was sure that others who followed would, someday, find Zarahemla.

The search continues. Various private and quasi-official expeditions have undertaken the quest. In 1951 the church sponsored the BYU-New World Archeological Foundation for this purpose; yet after publishing thirty-eight volumes of its findings during the next

22. The academy now was the university.

twenty-four years, "No statement of the landing places of these [Book of Mormon] people or the identification of any of the lands settled and cities established has ever been officially made by the Church or the Foundation," the publication *Brigham Young University Today* reported in December 1975.

BYU President Dallin Oaks authorized members of the faculty on Dec. 5 to exclude any student in violation of University dress and grooming standards from examinations at the end of the Fall Term. . . .

Faculty members were also given the prerogative to record failing grades for students in violation of BYU standards.

"We are all proud of BYU and the high moral principles for which we stand," the President said. "That is why faculty, students and administrators are deeply concerned over the . . . many violations of general grubbiness, moustaches below the corners of the mouth, sideburns of excessive length, and [with women,] mini skirts and other immodest apparel. The primary violations are young women wearing jeans and young men with hair length over their ears and shirt collars."

—BYU TODAY, February 1974

SALT LAKE CITY.—*A group called "Citizens for Decency" has vowed not to buy Sea and Ski suntan lotion unless the firm puts bigger bikinis on its billboard beauties.*

—San Francisco CHRONICLE, July 30, 1970

12

The Coach, the Culture, and Professor Koch of Vienna

IN THE ENTIRE WASATCH FRONT there was no more unlikely rebel than Eugene L. Roberts, director of physical education at Brigham Young University (not to be confused with the historian, B. H. Roberts). At the austere and straitlaced Y, Eugene L. Roberts was dedicated to building body, mind, and character. He was prominent in civic affairs, and had personally spark-plugged the Boy Scout program in Utah. He was a well-known author, a popular speaker, and honored for participation in church affairs. No breath of scandal ever touched this father of eight, whose personal life was beyond reproach and whose hobby was climbing mountains.

Yet a few intimate friends knew that Gene Roberts delighted in a secret life as a gadfly to the local establishment. He had a passion for that peculiarly American hoax indigenous to the West, the elaborate practical joke. Friends never knew when a series of strange events would entangle them, only to collapse in a house of cards. Yet it didn't stop there. Gene Roberts gleefully concocted hoaxes that involved the university, the town of Provo, and, in fact, the Mormon culture.

After his creation of the mythical "Harry Davidson Kemp," Provo quite literally was never the same. And after he concocted "Professor Koch of Vienna," neither was the local culture.

Harry Davidson Kemp proved that you *can* lick the city hall. Local citizens were highly pleased when this mythical "famous American journalist" supposedly arrived at Provo's sparkling mountain climate for his health. Because he required complete rest, Kemp remained in seclusion, reluctantly declining the many invitations to social affairs and requests for speaking engagements. In fact, only his old friend, Coach Gene Roberts of the Y, knew his identity and whereabouts. The public was delighted when Roberts persuaded the noted journalist to allow the Provo *Herald* to publish a series of articles in preparation by Kemp for eastern journals concerning central Utah—its magnificent scenery, its healthful climate, its hospitable people, and, Kemp admitted candidly, its need for improvement.[1]

Kemp's technique of criticism was the traditional Mormon "fist sandwich," a slice of wry between layers of praise. Snug in its

1. Roberts at first used the pseudonym "Harry Kemp," until the day that his fellow faculty member, T. Earl Pardoe, ran on to a poem by that author in a national magazine. Roberts was dismayed to discover that inadvertently he'd used the name of a living author. The actual Harry Kemp was an author and playwright, and published several volumes of poems. He also published two autobiographical books, "Tramping on Life," and, at the time he supposedly was in Provo, "More Miles" (New York: Boni and Liveright, 1926).

On discovering this, Roberts gave his pseudonym a middle name, to avoid a possible charge of plagiarism or defamation of character; thus "Harry Davidson Kemp." He told no one, not even Pardoe, who in the book, *The Sons of Brigham,* assumed that Roberts was the poet, author, and playwright, Harry Kemp.

mountain valley, secure in the belief that this was the chosen spot for the Lord's chosen people, Provo previously never had heard a discouraging word, until Kemp pointed out that "The Garden City" had weeds in the garden, ragged lawns, rank growth among the banks of the irrigation ditches bordering its dusty streets.

Housing was another target for Kemp's pen. Except for a few scattered mansions, such as the Knight, Mangrum, Smoot, Brimhall, Allen, and Taylor homes, Provo dwellings were going to seed. If a house was comfortable and weather-tight, people didn't seem to care if it needed paint, the front porch sagged, and there were gaps in the picket fence. Kemp was surprised that the modern city allowed new homes to be built which weren't "modern"—had no bathroom.

But why spruce up homes and gardens, with streets in such a mess? Except for University Avenue and Center Street, the only paving was on the highway in and out of town. Harry Davidson Kemp reported that his teeth rattled during a tour of the residential area as the Model T bounced through chuckholes and left a thick streamer of dust.

Nor did Kemp spare the university. The campus was divided between the original BYA buildings on University Avenue and the new construction atop Temple Hill almost a half mile away. With ten minutes between class periods, it was a mad scramble as hundreds of students hurried between the upper and lower campus, particularly in bad weather, for there was no paved path up the hill.

Harry Davidson Kemp changed all that. Conscious that the eyes of the entire nation were on Provo through these dispatches, the citizens pitched in with a typically Mormon cooperative effort on a massive program of city betterment. Joe Budro remembers the clean-up-paint-up campaign that gripped the city. Provo schools all joined the effort; bishops of the various wards exhorted their flocks and delegated the ward teachers on their monthly visits to make sure the program was being supported by every family. If the head of a household couldn't do it himself, or wouldn't, a gang of men from his ward arrived and did it for him. BYU students spent a hard week building concrete retaining walls and a paved path up Temple Hill.

Service clubs rehabilitated the city dump out east on Center Street. That treasure trove of Budro's childhood, prowled in search

of copper and brass worth 10¢ a pound to the junkman, became a
city park. The municipality burnished public buildings and grounds,
groomed parks. The most massive and expensive undertaking was
that the city embarked on a project of paving its residential streets.

With the city sparkling like a jewel, Harry Davidson Kemp expressed his approval, and, health restored, bade farewell.

Basically, Gene Roberts was a born rebel in the very heartland
of conformity. In an environment where all decisions were un-
questioned as the Lord's will, he bucked the official establishment
and, one way or another, had his own way in a surprising number
of cases.

He demonstrated this trait early. As one of the students of
Benjamin Cluff's horseback expedition to Zarahemla, Roberts was
among those who returned from Nogales. While many of the others
were called on missions, he resumed study at the Y and made
second-string quarterback on the football squad. And then,
abruptly, the school abolished football as being too rough.

Roberts was furious, particularly since football—and in fact
the entire athletic program—had been adopted only recently, after
Brimhall replaced Cluff as president. There had been a strong tradition of opposition to sports at the Y. The founder, Karl G. Maeser,
was "adamantly opposed to athletics," and had been supported in
this by George Q. Cannon and other church authorities. George
Goddard, Church Sunday School superintendent, protested that
"College yells and football games are damaging to the respectability
of such institutions," being hazardous to life and limb and "very
destructive" to the "religious tone that should characterize every
Latter-day Saint school of learning." Brigham Young, Jr., known
as "Young Briggie," called college yells "an abomination to my
spirit."

College debating had also come under attack as destructive of
character because students were required to argue positions which
were against their beliefs. The school had therefore banned both
athletics and debating. These activities recently had been restored,
but now once again football was banned.[2]

Roberts knew that protest by a student would be futile; it could
only land him on the carpet. However, as editor of the college paper
he had access to the power of the printed word. A contributor

2. BYU.

called "Owl" published several sharp pieces for the *White and Blue*, and this unprecedented criticism from within "created a sensation among students and faculty."[3] While the "Owl" pieces didn't get football restored, the hornets' nest they stirred had a lasting influence on Roberts' future. And he wasn't through. Though the Y no longer had a football team, Roberts organized the "Provo" team, which played the same schedule with the same student players except that now Roberts was first-string quarterback and captain. This was the last football team until Roberts himself restored the sport at the Y twenty years later.

Roberts also showed his spunk in religious matters. He was teaching at Provo in the Franklin grade school and engaged to be married when the letter arrived from Box B calling him on a mission without purse or scrip. Another letter in the same mail offered him a job editing a newspaper at $100 a month, an excellent opportunity compared to teaching, which paid only $65, and that for only the eight months of the school year. Of course it was unthinkable for a Provo teacher to reject a mission call; however, while a missionary traditionally "goes where the Lord wants me to go," Roberts distinctly didn't want to be stuck two years at Nauvoo, Illinois, guiding tourists about the abandoned Mormon city. It also was traditional for a missionary to kiss his girl good-bye, then live in suspense while away awaiting the "Dear John" letter.

Roberts had no intention of risking the loss of the beautiful Sytha Brown, so he promptly married her, then wrote Salt Lake saying he not only desired a foreign mission but wanted to take his wife along. Perhaps because such a letter was so exceptional, Gene and Sytha Roberts sailed for Liverpool in July 1906, aboard the White Star liner *Arabic,* with visions of treading the pioneer path of Heber C. Kimball, Brigham Young, Wilford Woodruff, John Taylor, Willard Richards, and a handful of other stalwarts who had made thousands of converts and established a shipping service to carry them to the gathering of Zion.[4]

This dream collapsed on landing in England. Pioneer days were over. The missionary program now fostered an "image." Whereas Brigham Young arrived in homespun, wearing a cap his wife had

3. Marva Hodson Gregory, *The Life and Educational Contribution of Eugene Lusk Roberts,* M.S. thesis, University of Utah, 1952. Hereafter, "Gregory."
4. Woodruff alone baptized some 8,000.

made from an old pair of pantaloons, Roberts found English missionaries must now wear dress suits and top hats. To him, they looked like professional clergymen, scorned by Mormons as "preaching for hire."

Roberts arrived just in time for a missionary conference at Bradford, where President Serge F. Ballif of the Swiss and German Mission called for volunteers to proselyte secretly in Germany, where missionary work was forbidden on pain of imprisonment. Tingling, Roberts looked at Sytha, to find her eyes shining. This was like the old days, when John Taylor had brought the gospel to France and Germany, holding secret meetings one jump ahead of the police.

The young couple registered at Stuttgart as "students" and for six months lived a cloak-and-dagger life bootlegging the gospel before danger of arrest caused a transfer to Switzerland. There, Sytha presented her husband with a baby girl.

On returning from his mission, Roberts went to Yale as assistant instructor to prepare for a career in physical education. As a teenager, he'd belonged to the Third Ward League, an athletic group, where he'd been coached in boxing by Willard Bean, known in the ring as the "Mormon Cyclone." Roberts picked up enough of the manly art that he subsequently gave some pointers to a husky Mormon kid getting started in the fight game, a bootblack named Jack Dempsey.

Near the close of the school year at Yale, Roberts considered several job offers. One was from George H. Brimhall, offering the position of director of physical education at the BYU for $1,200 a year. In reply, Roberts let Brimhall know he could begin elsewhere at $2,000. However, Brimhall knew the counter to that gambit. If it was gold he wanted, take it, Brimhall replied; but if he wanted happiness among his own people and treasures in heaven where neither moth nor rust doth corrupt, the Y was the place.

There were dire predictions that Roberts wouldn't last, when he announced that he was more interested in a program of physical fitness for Y students than in producing winning teams. Furthermore, he wouldn't proselyte athletes, nor allow alumni or the town to do so; there would be no jobs given for athletic ability, no scholarships, no subsidies of any kind, nor would athletes receive classroom favoritism. Also, there would be no paid coaching staff. He would personally coach every team of every sport, and direct the physical education program, with volunteer student help.

The basketball team greeted the new coach's methods with rebellion. Instead of telling them exactly what to do, Roberts stressed the development of "fundamental naturalness" with drills in passing, guarding, shooting, feinting. Roberts gained a truce only by making the whole team assistant coaches.

The attitude changed as the team won its first game, then the second and third, and went on to an undefeated season. Part of the success was due to the "renowned athletic directors," "famous coaches," and other experts—including the prestigious journalist, Harry Kemp—who just happened to see each game and who wrote detailed critiques to the Provo *Herald,* analyzing strong points and team weaknesses, while offering constructive tips for improvement. By coaching on the floor and through the press, Roberts fielded winning teams during his eighteen years at the Y, despite a college enrollment limited to 250 and a ban on recruiting.[5] In 1917, after taking the Utah Basketball League championship, the team went to the National AAU Tournament in Chicago and finished second.

An all-around athlete, Roberts could demonstrate by example. Joe Budro remembers watching him coach a pole-vaulter, at a time when Roberts was in his mid-forties. When the student didn't get the hang of things, Roberts took off his glasses and doffed the jacket of his business suit; then, still wearing vest, necktie, and street shoes, he took the pole and demonstrated. The student, stung by the fact that a man old enough to be his father had cleared the bar when he couldn't, took the pole and equaled the coach's mark. A contest ensued, the bar going up and up until Roberts bested the student.

Roberts coached Alma Richards and Clinton Larson to world records in the high jump. Richards won the Olympic championship in 1912, and three years later the National AAU Decathlon. Larson subsequently broke Richards' mark at the Pennsylvania Relays, then won first place at the Inter-Allied Games in Paris.[6]

---

5. At times it was even less. In 1921, amid rumors that the church would close down Brigham Young University, only twelve college students graduated. The Y was primarily a normal school. Below college level it had classes from kindergarten through the grades and high school, to provide teacher training.
6. Considering that it was illegal at that time to jump in any manner except "feet first," Richards' 6′4″ and Larson's 6′5⅜″ were exceptional marks; in fact, Richards held the world record for eight years.

Roberts was enthusiastic about the potential of the Boy Scouts and headed a group which urged the church to take the program under its wing. However, after presenting the case to a committee appointed to investigate the proposition, the coach was keenly disappointed when the committee chairman, B. H. Roberts, reported to the brethren that every objective of the Boy Scout program could be achieved by the existing teenage organization, the Mutual Improvement Association, and was thus unnecessary.

Roberts left the meeting at Barratt Hall in Salt Lake with mind churning. He wasted not a moment railing against the stupidity of the official mentality. *He* was at fault, for not presenting Scouting as something the church couldn't afford to do without. How to repair the damage? By the time he reached Provo he had the answer, and he was up early next morning hammering away on his Underwood.

His article said nothing about Boy Scouts—no use picking off the scab—but instead proposed organization of the Boy Pioneers of Utah, to preserve the memory of the pioneers. Here he plucked one of the most responsive heartstrings of Mormonism.[7] He invoked the vision of the Boy Pioneers hiking over old wagon and pushcart trails, reliving the heroic treks of their ancestors, camping as they did, listening to living pioneers tell stories around the campfire, keeping alive the old traditions.

On seeing the manuscript, B. H. Roberts did an about-face, not only getting "The Boy Pioneers of Utah" published in the church magazine, *The Improvement Era,* but lending his own eloquent pen in support of church sponsorship of the Boy Scout program, which was done.[8]

The following year, 1912, Gene Roberts found the answer to a dream he'd been vainly promoting ever since seeing the religious mountain pilgrimages in Switzerland during his mission. He wanted a similar group to climb up Timpanogos, highest summit of the Wasatch, which rose 12,008 feet into the sky at the north end of Academy Avenue. But Utah had no tradition of mountain climbing. To the wagon and handcart companies mountains weren't venerated—they loomed as back-breaking obstacles to be got over,

7. In his *Mormon Country,* Wallace Stegner likened reverence for the Utah pioneers to the ancestor worship of the Chinese.
8. Gregory.

around, or through. Provo citizens couldn't imagine climbing a mountain for *fun*. In the fall, yes, you went deer hunting. In December you hiked up Rock canyon for a Christmas tree. On Y Day students toted lime and water up the Y Mountain to whitewash the rocks forming the school letter.[9] You might prospect for minerals, go fishing in the canyons, search for a lost cow—but, climbing for fun? What could you do once you got to the top? Come down. Big deal.

After years of frustration, in a flash of light Roberts knew the answer: make it an *event*. Provo loved pageantry, cultural affairs, educational shindigs, and tradition.[10] Roberts began to publicize the Legend of Timpanogos, sacred mountain of the Indians, whose silhouette against the sky resembled a sleeping princess. He wrote "The Story of Utahna and Red Eagle," combining scraps of legend with a fertile imagination. Mary Hale Woolsey, who had written the lyrics of the song hit, "Springtime in the Rockies," did the words for "On the Trail of Timpanogos," to the music of Seldon Heaps. Roberts, President George H. Brimhall, and Professor Harrison R. Merrill wrote poems about the mountain.

The famous author, poet, playwright, and journalist, Harry Davidson Kemp, lent his prestige and his pen toward building the legend and promoting the hike. Artists painted Timpanogos as it appeared during all seasons (but always from the viewpoint of looking north from Provo). The mountain became such an object of veneration that Joe Budro's art teacher at Provo High spent sixteen years of devout study before daring to touch brush to canvas. Other artists were bolder, until virtually every house in Provo had either an oil or reproduction vying for space on the walls with other favorites, "The Lone Wolf," "The End of the Trail," or a Maxfield Parrish.

Timpanogos Cave, near the base of the north slope, became a National Monument, "abounding in coloration, odd forms, and curious resemblances,"

. . . the Dove's Nest, the Reclining Camel, Father Time's Jewel Box, Mother Earth's Lace Curtains, the Chocolate Fountain (well named),

9. This "Y" at 465' x 168' is claimed to be the largest school letter in the nation.

10. During Joe Budro's college days the Y had the tradition of each class wearing its own costume. This tradition was born and died in one year.

a seal, a dressed chicken, and scores of others. The "Heart of Timpanogos," bearing a remarkable resemblance to the human vital organ, is illuminated with a red light from behind; variations in opacity give it a lifelike appearance.[11]

Roberts carefully prepared the stage. People drove up Provo canyon, branched off at Wildwood up a steep road (which Model T's had to take in reverse) to the base of the mountain at Stewart's Flat, which Roberts had renamed Aspen Grove. They enjoyed an evening program of music, drama, and story-telling. They sat around a big campfire and ate a hearty barbecue dinner. They slept under the stars and next morning followed Gene Roberts up the mountain.

It became an annual event. The legends grew, the programs became more elaborate, celebrities attended; and when the Kiwanis Club threw its weight behind the Timp hike, Roberts knew he was in like Flynn.[12] Kiwanis improved the road to Aspen Grove. The National Park Service helped Y students build a trail up Timp. The event grew even beyond the dreams of its sponsor—now called "Timpanogos" Roberts. From a group of 22 the first year, there were more than 7,000 hikers the final year, and, with the Mormon love of superlatives, it was billed as the largest group climb in America.

Yes, there was a final year, and fortunately Roberts didn't live to see it. After the 1970 hike, with "ecology" the national hysteria and environmentalists in the saddle, the event was canceled. Hikers might tear down the mountain or something.

While Eugene L. Roberts received many honors and awards, he will be cherished in memory for his secret life as a prankster; and the climax of this career was the hoax of Professor Koch of Vienna. Professor Koch came into being because of a nagging doubt. Provo had long prided itself on being the cultural center of Utah; yet Roberts held some reservations. He enlisted the talents of Professor Koch, and the help of his old friend, Harry Davidson Kemp, to make sure.

It was quite true that Provo was mad about cultural events.

11. *Utah, a Guide to the State,* American Guide Series (New York: Hastings House, 1941). Hereafter, "Utah."
12. In Provo they said Kiwanis ran the town, Rotary the business, and Lions had the fun.

The Coach, the Culture, and Professor Koch of Vienna

The Y sponsored the Lyceum series, which brought poets, dancers, novelists, singers, and performing groups to Utah valley. Will Durant, Carl Sandburg, Sergei Rachmaninoff, and Robert Frost appeared at the Y. Professor Herald R. Clark, in charge of the program, read the New York *Times* to find where notables and performers were traveling, and if within range brought them to Provo—the Minneapolis, Los Angeles, and Boston symphonies performed, the French National Orchestra and the New York Philharmonic. Soloists included Jascha Heifetz, Fritz Kreisler, Clifford Curzon, Helen Traubel, Bela Bartok, Artur Rubenstein, and Ezio Pinza.

But enthusiastic as the response was, and regardless of packed auditoriums and the critical acclaim of the *Herald*, Gene Roberts wondered if the people really appreciated the events or liked to appear as if they did. The Y cultural programs were the *thing* in Provo; you had to go, had to be seen; you just didn't rate socially if you couldn't toss off references to the brilliance of Heifetz as compared to the warmth—the *heart*—of Kreisler. But Roberts had noticed that the comments were strangely parallel to the *Herald* reviews, and he had observed some of the most cultured citizens napping during the most inspiring performances.[13] Roberts discussed his nagging doubt with his friend T. Earl Pardoe, chairman of the BYU Speech Department, and *confrère* in the Boy Scout, Timp hike, and other projects. Pardoe also held reservations. So Gene Roberts concocted Professor Koch of Vienna to make sure.

The townspeople first learned of Professor Koch through a dispatch from Harry Davidson Kemp, now touring Europe. Kemp said that the famous pianist, whose revolutionary percussion style of play had taken Europe by storm, would tour America and appear at the Y. Meanwhile, Kemp poured coal on the cultural fires with dispatches of Koch's brilliant performances at Rome, Hamburg, Moscow, Prague, and other cities. Then came disheartening news that Professor Koch, exhausted by the European tour, had canceled the American visit.

When all seemed lost, Coach Eugene L. Roberts sent an appeal through Kemp for the professor to reconsider. Then came the electrifying news that Professor Koch would indeed arrive at Provo. He had heard much of the beauty of Utah valley, of the great

13. A sister of Joe Budro's never missed an event and slept through every one.

183

mountain Timpanogos, while the unparalleled hospitality and deep appreciation of music at Provo was known to artists throughout the world. Rather than disappoint such an audience, and because of his friendship for Harry Davidson Kemp, he would come to America, but for one performance only, at Provo!

And it would be on a basis of friendship. He would waive his customary $3,000 fee.

With the stage set, Roberts visited his friend Al in Salt Lake. Al was organist for his local ward, was active in amateur theatricals, and had a talent for comedy. He howled with delight on hearing of the hoax and agreed to work up a routine. Roberts suggested that Al begin the concert with a serious composition, then gradually turn it into burlesque until by the end of the concert it would be broad slapstick.

"About halfway through they begin to grin, and we end with a belly laugh," Al said.

"I'll bet they take the whole thing straight, as art."

"But after all, Gene, these people have heard the best artists in the world. They know good music."

"Professor Koch's percussion style is something new. And who would be first to say, 'But the emperor has no clothes'?"

"Aw, Gene—they'll break down before I take off the wig and beard at the finale."

"We'll see," Roberts said.

While Harry Kemp beat the publicity drums, Al worked up a routine which, in rehearsal, had Roberts screaming.

The actual arrival of Professor Koch presented ticklish problems. The great man demanded absolute privacy; no reception; no interviews. He would arrive at Salt Lake incognito, where Kemp's friend Eugene L. Roberts would meet him and drive him to Provo for the performance.

When Roberts arrived at Salt Lake to pick up Al on the day of the show, he found the man in a blue funk. "I can't do it, Gene."

"You've got to," Roberts protested.

"Look, I'm organist for the ward. My wife is counselor in the Relief Society. A thing like this—I just can't."

"It's only a joke, Al."

"Think of yourself, Gene. People won't think it's funny. You could be called on the carpet. If this backfires, you could lose your job at the Y."

"But the house is sold out. What'll I do?"

"Tell them the professor canceled out."

"After all this buildup? He's *got* to show."

"All right, Professor," Al said, handing him the beard and wig. "Good luck."

When Professor Koch stepped onto the stage that evening, he certainly fit the image of the eccentric genius. Thanks to the apprehensive help of T. Earl Pardoe, it was an excellent job of makeup and costume. The professor wore a bright red necktie with a rusty full-dress suit, and on his feet were tennis shoes. He peered through thick glasses and seemed so shortsighted that he stumbled over the piano stool. This opening pratfall brought only gasps of concern. The professor announced in a thick accent that he would interpret the deep meaning of the first composition he had ever played. He sat down, raised his hands over the keyboard, then paused. He wound the circular seat of the stool higher. Once more he got ready, but again stopped to whirl the seat lower. After several adjustments he began playing "Chopsticks."

Upon completion of the first number, the professor arose in dead silence and took a bow. Then the applause came like thunder. The people of Provo certainly wouldn't disagree with renowned European critics who had recognized the subtle artistry with which the professor gave depth and meaning to an apparently childish rendition.

From that point, Roberts had to improvise. "Chopsticks" was his entire musical repertoire. So for the next number Professor Koch demonstrated the percussion technique which had taken Europe by storm, beating the keyboard with clenched fists and elbows. As the audience well knew, the percussion method was acclaimed by cultural centers of the Old World as an entirely new dimension in piano playing. Provo could do no less than show it was hep with lusty applause.

After a brief intermission, Professor Koch came onstage wearing boxing gloves. This gave an added dimension to his fist technique. The audience cheered the performance.

For the final number, it was apparent that the tennis shoes weren't merely an eccentricity of dress. Professor Koch sat atop the piano and stomped on the keys. The audience gave him a standing ovation.

At the curtain call, the professor took hold of his beard. Then Gene Roberts hesitated. He realized, as Al had, that he just couldn't do it. These were his own people. Yes, they had their little conceits, but who didn't? Yes, they had been bewildered by the performance, but felt obliged to show appreciation. He knew, also, how thin a line he had walked. The voice of a single child, saying "But the emperor has no clothes," would have toppled the entire structure. With applause beating in his ears, Professor Koch brought his fingers from the beard to his lips. He blew a kiss and was gone.

Many years later, Eugene L. Roberts attended a performance of Joe Budro's play, *The Square Needle,* at the Las Palmas Theater in Hollywood, and after the show told him the story of Professor Koch of Vienna. While this might be the first time the hoax has been written, there were some who smelled a rat at the time. One was the *Herald* editor, Ernest Rasmussen, who did not review Professor Koch's performance. He and others wondered why he and Roberts were never seen together, where the coach was on the night of the performance, and how Professor Koch got out of town. Yes, they'd been hoaxed, but as the people of Provo got wise, laughter swept through the town. They had the westerners' appreciation for the practical joke and certainly this was one in the grand tradition.

At this point some specialist in cultural trivia might arise to point out that it wasn't Joe Budro who wrote *The Square Needle,* but that Samuel W. Taylor actually was the author. This being true—who was Joe Budro?

Joe Budro was another mythical character of Provo. When Sam Taylor was a student at the Y he worked the swing shift as night clerk at the Roberts Hotel (built by the coach's uncle). Students arriving in Provo at the beginning of each college quarter would stay at the Roberts a day or so while finding permanent accommodations. There was considerable coming and going; and, for reasons best known to the ones involved, all the male students from southern Idaho signed the hotel register with the same name, "Joe Budro." Well, each morning the *Herald* would phone the hotel to find out who was in town. Joe Budro visited so often that the paper listed his arrivals, and, in fact, he became a person of local note.

The Coach, the Culture, and Professor Koch of Vienna

As for the night clerk, Sam Taylor joined the club. Henceforth, as Joe Budro he left a signature on guest books and registers at weddings, receptions, funerals, at national parks, at Timpanogos Cave, at the gorge of Hole-in-the-Rock, and wherever else people signed their names (except that he avoided restroom graffiti).

Because Taylor believed firmly that a reporter should keep out of his own publicity, Joe Budro's name and picture appeared in news items for the church press over the years, and in a book he helped write concerning the history of the Mormons in the San Francisco Bay area.[14]

Like Kilroy, Budro was there. And, as a final personal note, Taylor's daughter joined the club, as Josephine Budro.

14. *A Vineyard by the Bay,* by various authors (San Mateo: San Mateo Stake of Zion, 1968).

In our lovely Deseret,
Where the Saints of God have met,
There's a multitude of children all around;
They are generous and brave,
They have precious souls to save,
They must listen and obey the gospel's sound.

That the children may live long,
And be beautiful and strong,
Tea and coffee and tobacco they despise;
Drink no liquor, and they eat
But a very little meat;
They are seeking to be great and good and wise.

They should be instructed young,
How to watch and guard the tongue,
And their tempers train and evil passions bind;
They should always be polite,
And treat everybody right,
And in every place be affable and kind.

They must not forget to pray,
Night and morning every day,
For the Lord to keep them safe from every ill;
And assist them to do right,
That with all their mind and might,
They may love Him and may learn to do His will.

—SONGS OF ZION, No. 114

13

The Closet Budro of Happy Valley

IDA SMOOT DUSENBERRY was a younger sister of Reed Smoot. In 1876 he was one of the twenty-nine students in the first class attending Brigham Young Academy. Two years later, at the age of five, Ida became a pupil of the Kindergarten Normal Training School at BYA. She continued her education at that institution until graduating with a college degree.

Reed Smoot had become a U.S. senator, and the school a university, when Joe Budro began kindergarten at BYU, with Ida

Dusenberry his teacher. Budro wasn't really too fond of kindergarten; despite his angelic disposition and exemplary conduct, Mrs. Dusenberry would each day tie him up with a rope and lock him in a black closet. Budro never complained, though the curriculum did seem monotonous. Each afternoon when his mother asked what he'd learned, he'd say truthfully, "To take little bites." This was all there was time for, outside the closet, during the school year.

Being of modest nature, Budro never told his mother that he was receiving special attention. She was baffled when he refused to continue his education at the Lord's school. He enrolled in the first grade at the Parker public school, where his teacher was Edith Young, Brigham's granddaughter. Miss Young didn't have the rope and closet, but she did have the Robins and Bluebirds. Budro found himself in the Bluebird ghetto until nearly Christmas, when she discovered he'd memorized the first-grade reader and was reading *Black Beauty* behind it.

In the second grade, however, Miss Andelin again consigned him to the Bluebirds, until she found the reason for his inattention. He was devouring a Horatio Alger book a week in class. Then in the third grade Miss Bean cast him to the Bluebirds until the day he spelled the class down. At the end of the year she told him that if only one student could be promoted it would be him. Yet Jimmie Hickman, the next year, not only relegated him to the Bluebirds but put him on Poverty Row.

By this time the twig was bent. Budro accepted the fact that life was a matter of the Robins and Bluebirds, and that he never could expect to get along with the establishment. Nothing in later life would change this concept.

The Provo region was called Happy Valley, being remote from the wicked outside world, its people serene in the security of the only true gospel. For centuries theologians had wrestled with the question, What is God's will? The Saints of Happy Valley had the big answer, and if a minor question arose, the official Word could be had from Salt Lake by return mail.

Most backyards had a barn, cow, chicken coop, and pigpen. Budro drove Daisy and Buttercup to and from the First Ward Pasture morning and evening and learned the facts of life early when they pined for romance and he took them for a visit with Brother Smoot's bull.

Provo was "The Garden City." Each home had its vegetable patch, a couple of fruit trees, perhaps a stand of raspberries or strawberries. Each week it had its water turn from the irrigation ditches lining the streets. If the man above you didn't release the water in time; well, if there was one source of continual conflict in Happy Valley, this was it. In an earlier day, a man might take his rifle along with his shovel, if the ditch was dry.

At conference time in April and October the adult Saints boarded the Orem Electric line for Salt Lake to receive the inspired word from the Lord's prophets and take advantage of the conference sales. An intrepid few drove their cars the 45 miles of dust and chuckholes; and one, Walter Cox, a small and dapper man, put a flower in his buttonhole and walked to conference.

Women did their style shopping at conference time, and merchants reaped a semiannual harvest. It was also whispered that the soiled doves of Second South Street did a brisk business at this time. They were openly scornful of johns who bought girls' favors but insisted on keeping their garments on, evidently as protection against evil.

Budro wore a mask to school during the great influenza epidemic of 1918. Because of the scourge, there was no public funeral when Church President Joseph F. Smith died. The new president, Heber J. Grant, was thrilled by "the splendid editorial that appeared in the *Tribune,* when President Smith passed away," in contrast to the "many lies which appeared in that paper soon after he became President." Grant wrote to Reed Smoot that "I believe we are entering upon an era of good will for our people."[1]

Grant went to work to foster the era of good will through an aggressive public-relations program designed to present a new image of the Saints to the world. He altered the belligerent tone of the missionary lessons, claiming they made enemies rather than friends. He stiffened the attitude against plural marriage, actively helping civil authorities to bring such lawbreakers to justice. He used the church's growing financial clout, and Senator Smoot's increasing political power, to foster favorable publicity and suppress anything negative.

On an early Sunday morning Budro and other boys waited at

1. MFP, 5:168.

the Orem station, to begin their paper routes. When the bundles were tossed off, the *Tribune* carried black headlines. The screen's most popular actor, Fatty Arbuckle, was involved in the sordid death of a girl at a wild party. At this time Budro was looking forward to the beginning of a new serial at the Columbia, "Riders of the Purple Sage," based on the Zane Grey novel about the Mormons, which the church considered "scandalous." But he never saw the serial, nor did Fatty Arbuckle again appear on the screen. At Grant's urging, Reed Smoot persuaded Will H. Hays of the Motion Picture Producers Association—the Hays Office—to ban both. Grant wired congratulations to Smoot:

THE PRESIDENCY APPRECIATE HIGHLY WHAT MR HAYS HAS DONE IN SUPPRESSING THE ARBUCKLE AND OTHER IMPROPER FILMS.[2]

The Columbia, however, struck back. In defiance of local ordinance, it ran a motion picture on Sunday, which attracted Budro and a full house of sinners. The manager was promptly arrested, but showed another movie the following Sabbath. On appeal, the blue law was stricken down, amid dire predictions that it was the entering wedge of Gentile abominations.

Heber J. Grant continued the unending battle to keep Mormon women from wearing fashions of the wicked outside world. Brigham Young had spurred the formation of the Young Ladies Retrenchment Association, dedicated to the avoidance of the frills, flounces, and follies of foolish fashion. In fact he had tried to put females in uniform, the Deseret costume. But Brigham met defeat when the young ladies forgot their high resolves as it became apparent that the young men were attracted to giddy girls who did adorn themselves with frills and flounces.

By 1918 the demands of fashion seriously conflicted with the style of undergarment worn by women who had been through the temple. A circular to bishops declared:

The Saints should know that the pattern of endowment garments was revealed from heaven, and that the blessings promised in connection with wearing them will not be realized if any unauthorized change is made in their form, or in the manner of wearing them.

2. MFP, 5:198–203.

"The garments," the circular specified, must be "of the approved pattern; they must not be altered or mutilated, and are to be worn as intended, down to the wrist and ankles, and around the neck."[3]

But, like Brigham Young, Grant found that fashion had more clout than revelation from heaven, and was forced to compromise. Each change of the original pattern, however, was met with cries of outrage from hardshells, who claimed the sacred garment was being mutilated to a flimsy rag.

Some, even today, will wear nothing except the original pattern, to neck, wrists, and ankles. They also adhere to the tradition of never taking them off completely. Even while bathing, one leg is draped over the bathtub with the garment dangling from the ankle, and the new pair put on the other leg before the old is removed. During Budro's childhood a devout sister used to frequent the public swimming pool at Pioneer Park wearing her garments to wrists and ankles, and her swimming suit over the top.

As adherence to the original pattern became associated with dissident groups, this became a matter of official displeasure, until, as with plural marriage, there was a complete reversal of attitude. A most serious charge against a Mormon called before his stake high council accused of unchristianlike conduct, is that he doesn't wear the officially-approved garment—specifically, today, that he wears strings.

Perhaps in reaction to the ribald Gentile attitude toward plural marriage, the new image emphasized strict sexual morality, adultery became a sin second only to murder. Grant also placed enormous importance on the Word of Wisdom, until it became a question of whether a cigarette or a cup of coffee was worth more than the gospel; it had to be one or the other.

The Saints were exhorted to remain unspotted from the wicked outside world, to be in it but not part of its iniquities and abominations. Budro was fully aware of the insidious lure of evil, because from earliest memory he was tantalized by the exquisite bouquet of coffee in the kitchen, as his mother prepared the poison for Gentile boarders. He never had it at home, of course, but when, his moral fiber undermined, he ordered it at a café, he drank with

3. MFP, 5:110.

his left hand to put his lips on the rim at a place uncontaminated by the ungodly.

The very emphasis on the Word of Wisdom became a challenge to some, who went to no end of trouble to flout it. Budro's cousin Alvin constructed a special room in the basement, its door secured by a Yale lock, as a smoking retreat. The room had no furniture, not even an ashtray; the floor was an inch deep in cigarette butts. When Alvin entered his smoking room his wife stood upstairs at the window, ready to thump on the floor with a broom handle if visitors turned in the gate. Alvin, incidentally, was a prosperous business-man.

Budro's brother Raymond married a cold-water Mormon who lived in fear that he would fall victim to his family's weakness for coffee. During the depression she made him quit a traveling job paying $25,000 a year, because he might get the coffee habit on the road. What she never did know was that he had the habit when he married her, and contrived to maintain it. He had his cold-water breakfast with her at home, then hastened downtown for coffee and a doughnut at the Provo Bakery to top it off. He and his wife liked to drive up Provo canyon to his sister Lillian's for a visit. Lillian always had the coffeepot on, and when Raymond's car turned into the lane she knew what to do. Soon after arrival, Raymond would go to the bathroom, open the medicine cabinet, and enjoy a steaming cup of poison.

While Raymond sustained the Salt Lake authorities in their positions, one of them was personally obnoxious to him. This man (call him "Brother Jonas") in turn disliked Raymond; the two clashed on several occasions. As Brother Jonas lived on and on beyond his allotted three score and ten, Raymond wondered if he was so ornery that even the Lord didn't want him. "So I made a deal with the Lord," Raymond said. "I promised that if he'd take Brother Jonas, I'd quit coffee. Next morning the radio announced his death, and I haven't wanted a cup since."

At the counters of the Provo Bakery and Sutton's Café, Saints could sit around for hours howling over Word of Wisdom stories. One concerned a former bishop who explained, "I never take a highball except with members in good standing. Gentiles just wouldn't understand." But the classic was about the BYU prof who took a brisk walk each morning from the campus to Sutton's during an open class period for a cup of Postum. The waitress always put the can beside the cup to avoid the appearance of evil. This went on for some twenty years, until one day there was a new waitress. The prof ordered Postum, she gave him Postum, and he was so infuriated that he never went back.

Professional wowsers toured Mormon country during Budro's tenure at Provo High.[4] These zealous upholders of Zion's mores dedicated their lives to terrifying teenagers regarding what, in those simple days, were the two major threats to LDS youth, the cigarette habit and the solitary vice. The Sex Maniac, as students called the sin-stomper who threatened debility, nervous collapse, loss of memory, pimples, rotting of the moral fiber, insanity, eternal damnation, and hair in the palm, would point to the east, where the Utah State Mental Asylum at the base of Y Mountain marked the end of Center Street. There, he thundered, was the end of the line for the pitiful victims unable to conquer the pernicious habit.

Fortunately, Budro had acquired a more scientific attitude at the age of eleven when he'd become yard boy at the Provo General Hospital and spent more time absorbing the medical library than watering the lawns. But the Sex Maniac also tilled stony soil among Provo High boys, who explicitly detailed the delights of erotic fantasies in bawdy verses they improvised for Glee Club songs. Their words for "My Spanish Guitar" actually were rather good, though unprintable in that milieu.

On being called on missions, young men were grilled on the subject. If they admitted to solitary guilt they were required to conquer themselves first. "I told the truth the first time," one told Budro. "But I wanted to go, so next time I told him what he wanted to hear."

At this time cigarettes were called coffin nails, and a standard attraction among the Freaks of Nature exhibited by carnival side-shows was the Cigarette Fiend, portrayed as a living skeleton with four cigarettes in his mouth and more in each hand. The concept was so menacing that a girl at Provo High who got into trouble refused a shotgun marriage because the father of her child smoked.

During his lecture the other wowser, known as the Cigarette Fiend, asked for four volunteers from the high school audience,

4. As defined by H. L. Mencken, who was Budro's ideal, a wowser was a person haunted by the fear that someone, somewhere, might be happy.

then opened a cardboard box and took out a scrawny alley cat. As four huskies from the football squad each held a paw, the Fiend injected a nicotine solution from a cigarette into the cat with a hypodermic needle. Budro's sympathies were all for the cat, which yowled, writhing and twisting in agony, then began to subside as the poison took effect. He wasn't impressed, knowing that various foreign substances—milk, for example—would have the same effect if injected. Also, the lecture was wasted on him, because after smoking for seven years he'd quit at the age of twelve for fear it might stunt his growth (alas, too late; he remained the runt of the litter). He felt only outrage at the callous brutality of the Cigarette Fiend, who, as the four huskies held the comatose cat, thundered that cigarettes were the Devil's kindling wood, lighting the fires of dissipation—liquor, gambling, loose women, social disease, the gutter, and early death.

And then in the midst of this tirade, the cat began to revive. It yowled, tail stiff and hair on end. As it gained strength it pulled the four huskies to and fro as they struggled to hold it. Then one claw came free and quickly slashed at the other hands. The cat dropped to the podium floor and bounced as if on springs as the huskies and the Cigarette Fiend sought cover. The cat bounded onto the lectern, and then with a mighty leap sailed through the opening of a high window, while the auditorium rocked with cheers.

Subsequently, Budro felt much the same emotion at a Mexican bullfight, when the bull gored the man. Or when his cat, Sally, with young kittens, learned the trick of lurking on a high windowsill and dive-bombing unsuspecting dogs who came sniffing around her food dish. They uttered a wild cry as she landed and streaked away yelping in terror as she rode them off her property with claws slashing.

At this time BYU enjoyed an ambiguous status among Provo citizens. It was both the Lord's university, and, by reason of this fact, a type of reform school. If a teenager was running wild in a Mormon hamlet his parents, generally on their bishop's advice, shipped him off to the Y to profit by its spiritual climate. Particularly in the period of Budro's childhood, when enrollment was small, Provo citizens at times wondered if the number of delinquents wasn't contaminating the spiritual climate. One student, a returned missionary, was dismayed to have his rubbers stolen from the hallway outside a classroom. When it happened again, he made complaint to President George H. Brimhall. Brimhall assured him that there was some mistake; certainly nobody in the Lord's university would stoop to petty thievery. Perhaps the rubbers had merely been misplaced. However, a third pair of rubbers vanished. In looking for them, the student discovered a pair in a hallway with the name "George H. Brimhall" inked on the inner lining. He walked away in them and never again had the rubbers taken.

As a freshman at the Y, Budro was aware that several of his peers were majoring in banking at Bullock's pool hall and were also smoking, imbibing home brew, playing penny-ante poker, and chasing fast girls. The wildest boy of the freshman class was called on a mission at midterm. He returned two years later serious, devout, devoid of bad habits, and with a roach in his hair. The reformation of the missionary experience was sometimes viewed with mixed feelings by the parents. "Ralph's going to give us a hard time for awhile after he gets back," the mother of a missionary said. She and her husband smoked. "Until," she added, "he becomes human again."

The mission didn't always reform. Budro visited a friend scheduled to leave for the mission field to find him kneeling, not in prayer but to blow smoke up the fireplace. And while the record of conversions speaks well of the labors in the Lord's vineyard, a surprising statistic indicates that perhaps the missionaries aren't converting themselves. A church official, Paul Dunn, stated that six out of ten fell away from church activity after returning.

After hearing discussions of this over a period of years, as a serious problem—freely mentioned by speakers touring the stakes with the "Education Week" and "Know Your Religion" programs —Budro was boggled by an official survey undertaken because "stories have persisted in the Church claiming that a high percentage of returned missionaries became inactive." The survey indicated it wasn't so, 97 percent of them attending at least one sacrament meeting each month, 89 percent having a current church calling, 95 percent being married in the temple.[5] So either men in a position to know hadn't known what they were talking about, or there was

5. *Ensign*, February 1978. This report was a blow to a friend of Budro's, who at the time was busily at work writing a book about the serious problem of returned missionary dropouts.

a joker in the survey, something as neat as the way the polygamy problem was solved by calling it bigamy.

As Depression blighted the land, Budro was fortunate to find a part-time job as night clerk at the Roberts Hotel while attending the Y. Hours were six to midnight, seven nights a week, which left scant time for study. However, the pay was good, $30 a month plus a free meal (the only one he ate). There wasn't much to do except manage the desk, run the switchboard, tote suitcases upstairs as bellhop (no elevator), keep the company books, and, before leaving each night, mop the lobby.

He found time to drop in at the Provo Public Library each month to enjoy H. L. Mencken's caustic view of Americana in the *American Mercury*. He never forgot the bitter winter day when he entered the welcome warmth and at the golden oak table opened the *Mercury* to find the same jaundiced view of Mormon country that the magazine had taken of the Bible Belt. For the first time in his life, Budro saw the Saints depicted with detached urbanity from the viewpoint of the outside world in Bernard DeVoto's "The Centennial of Mormonism: A Study in Utopia and Dictatorship."[6]

"Although America had been able to devise but one soup," DeVoto said, "it had invented a hundred religions."

Some subtlety of climate, racial stock or social organization on the frontier of New England and New York made the air fecund. A circle described on a radius of one hundred and fifty miles around such a center as Pittsfield, Massachusetts, would include the birthplace of ninety percent of the American sects and of an even greater percentage of their prophets. Many prophets before Joseph Smith revealed God's will within that circle, and many more came after him.

Budro had been taught that God had reserved the Western hemisphere specifically for the purpose of founding Mormonism. Columbus was led by divine guidance to discover America; the colonists were specially selected for their mission; the Revolutionary War threw off the yoke of Europe, where religious freedom was impossible; the United States adopted a constitutional form of government, which guaranteed freedom of speech, religion, assembly,

6. January 1930.

and the press. And, with the way prepared, Joseph Smith restored the true gospel.

Every step was foreknown by God the Father and is part of his great plan to bring about the salvation of his children. He has prepared this land for centuries for the restoration of the gospel.[7]

"But if there was nothing singular in the Restoration and the ensuing birth of the Church of Jesus Christ of Latter-day Saints," DeVoto wrote, "there has been something remarkable in its survival."

Consider: Of the scores of True Churches that the four millennial decades produced, hardly a handful remain today. . . . They came in sudden glory, the sky opening up to the immemorial thunderclap, the awful Voice proclaiming that the hour had struck and summoning all kindreds, tongues and peoples into judgment. They end with a group of gray-beards kneeling while a priest of the eternal mysteries prays for a miracle that will pay off the mortgage on the meeting house.

"Why has one True Church survived while scores of others have perished?" DeVoto gave this axiom:

Mormonism is a wholly American religion, and it contrived to satisfy needs which are basic with a good many Americans and which none of its competitors managed to supply. Otherwise, one may be sure, 1930 would have found it as dead as the creed of the Icarian communists who took over its deserted city of Nauvoo.

"The story of Mormonism is one of the most fascinating in all American history," he stated. "Yet no qualified historian has ever written a comprehensive treatise on Mormonism." Totally rejecting the veritable flood of material issued by the church press, DeVoto listed only two books worthy of notice, W. A. Linn's *Story of the Mormons,* and M. R. Werner's *Brigham Young;* though Linn's was outdated "and is the work of a man who had no historical perspective," while Werner "did not master the Mormon point of view."

Though the internal literature was worthless as history, "The

7. "The Great Prologue: A Prophetic History and Destiny of America," a manual for family home evenings, 1976, adapted from Mark E. Petersen's book, *The Great Prologue* (Salt Lake: Deseret Book Co., 1975).

best way to understand Mormonism is still to read its holy books and its periodicals," DeVoto concluded, "and the best way to answer our question, to determine why Mormonism has survived, is to read the sermons of Brigham Young."

The church survived because of three important forces: "the frontier environment, the martyrdom of Joseph Smith, and the leadership of Brigham Young." DeVoto described Mormonism as "a magnificent catch-all of the dogmas and doctrines which had agitated the devout" on the frontier.

It was at once millennial, restorationist and perfectionist. It combined in one daring blend the frontier's three favorite avenues of salvation: salvation by the Last Judgment, salvation by return to apostolic Christianity, and salvation by perfect and present identification with the will of God.

Budro had been nurtured from infancy on stories of the persecution of the Saints of early days by wicked Gentiles. Yet DeVoto claimed that the church invited trouble, because "almost from the very beginning Mormonism ran counter to sentiments, ideals, institutions, and ways of life that were fundamental forces of the frontier."

These were not so much the religious teachings. . . . Rather they were economic, and especially social. The difference can be seen as early as Kirtland. The Mormon real-estate speculations and wildcat banking of that period could have occasioned no such antagonism if the peculiar people had not also been a unified people, . . . a society governed by one man who was answerable to no one but God and who was little short of omnipotent in the management of his people's property.

"The principle thus established was proved to the hilt in Missouri and Illinois," where the Mormons antagonized the natives "by the overbearing smugness that characterizes every chosen people."

A more important offense was their political unity, the certainty with which their leaders could turn any election, and thus secure any privileges desired, by voting thousands of men as one. But the decisive offense was the economic power that could be wielded by a cooperate hagiocracy—a people who held a great part of their wealth in common, undertook collective enterprises, excluded the ungodly from their businesses, and obeyed the orders of their leaders. The frontier could not tolerate it—and did not tolerate it. The sixteen years of the Missouri and Illinois settlements . . . proved conclusively that Mormonism could not exist in the American system.

"To this period must be traced the characteristic Mormon state of mind, that of the Lord's chosen persecuted by the children of evil," DeVoto stated. "It was reinforced for seventy years."

Throughout all that time the Saints had a sense of present martyrdom, and it was the most important single fact about them, the strongest single force in their survival. They have it today. . . .

"And of this, the most decisive element was the actual martyrdom of Joseph and his brother Hyrum," he concluded. "The blood of the martyrs became once more the seed of the Church."

Brigham Young's leadership "marks a decisive change in Mormonism," DeVoto pointed out.

Whatever else Smith was, he was primarily a prophet, a religious leader. . . . Young was primarily an organizer of the kingdom on this earth. . . . Under Young [Mormonism] became a religio-economic social system, based on cooperative enterprise, subordinating religious ecstasy to practical achievement. . . .

"Live your religion," was his unvarying counsel to the Saints. And by "live your religion" he meant: take up more land, get your ditches in, make the roof of your barn tight, improve your livestock, and in so doing glorify God and advance the Kingdom.

Budro had been indoctrinated with the belief in the power of the priesthood, the awesome ability to speak in God's name. DeVoto saw the priesthood under Joseph as "a system of stairways and corridors through the crazy-quilt glories of the Mormon apocalypse."

Under Young, however, the priesthood became the commissioned and noncommissioned staff of the social army. They were the great and the small leaders of Israel, the channel of direction and control, the overseers, the department managers, the adjutants, the deputies and the police.

200

"That," DeVoto concluded, "is the principal part of what has survived as Mormonism."

The settlement of Utah was "the accomplishment of a cooperative society obedient to the will of a dictator," he wrote. Parallels were obvious "between Mormon and the European dictatorships." The Saints had their myth of being the chosen people, destined to dominate mankind.

Dedication to that destiny implied their . . . cheerfully accepting a rigorous and sometimes savage discipline in which the individual counted for nothing against the group. Opposition to the priesthood has always been as inconceivable as individual defiance of Hitler or Stalin.

"Effective government, too, required a sedulous attention to Israel's young," he said, with "a succession of schools, classes, clubs and training corps . . . from the age of three until they are admitted to the priesthood, which condition their reflexes as effectively as the corresponding institutions of Russia and Italy."

Furthermore, a steady necessity was the perpetuation of and appeal to the persecution-neurosis. Israel has always been told that every man's hand was against it, that it must always work unanimously toward the righting of that wrong, that any faltering would insure victory for its enemies.

As with other dictatorships, there was a system of infinite promotion and reward for the orthodox and faithful, while the worse sin was nonconformity. "And finally," he said, "Mormonism repeats the experience of all absolutisms: a dictatorship must rest on the interests of a ruling class and comes to be a mechanism by which an elite exercises power over a society."

Under this oligarchy, the cooperative society "was governed in the interest of the elite," he claimed.

Mormonism was developing not in the direction of Rochdale, New Harmony, the Oneida Community, Brook Farm, the United Order of the Kingdom of God—but in the direction of Standard Oil.

He cited as an example that in *Who's Who* Heber J. Grant listed his positions in business enterprises ahead of the fact that he was LDS Church president. "The list shows the final emphasis and values of Mormonism, but it merely hints at the economic power that is vested in the hierarchy. That power is absolute over the business and finance of Utah."

In the change from pioneer values to modern Mormonism, the decisive period "was that between the Woodruff Manifesto of 1890," DeVoto said, "and the adoption by the United States Senate in 1907 of the minority report . . . which confirmed Reed Smoot. During that time the Church learned not only that it must outwardly conform to the requirements of the American system but also that it would lose nothing by doing so."

The new generation of leaders heard but impatiently the grandsires who preached fidelity to prophecy even though it should destroy the church. Israel capitulated to the United States, has never violated the bargain then made, and has had no reason to regret it.

"Splendor dies with that hardheaded decision," he said.

Reed Smoot rising to power in the Republican Party, becoming chairman of the Senate Committee on Finance, consulting with his peers to force the nomination of Warren G. Harding—Reed Smoot is the perfect image of modern Mormonism. . . . God had brought His people into the glory promised them. His house, it was already recorded, had many mansions; of them the one that had proved most durable was the countinghouse.

"Theologically, Mormonism is a creation of the American Pentecost," DeVoto said. "Philosophically, it is a solution of a problem which American thought has grappled with for three hundred years: how to identify spiritual grace with the making of money."

Historically, "Mormonism is the fulfillment of a social ideal," he said, "the achievement of Utopia. It is what happens when Utopian dreams work out in a free society."

Nearly any statistical index you may choose—literacy, school system, good roads, public health, bank savings, *per capita* wealth, business solvency, ownership of land free of incumbrance, infrequency of divorce or infanticide, infrequency of crimes against persons and property— will show that the Saints are better off than the average of their neighbors. And the state has always taken care of its poor. . . . The Church has developed agencies for finding the gifted, the useful, clearing the way before them, and bringing them to a better functioning in Israel. The agencies and the institutions are there, and the priesthood is there, overseeing the people, going among them and counseling them, sharing their problems, working with them toward the answers.

"That, heaven knows, adds up to an impressive total," DeVoto conceded. "But there is something that counts much more: the Saints are members one of another." In reading the article, Budro hadn't entirely agreed with all DeVoto previously had said; here, however, he pinpointed the very essence of Mormonism. It was more than a religion, it was an attitude and a way of life. "They form a community with recognized objectives, the realization of which every member has an active part," DeVoto said; and, having grown up in Utah, he knew.

Here is the fellowship of common endeavor—the sense of sharing a social vision, the communion of men bound together in a cause—that is gone from the Christian Church and from the modern world. It is what Stalin and Hitler and Mussolini have tried to invoke; it is what ardent and generous and despairing people hold out as our only hope, our only defense against chaos.

"The Saints have had it from the beginning and they will never lose it," DeVoto said, as Budro tingled with the knowledge of recognized truth. "Yes, Utopia exists in the Wasatch valleys. And its idiom is completely American. This is the fulfillment of our prophets' dreams."

But Utopia had been attained at a stiff price. One requirement was "a ruthless destruction of the individual," coupled with the absolute demand for conformity.

Day by day the priesthood is there, with powers not only of excommunication from eternal glory but of boycott, espionage, monopoly, price-cutting and the big stick. Refusal to "sustain the Presidency" in any way is inconceivable. The Saint in business "accepts counsel"—that is, does what the priesthood tells him to do—quite as inevitably and as thoroughly as he does in matters of doctrinal orthodoxy. . . . Utopia can tolerate unorthodoxy in behavior or in idea no more than it can tolerate disunion in belief.

"This implies that the culture of Utopia, though it be vigorous, must be comfortable and mediocre," DeVoto declared. And, reading the words, Budro understood the reason for what Mormon scholars termed the "lack of maturity" of the LDS people in the arts. It was no accident that Mormonism had been unable to produce great literature, music, drama, architecture, sculpture, or painting; the creative talent withered in a culture that judged art by its faith-promoting content. "In Utopia talent must string along or it must get out," DeVoto said flatly.

"What has Israel produced? Business men, politicians, bankers. . . . Its genius finds expression in that kind of man; its elite are a business elite exclusively. Its scholars, scientists, artists, thinkers, all its infrequent talent, it has plowed back into the Kingdom."

In fact, "In Utopia the fate of the superior person is tragic," he said.

The sensitive, the intelligent, the individual, all those not gifted for the increase of kine, have always got out, for Utopia is death to them. They have not been numerous; the elite reproduces itself in kind.[8]

Surveying Mormonism at the end of its first century, DeVoto said that it was, aside from doctrine, "a set of cooperative institutions strictly limited and managed in support of an elite, and, beyond that, effectively an identification with industry and finance."

Martyrdom, years of suffering, the colonization of the desert and the dream of millennial justice come out by the same door as any private enterprise in stock-jobbing. . . . At arm's length you cannot tell Utopia from anything else. It has blended with the map; it has joined hands with the damned.

"There it is: what has actually survived from the Newness and the Striving," he concluded. "That is the way the dream and the world are made flesh. Mormonism is the millennium that comes through."

The Budro who closed the *American Mercury* and left the library was a different person from the one who had entered. He

8. In 1966 only fourteen members of the National Academy of Sciences lived and worked in the six mountain states, Montana, Wyoming, Idaho, Utah, Colorado, and Nevada—the Deseret region. Four were in Utah. See "The Costly 'Brain Drain,' " *Deseret News,* August 6. The academy had 740 members.

didn't feel the bitter cold of early darkness as he walked the three blocks to the Roberts Hotel. For the first time in his life he stood apart, looking at his people from an outside viewpoint.

The Salt Lake *Telegram* had published an editorial urging the Saints to mine the fabulous lode of literary material in the history and culture of the Peculiar People which lay virtually untouched. Why leave it to be distorted and sensationalized by Gentiles? The true literature must spring from the Saints themselves.

Budro had been stirred with ambition by this. But now he realized that the literary lode would never in the future be mined by conformists, positive thinkers, and apologists any more than it had been in the past. Mormon historians were primarily lawyers, proving a case. Mormon authors wrote primarily for approval by Salt Lake, for without it they couldn't publish in the managed press. The literature that would come from his people, Budro now knew, could only be written by those who could stand apart with a sympathetic but objective standard of judgment. It would be published in the commercial market for regular trade channels, not by the internal press for church outlets.

It hadn't yet been done. Could he qualify?

While gaining a liberal education at BYU in the humanities, Budro received a literal course in human nature at the Roberts Hotel. On his first night at the job the hotel owner warned him never to accept a check from a promoter or politician and to beware of do-gooders. He was particularly warned to watch out for the Bible salesman in Room 11. True enough, the affable salesman was caught with his hand in the till by a police stake-out, which solved shortages in the cash drawer. The Roberts was strict about men having girls in their rooms; yet Budro discovered that even among the fairest flowers of Zion love would find a way, generally via the back stairs.

Then there was George's last trip. George was a canned-milk salesman who had stayed overnight at the Roberts once a week for thirty years. Now he was retiring. Tears welled in the eyes of all present as he wrote a check for room and meals, shook hands around, picked up his Gladstone, and went out. The check bounced, as did every one he wrote on the route of his final trip.

The noble experiment of prohibition had made drinking fashionable and smart, even in Provo. The bootlegger was a quasi-respectable fixture of society. Every grocery store sold malt extract and bottle caps for a nation of amateur brewmasters. Budro and his cousin Alvin had their home-brew equipment, a five-gallon crock and a bottle capper, and they put on a batch in Alvin's basement smoking room. When it was ready they bottled it, then impatiently waited a week for it to age properly. The great and suspenseful moment was the uncapping of the first bottle. Would it be wild? Would it be green, still sweet? Would it be flat? Or would it be just right?

As Budro reached for a bottle to find out, he froze in a crouch, stricken with an excruciating pain in the hinge of his back. He couldn't stoop further, and he couldn't straighten up. Had the Lord smitten him in the act of sinning? Or, more likely, was it related to a hard fall he'd recently taken on skis?

Incidentally, the batch was wild.

Budro took a bottle to school in his briefcase, and late that afternoon at the *Y News* office he and the editor sampled it. This took a bit of doing, because it was dark outside and two large windows gave an excellent view of the interior for students and faculty passing by. Also, there was no lock on the door. However, risk seemed part of the game. Instead of turning off the light, they stood close to the narrow section of wall between the windows, and uncapped the bottle. Whew! The brew was warm and well shaken from a day in the briefcase. It shot out of the bottle and over ceiling, walls, and windows. As the two tried to cap it with their thumbs and deflect the geyser to their mouths, they were thoroughly drenched. They did manage a couple of swallows apiece, bitter with yeast, but that wasn't the point. The point was to live dangerously.

At the hotel Budro took ice and ginger ale to the rooms on request, but if asked where to buy a bottle he professed ignorance. Of course, as night clerk he came to know bootleggers who supplied guests and discovered that several enterprising BYU students were working their way through college in this manner. This seemed interesting enough to mention in a column he was writing for the college paper, and he received a quick lesson in the power of the written word. The ink was hardly dry on the *Y News* when he was on the carpet.

His valiant stand regarding the inviolability of reporter's sources of information fell on deaf ears. *Who were the bootleggers?* On refusing to identify them, he was suspended. When allowed back in school, the next column picked off the scab; out again. The pattern repeated itself, until after the sixth suspension, Budro had been tied in the closet once too often. He finally began to suspect that they didn't like him at BYU. Being a sensitive soul, he never went back.

14

Bishop Koyle,
the Angel, and
the Dream Mine

ON THE 17TH OF SEPTEMBER 1894 a party of six men climbed the face of a mountain east of Spanish Fork, Utah. The leader, John H. Koyle, selected a spot he had seen in a dream, and they started to dig. They didn't find paying ore.

Forty-nine years later, when Joe Budro interviewed Koyle in 1943, the Dream Mine was still in operation. Koyle had blasted tunnels and shafts totaling almost a mile and a half into the rock of the mountain. A $60,000 flotation mill of gleaming white concrete had been erected to process the ore, which hadn't yet been found.[1] In 1972, long after Koyle's death, operations continued. No ore had been discovered. However, a letter from the man currently in charge said,

1. See Samuel W. Taylor, "Time and the Dream Mine," *Esquire,* May 1944. The magazine editor with exquisite tact blue-penciled all reference to Mormonism, which made the article read like a biography of Joseph Smith that failed to mention that he founded the Mormon Church. In this chapter the author has again placed Koyle and the Dream Mine among the LDS people, for this is the only way the story can be understood. The material also has been updated.

208

Bishop Koyle, the Angel, and the Dream Mine

About 27 years ago I remember a statement of Bishop Koyle's in which he told me of a dream he had about the death and burial of Pres. Harry S Truman. He said this would mark the time when the Dream Mine would turn out.[2]

When this sign proved a false alarm, another carrot kept hopes high as mining continued.

If the Dream Mine was a con game, it was a strange one, for all the money went into the hole in the mountain. John Koyle began digging a poor man. When Joe Budro interviewed him forty-nine years later, Koyle was still a poor man. The mine had been financed entirely by the savings of hardheaded and thrifty Mormon stockholders, who numbered around seven thousand at that time. After almost a half century of frustration, the stockholders weren't at all perturbed by the lack of the usual incentives for investment. On the contrary, they were filled with almost rabid enthusiasm, and at the weekly meetings held on Thursday nights in the full basement of Koyle's house there was singing, rejoicing, and the fervent bearing of testimonies to the Dream.

True, an occasional discouraged Dreamer, as stockholders are termed, may have unloaded his holdings at a quarter to four-bits a share; but the purchaser would not be a true Dreamer, for those firm in the faith wouldn't dream of buying stock except from Koyle himself, at the unvarying price of $1.50 a share. Inasmuch as the mine's only source of income came from the sale of new stock, it wouldn't help the cause to buy resold stock, at however much a bargain.

Koyle agreed that the story of the Dream Mine was a good one; but it was too bad, he informed Joe Budro, that he couldn't tell it. Not yet. The story could be told in a few weeks. Big things were breaking, but the time hadn't come to reveal them. Scoffers had told Budro that big things had been breaking with clocklike regularity for forty-nine years; but John Koyle declared that this time every problem had been solved and every obstacle overcome. Another boom was on. Enthusiasm was so high that, despite long-standing opposition by church authorities at Salt Lake, a prominent sociologist, Dr. Lowry Nelson, had said that in the entire history

2. Norman C. Pierce to Samuel W. Taylor.

of Mormonism the Dreamers were "the largest social group movement in the Church."

The Dream Mine did produce a certain ore. Scoffers said it was worthless. Dreamers said it was extremely rich. On the face of things, it would seem that the thing could be settled once and for all by assay. Indeed, assays had been made, and according to them the ore was without value. When the Utah State Securities Commission called in a prominent geologist, Dr. Frederick J. Pack of the University of Utah, to investigate the Dream Mine, his report concluded that "evidences of commercial mineralization are wholly lacking," and that "The 'ore' bodies recently discovered are shown by assays to be worthless."[3] In fact, Pack added as the controversy continued, "You can get more values out of the dirt sweepings on the main streets of Salt Lake City than you can out of ore from the Dream Mine."[4]

This didn't deter Koyle in the slightest, nor dampen the enthusiasm of the Dreamers. Koyle simply claimed, and his disciples believed, that this ore was an unusual combination of valuable metals and that all the values were burned out of it by ordinary methods of assay.

The Dream Mine story would be incredible, except for factors peculiar to Mormon country. There is the belief in dreams, visions, inspiration, visitations—guidance from the spirit world. The church itself was founded on such manifestations. There is the folklore regarding the Three Nephites, immortal beings from Book of Mormon times who appear from nowhere to perform good deeds and miracles to worthy Saints, then vanish. To scoffers, Dreamers could always point to Jesse Knight, a Mormon who was guided by a voice from beyond to discover fabulous wealth in an area which geologists had declared worthless—in fact, he named his first big strike the Humbug in recognition of expert opinion. And last but not least was the belief that the Dream Mine was destined to strike it rich

3. *Deseret News,* January 20, 1933.
4. Norman C. Pierce comments that the geologist was "the same Dr. Pack, in fact, who taught each of his classes in geology that oil in commercial quantities would never be found in Utah because the earth was so fractured thruout the state that about all of the oil had escaped, most of it having gone down the Colorado River.—Yet the nation's biggest oil fields are now in Utah." See *The Dream Mine Story* (Salt Lake: The author, rev. ed., 1972).

just in time to rescue Zion by saving the church in its hour of dire need, while at the same time making the stockholders wealthy and honored as redeemers of Israel.

Such a combination was hard to beat, as both the church and the State of Utah had discovered in vainly trying to close down operations of what, to the officials, was a con game.

The man who had bested the awesome opposition of church and state for almost a half century certainly didn't look the part of the flamboyant, spellbinding snake-oil salesman. Joe Budro interviewed an unprepossessing man of seventy-nine, stooped from a lifetime of hard work, arms hanging forward from the bent frame, powerful hands gnarled from long years of labor with pick and shovel, double-jack and drill steel. He wore a faded blue shirt, worn dungarees supported by yellow suspenders, heavy farm shoes. His eyes were dimming now, yet except for a grizzled moustache his hair was black. The long conflict had left his face curiously smooth and unlined. He exuded the calm serenity of a man with a mission, directed by celestial beings.

Koyle sat in a rocking chair at his modest frame house (which the Dreamers had built for him) located amid the scrub oak and sagebrush just below the magnificent mill that was a monument to his life's dream. He spoke in a thin voice, almost a monotone, his manner entirely devoid of theatrics or the emotionalism of a zealot. He talked about crops, the labor situation, people in the vicinity. Joe Budro was in uniform, and they discussed Hitler and World War II. Koyle couldn't talk about the Dream Mine, he said; not for a few weeks. Budro didn't have that much time. His company was alerted for overseas. He'd secured an overnight pass for the interview, and then he'd be en route for Europe. No matter, Koyle said. People had doubted him too long. Couldn't talk. This time he'd show them.

And the interview continued into the night for four hours as Koyle's voice droned on steadily with the story he couldn't tell.

Yes, he started it back in Ninety-four, Koyle said. And some people still doubted he'd got paying ore. He smiled slightly behind the scraggly moustache, and there was a change. The voice remained quiet but gained timbre. A glow lighted the eyes. His face radiated confidence. The ore was there, yes, sir. Pure tungsten made a filagree on the face of the vein; you could pick it off with your fingers.

From time to time, Budro had been told, enthusiasm had reached a fever pitch among Dreamers as new metals were reportedly found in the ore. Today, Koyle stated, there were thirty-three metals in it, including breathtaking quantities of gold, silver, platinum, and lead.

Scoffers had claimed that when Koyle needed more money he simply "discovered" a new metal in the ore. Budro's brother, Raymond, who lived nearby in Spanish Fork, had gone through the mine, and at the ore bins in the mill he asked Koyle to select a choice specimen for assay. "Don't send it to Salt Lake; they're against me," Koyle cautioned. "And remember, this ore has got to be assayed the right way." Raymond sent the specimen to Denver with Koyle's specific instructions. This assay found nothing except a trace of gold.

The big trouble, Koyle explained to Joe Budro, was that the ore was too rich. All of its thirty-three metals had different melting points. Under ordinary smelting methods, you'd lose most of them —they'd vaporize and go up the chimney. But now he had that licked, he said. Never mind how. Just wait a few weeks. Then he'd have something to tell.

Hadn't it been difficult to keep going all this while in the face of opposition? Budro asked. Koyle smiled in triumphant memory. Yes, he'd had a fight of it. But they'd all come around begging for stock when it's too late, and there won't be any for sale. He knew what'd happen. He saw it all from the beginning, when an angel took him inside the mountain, and showed him everything, before he began to dig.

A dream? Well, you might call it that. He was guided, same as Jesse Knight. Uncle Jesse was told to dig through unpromising formation until he broke into a cavern, its roof glittering with beautiful crystals.

The bottom of the cave was solid carbonate lead-silver ores that could easily be dug with the toe of a boot. The average width was about thirty feet and from forty to fifty feet in thickness. One could walk in the cave a distance of one thousand feet on top of this clean rich sand carbonate ore that was free from waste, resembling in a way wheat in a bin ready for harvest.[5]

Jesse Knight had believed that he was guided for a purpose. He really didn't own the wealth, but only had stewardship of it, to use for the good of the church and his people. And John Koyle's mine was for a similar but even more vital purpose.

At the Thursday night meetings in his basement Koyle had told the story many times. How he awakened in the night to find a heavenly being there, dressed in white and radiating a brilliant illumination. This personage conducted Koyle in spirit to a nearby mountain, then inside it, pointing out the different formations to be encountered until they reached a large chimney of white quartz rich with a leaf gold. They followed down this chimney to a vast body of ore, and nine large caverns filled with treasure, which had been mined by the ancient Nephites during Book of Mormon times. The Nephites had left relics of their civilization—implements, ornaments, and artifacts—and one room held sacred records engraved on plates of gold and brass. Another room was stacked with large vases holding gold coins.

The angel said the treasures had been lost to the Nephites because of their iniquity, and that they also would be shut off from Koyle and his associates if they became lifted up in pride, hardhearted, stiffnecked, and began using the wealth for their own self-gratification.

As they stood in the cavern, "The messenger then showed me how this great wealth could be lost to us," Koyle said. " 'Look!' he commanded, and immediately there followed a tremor of the earth, shifting rock in front of us." The rich ore, which had been there but a moment before, could no longer be found. " 'Now you can see how easily the riches can be taken from you,' the messenger said." But, if used for the right purpose, "There is much more here than you can take out in several generations," the angel promised.[6]

5. Jesse William Knight, *The Jesse Knight Family* (Salt Lake: Deseret News Press, 1940). It should also be remembered that the richest strikes in Utah had been made at places considered geological impossibilities. These included the mining districts of East Tintic, Mercur, Silver Reef, and Big Indian.

6. Pierce. This visitation was, of course, strikingly similar in some respects to the appearance of the Angel Moroni to Joseph Smith. The angel led Joseph into the Hill Cumorah, and showed him the golden plates from which Joseph

Koyle and his volunteer crew had been digging awhile, following the strata in a slope toward the east, when an eminent geologist and mining engineer came for a look. "You'll never find anything on the east slope," he predicted.

Koyle continued digging. Presently, just as he had predicted, the slope switched toward the west. At this time certain members of the crew wanted to follow the slope directly west. Koyle knew he should go diagonally. There was an argument, and he closed down the mine. Two years later, after apologies indicated repentance, he continued digging. Since that time there had been no question of who was boss.

After fifteen years of mining, Koyle decided to put things on a business basis in 1909, and organized the Koyle Mining Co., with a public stock issue. Men who'd worked in the mine got stock in payment, three shares a day. The public was offered stock at $1.50. Koyle predicted that when the mine came in, stock would be worth $1,000. He advised investors that 100 shares was sufficient; no need to be greedy.

The stock offering brought trouble. The geologist, who had kept an eye on the operation, was Apostle James E. Talmage. He was concerned with the plight of innocent investors, particularly when they bought stock because of dreams and visitations with expectations of redeeming the church in its hour of need. This opposition was potent because Talmage was a member of the Twelve while Koyle was now bishop of the Leland Ward and as such should obey counsel from above. Talmage pointed out that there was no iron, no slate, and no igneous rock, all of which should have been present. Koyle roamed the mountain with him and found a huge slate bed. He pointed out acres of igneous rock outcroppings. In the mine he indicated a vein of iron.

"It's the wrong color," the geologist said.

Koyle tested a sample. "It assayed fifty percent iron. It was the wrong color because it was burned," he told Joe Budro. "And that means there was a fire in the earth. And that means there's metals. The iron is the mother and the igneous rock is the father,

---

translated the Book of Mormon. Koyle was convinced that it was the same angel who took him into the mountain to show him ancient treasure and more sacred records.

and the offspring is my ore." He didn't know what part the slate played; but he'd leave that to the geologists.

They tried to stop him. Koyle was hauled into court. Arrayed as witnesses against him were more than a dozen stockholders smarting at being fleeced. They had the sucker's rabid yen for revenge. With such witnesses, Koyle seemed doomed. He remained unperturbed.

"When they got on the stand, they changed their tune," Koyle said, grinning. "Instead of testifying against me, they began whooping it up for the Dream Mine. Regular testimony meeting in court. Case dismissed. Knowed it would be, from the start."

What caused the hostile witnesses to find their faith restored in his presence? There was no outward sign in the stooped figure with his worn work clothing to hint at his uncanny charisma; yet Joe Budro felt it. In his presence, under the influence of his hypnotic sincerity, it was impossible to doubt the destiny of the Dream Mine. With this gift he had kept the unshaken faith of thousands of Dreamers for forty-nine years. He had had both church and state arrayed against him. At one time seventeen deputies were hunting him. Yet he was still going strong; and right now, he told Budro, the Dream Mine was on the brink of the biggest boom of all.

Things got tough, at times. But when Dreamers began wondering about dividends or muttering about court action, Koyle would revive them. He'd find a new metal in the ore or run onto a sign inside the magic mountain—a blaze, as it were, to show he was on the right trail. For instance, a hog's back in the rock formation. He'd predicted it would be there, and here it was. Again, a map of North America was revealed in the strata as foretold. Faults made perfect north and south walls to the mine for 100 yards—just as he'd said they would. John Koyle knew where he was going.

Opposition increased. In 1913 Talmage prepared an article, "A Warning Voice," which was issued over the signatures of the First Presidency.

We feel it our duty to warn the Latter-day Saints against fake mining schemes which have no warrant for success beyond the professed spiritual manifestations of their projectors and the influence gained over the excited minds of their victims. We caution the Saints against investing money or property . . . [in] fanciful schemes to make money for the alleged purpose of "redeeming Zion." . . .[7]

This, among the Saints, was considered the inspired word of the Lord. Yet despite the crushing pressure of this disapproval, Koyle kept on. He'd had what he considered even more impressive evidence to continue.

The shaft was now 1,400 feet deep, and it was back-breaking work to raise the muck to the surface by means of a series of eleven winches. In a dream the night of January 5, 1914, he was instructed to drive a tunnel lower down in the mountain to intersect the bottom of the shaft. Once again he was taken inside the mountain, shown the signs and formations to be encountered.

Koyle was his own surveyor for the tunnel, which had to be started at the correct spot and aimed at a gradual incline to drain away the water encountered. He climbed up the other side of a ravine, and, clinging to a bush with one hand, sighted across to spot the place to begin the tunnel.

Five days later, Koyle was lying awake in the early morning when he felt a powerful presence, and two personages walked through the wall to his bedside. They were two of the Three Nephites, who had custody of the ancient mine.[8] These immortals, who were to roam the land until the Second Coming, reassured Koyle that his tunnel was correctly situated and aimed, but warned him of opposition to come. They counseled him to hold the faith, promising that he would always find a way to continue operations and that everything would come out as foretold. Then they walked away through the wall.

Koyle kept on with the tunnel, insisting on a ditch along one side to carry away the water. What water? The shaft they'd dug was bone dry at 1,400 feet. Never mind, Koyle said, just make that ditch; there'd be water. The workers grumbled about the ditch as they bored 2,000 feet into the mountain with nary a drop. Then

7. To give the widest possible circulation to this message, it was published in the *Deseret News,* August 2, 1913, and at three subsequent dates. It also appeared in the church magazine *Improvement Era,* and was sent as a letter "to be read in ward meetings, or stake conferences, or other similar gatherings of the people."
8. For legends of the Three Nephites, see Austin and Alta Fife, *Saints of Sage and Saddle. Folklore among the Mormons* (Bloomington: Indiana University Press, 1956).

at 2,400 feet the water gushed forth, filling the ditch—clear, pure, icy water. This, in the desert, was the most valuable strike of the Dream Mine.

The tunnel was now 3,400 feet long, Koyle told Budro, and at the back end you could still see daylight from the front. Pretty fair engineering job, at that.

Apostle Talmage, backed by the church and with clout in the state, continued opposition. Koyle, however, always knew beforehand what was up, and kept a jump ahead. This baffled Talmage. Koyle's foreknowledge this time had nothing to do with dreams— a secretary at Talmage's office happened to be a Dreamer.

A few months after issuing "A Warning Voice," the church lowered the boom. John H. Koyle was released from the office of bishop, and told to shut down the mine if he wished to retain church membership. He obeyed. For six years he waited patiently until there was a change in church leadership; then he resumed operations.

Talmage, however, also renewed his campaign to protect innocent stockholders. The State of Utah joined in, together with the Federal Securities and Exchange Commission. Koyle found his company prohibited from selling stock. Inasmuch as this was his only source of capital, he seemed to be stopped cold. But Koyle took the situation in stride. He called in his Board of Directors and told them what to do.

"Issue me some stock," he directed. "Fifty thousand shares of special stock." The directors did as directed. This was Koyle's personal stock, and there was no law against a man selling his private stock. The Dream Mine continued operations.[9]

Koyle was a man given to predictions, and the number of things that came to pass is astounding. He accurately foretold the time of the 1929 stock market crash and when World War II would end. One of his more outlandish statements came when, pointing to a desolate spot on the sagebrush desert, he said, "There'll be a big manufacturing plant right there, someday." The place was isolated, on rocky ground above irrigation level, far from habitation; while lower in the valley there were many better sites. But war came, and as Budro interviewed Koyle, through the window

9. Austin and Alta Fife reported that by 1956 a total of three-quarter-million dollars' worth in stock had been issued. *Saints of Sage and Saddle.*

he could see a powder mill in the moonlight, located on that spot. Isolation was a prime requisite for that industry.

Another prediction looked ahead some thirty years to the "end of the Republican elephant," clearly indicating the debacle of Watergate. Koyle said that at this time both the president and vice president would die—which they did, politically.[10]

Another prediction concerned James E. Talmage, who had continued to do his utmost to close down the Dream Mine. Talmage wrote articles against the mine; he delivered a blistering speech in Koyle's own stake; he enlisted the stake president and others in the campaign to stop Koyle.

In this unequal struggle, Talmage had the advantage of high church position. He was a geologist of stature; Koyle was guided by dreams. Talmage could point to the many years of futility as the Dreamers poured their savings down the rathole of the mine; Koyle could only reply that the time wasn't yet ripe for the redemption of Zion.

The day came when Koyle's infinite patience was strained. "The time will come," he declared, "when that man will come to me and ask forgiveness."

A short time later, Talmage died. For a while, Koyle admitted to Budro, even the most faithful Dreamers sort of doubted him. They kind of wondered. But Koyle stuck by his statement. And sure enough, Koyle allowed, the geologist *did* appear to him one night, in spirit form. Apparently Talmage had gone just so far and no farther on the other side. He couldn't take another step without seeking forgiveness from John H. Koyle.

"Sure, I forgave him," Koyle admitted. "Didn't want to cause him no trouble over there."

Came the depression. Nobody had a nickel. Nobody would invest. Mining was particularly hard hit. World-famous workings were closing down. Mining stock could hardly be given away. Things looked black for the Dream Mine. For seven weeks Koyle couldn't meet the payroll. Dreamers wanted action, not prophecy of the future.

Koyle explained that there was plenty of rich ore, but it was

10. See Pierce, *The Dream Mine Story.* The book, containing this prediction, was published in November 1972, at the very time President Nixon had won a landslide victory at the polls and was at the height of his popularity.

of this special kind, with all those metals mixed up in it. You heat it and a black smoke comes off, the metals going up the chimney. There was no plant in the world that could handle it.

"We've got to build our own flotation mill," Koyle told his directors. They threw up their hands in horror. Koyle realized that it was no use trying to talk to them. "I was afraid to tell 'em," he admitted. So without a word he set a crew to building the mill on his own hook.

This was in July 1932, at the very bottom of the depression. By November the mill was finished, and the $40,000 in construction costs had been paid in cash. Then he installed $20,000 worth of machinery and equipment. How? Koyle smiled. "The money it come." And that's all he'd say. He wasn't talking; not yet. It wasn't time to tell the Dream Mine story.

What actually happened, of course, was that the prospect of the Dream Mine proving a bonanza during the depths of the depression, when it appeared that the church would be in its hour of need, rallied support from old Dreamers and attracted thousands of new ones.

He built the mill in typical Koyle fashion. When construction was underway and things were too far along to recall, the directors demanded an architect. The contractor refused to do another tap without blueprints. "I didn't need no blueprints," Koyle told Budro. "I knowed what I wanted."

But he did compromise. He hired a good architect, Alexander Pope. The builder meanwhile agreed to go on with the work while awaiting finished specifications. "By the time the first section was finished, the architect he come around with the blueprints for it," Koyle recalled, grinning. He had meanwhile started the next section, and Pope hurried to catch up. How much influence the architect actually had might be impossible to say, but the finished mill was truly magnificent. It looks like no other flotation mill in the world. Gleaming white with modernistic horizontal window lines, it looks like a high-rise luxury apartment house built against the mountain, or a rich man's castle. Koyle was justly proud of it.

However, there was one minor flaw in the design: the mill couldn't process the ore. The only shipment that actually brought a return sold for $103.03, and this victory was clouded by allegations that men promoting a new process had salted the ore of that batch. When charged with rigging results, the promoters picked up and left.

Disappointment? There's a time for all things, Koyle explained. He was not to be rushed. Certain other ore had to be found to mix with the original ore, to make it workable. Also, the operation was not merely a mine. It was fulfillment of prophecy. It would bring the redemption of Zion in the hour of need.

All the Dreamers knew—and had known for forty-nine years —that the time was near. And now, at last, Koyle told Budro, the time was at hand. The very last obstacle had been overcome, right now, this very week.

Koyle sat there in his rocker, a slight old gentleman of seventy-nine, getting frail but supremely confident. He was sorry, but he couldn't talk. Just sort of rambled tonight, he said, jumping around purposely so that Budro wouldn't get the real story. But pretty soon he'd be able to tell it. Until then, he couldn't say a word.

As he shook Budro's hand goodnight, his voice again was thin, the eyes dim.

Yep, the story of the Dream Mine would be a good one, when Koyle got ready to tell it.

Budro went to his brother Raymond's house and sat up all night beating out an article on the Dream Mine. In the morning Raymond drove him to Salt Lake, to see him off for overseas.

"What's the new discovery that will bring the Dream Mine in next week?" Budro asked.

"There's a new machine, a different process, a discovery, a gimmick every week," Raymond said. Then he added, "The machine he needs is the one that puts the gold *into* the ore."

Budro was in Europe, fighting the war with his typewriter, when the Dream Mine article appeared in *Esquire*. Raymond wrote that the piece was something of a minor miracle, in that both sides of the controversy proclaimed it a masterpiece—Salt Lake for exposing the Dream Mine as a fraud, and Koyle for proving it wasn't. Koyle read it aloud at the Thursday night meeting.

The war was over, and Budro was back in the ZI[11] when Raymond reported the next development.

11. ZI—military for Zone of the Interior, the United States.

The High Council met under direction from above, and pinned old man Koyle to the cross. They gave him his choice of signing a "voluntary statement," which repudiated all spiritual claims to the Dream Mine, or being cut off the church. He signed.

The old man is feeble now—83 years old—and was very slow to comprehend and react to questions. There was considerable weeping and pleading on both sides. Quayle Dixon [secretary of the mine] finally persuaded the old man to give in and sign. They were in session from 6 P.M. to I A.M.

The following day, January 8, 1947, the *Deseret News* published a three-column reproduction of Koyle's repudiation on the front page.

"John H. Koyle regretted deeply what he had done," Pierce recorded in *The Dream Mine Story*, "and repented of it at once."

Work at the mine continued faster than ever. In a few weeks they resumed their Thursday night meetings also, and his faithful followers came out in strength, still true to him. . . .

Raymond was a member of the Palmyra Stake High Council which summoned Koyle before it for trial on the charge of holding unauthorized church meetings. The specific charge was that Koyle had promised to discontinue holding the Thursday meetings on a religious basis, but that on April 1, 1948,

About 100 persons were present, . . . that they did bear their testimonies, sing the songs of Zion, and that certain speakers quoted from the scriptures.

Koyle also was charged with telling of former church officials who had opposed him in life returning in spirit form after death to beg forgiveness. "Each statement he admitted," Raymond wrote.

When the high council announced the verdict of excommunication, "The old man told us all off. It really stirred me. He called down the judgment of God upon all of us in a very eloquent manner. I admired his spunk. I didn't sleep that night at all."

A year later, on May 17, 1949, John H. Koyle went to his reward. Quayle Dixon took control of the Dream Mine, and with his associates continued keeping up the assessment work year after year, which required an annual investment of some $25,000 in cash and labor.

The charisma of the leadership was gone, but the legends of Koyle grew with the years. His predictions became prophecies, and Norman C. Pierce gathered and assembled them with the reverence of one compiling scripture. In studying the legends, Pierce decided in 1971 that "a series of signposts" pointed toward the time when Bishop Koyle would return from the dead, the Three Nephites would be on hand, and "the Light Complexioned Man with White Hair from north of the mine" would finance the first shipment of rich ore after the Three Nephites had caused an earthquake to open up the ancient treasures.

Pierce was himself of light complexion, and his formerly fair hair had turned white. He lived at Salt Lake, north some 60 miles from the Dream Mine. He felt that, quite obviously, he had been called by prophecy.

His wife wasn't at all convinced. She was apprehensive as he worked on the Dream Mine book. Then at October conference, 1972, a new church president, Harold B. Lee, counseled the Saints to beware of impostors, manipulators, extremists, and self-styled visionaries in their midst.

He particularly warned against "mining schemes which have no warrant for success beyond the professed spiritual manifestations of their projector and the influence gained over gullible minds of their victims."[12]

Mrs. Pierce laid down an ultimatum to her husband: if he published the book, she'd divorce him. He did, and she did.

In sending a copy of the book to Joe Brown, Pierce wrote that he was moving to Spanish Fork, "where the action is." A few weeks later, February 14, 1973, Pierce mailed a supplementary sheet of predictions with the notation, "This is it! All the signposts are in place."

But as this is written, Pierce's prediction remains unfulfilled, as have all the others since 1894. No man knows the day or the hour when Bishop John H. Koyle's far-elusive dream will come true.

However, in remembering what Raymond said in 1943, on

12. San Francisco *Chronicle,* October 9.

the morning he drove Budro back to Salt Lake after the interview with Koyle, the question must arise: Does it really matter whether or not the Dream Mine predictions are literally fulfilled?

As the car rounded the Point of the Mountain and headed north along the Salt Lake valley, Raymond said, "It's easy to scoff at Koyle. I do understand church opposition, and those who claim he's running a con game. But do you realize the joy and happiness that he's brought to thousands of Dreamers? You should see one of those Thursday night meetings as they whoop and holler for the glory and the power forever amen. Koyle really puts on a great show, and it doesn't cost much. He advises people to buy just a hundred shares of stock—not to be greedy. That's a total investment of a hundred and fifty dollars. And for a hundred and fifty bucks he makes you a millionaire."

"Millionaire?"

"Wealth isn't a matter of having money," Raymond said, "it's an attitude. You can only eat so much at each meal. You can ride in only one car at a time. You can sleep in only one bed. Beyond that, wealth is simply knowing that you've *got* it. And the Dreamers have *got* it. They're all rich. They'll redeem Zion and save the church. They'll be honored and revered when those against them will come on hands and knees begging forgiveness. They get all this for a hundred and fifty dollars. It's a bargain."

As a final footnote, when Budro wrote to Norman Pierce in April 1977 for an update of the latest scoop on the Dream Mine, he learned that Pierce was indeed where the action was. He had joined Bishop Koyle and old-time Dreamers dating back to 1894 in the Thursday night meetings at the great Dream Mine in the sky.

Poulson? Ouch! He was a mental case.

—FORMER STUDENT

He influenced me more than anyone else in my life.

—FORMER STUDENT

You loved him or hated him. There was no middle ground.

—FACULTY MEMBER

After a quarter century, I still quote him every day.

—FORMER STUDENT

Students came back to see him, by the hundreds, every year.

—FACULTY MEMBER

15

The Secret Quest of the BYU Bogeyman

CERTAINLY he fit the stereotype of the preoccupied professor. He rode a bicycle along Provo streets with slow deliberation, ancient hat perfectly straight, steel-rimmed glasses halfway down his nose. He looked neither right nor left. After dismounting he'd go about town and the campus forgetful of the black clips on his trouser legs. He ignored the whims of style, wearing his gray suits threadbare. His neckties were outdated enough to be weird, and he'd never learned how to knot them. His hair could always use a comb and his shoes a shine.

Everyone knew him by sight and reputation—Professor M. Wilford Poulson, irascible ogre of the BYU, and the tightest man in town. Freshmen arriving from the far corners of Deseret had heard of his ferocious reputation. They avoided his classes like the plague. He was, without doubt, the most unpopular teacher in the history of Brigham Young University.

And, people said, tighter than the bark on a tree. When investing in a toaster or waffle iron, he shopped every store in Provo—and woe to the clerk who misrepresented the product. He read the fine print of the guarantee, and filed it away for future reference. And did you hear how Poulson backed the Utah Power and Light Company into a corner because of a 14¢ overcharge? He must have plenty stashed away, people said. While BYU salaries weren't high, and he had six children, other faculty members drove cars, dressed well, had better homes.

Such was the reputation of M. Wilford Poulson. Yet one of his own precepts, which Budro never forgot, was that whenever everyone was in agreement on something, it was sure to be a fallacy.

Yes, it was true that he sacrificed popularity in the classroom; but it was for values which many of his students came to appreciate only years later. He undoubtedly was a martinet; yet he was never harsh with those needing help. His particular victims, as a matter of fact, were the very students who got by without half trying in other classes.

Yes, he was very careful with money. Yet only his family, and an extremely few intimate friends, knew of the secret quest that had absorbed every spare dollar and hour of his adult lifetime. They said nothing about the contents of his basement, because his position at the university, his church standing, and social status might well depend upon their silence. The high windows of the basement were covered with tarpaper. He carried the only key to the door.

The Y was a small school when Budro entered its hallowed halls, and Professor Poulson was the entire psychology department. And that was the rub. One of his courses, Psychology 11, was necessary for graduation. For normal students, Psychology of Education also was required. So Poulson didn't have to be popular. All he had to do was wait.

There was one escape hatch, pioneered by a student (call him Anderson) who was brilliant, charming, handsome, a returned missionary, member of a prominent family, a student-body leader, and exceptionally articulate. With these attributes, he found it easy to get straight A's. But not in Poulson's class, where Anderson found himself in the unfamiliar role of the class goat. Baffled and hurt, he had a private talk with Poulson, who told him bluntly that he was an apple-polisher. Maybe in other courses he could parlay a smattering of knowledge, an agile mind, a glib tongue, and a warm personality into an A grade. "That won't work in my classes, Brother Anderson."

Stung and infuriated, Anderson made a mistake—he mentioned his family's influence. That did it. Poulson rode him mercilessly from then on. Anderson flunked Psych 11. He took it the following year, and flunked again. Deciding he'd had enough of that wormy apple, Anderson took a course by extension from the University of Utah for the credits necessary to graduate.

This method of avoiding Poulson became so popular that the university issued a rule against it. Didn't look right, BYU students taking correspondence courses from U. of U.

There was no escape route for Budro. For two years he avoided the inevitable, while listening to stories of the Poulson legend, his tyranny in the classroom, and eccentricities outside it.

Painfully honest himself, Poulson demanded absolute integrity from others. His battle with the Utah Power and Light Company over the 14¢ overcharge was typical. He indignantly refused the company's offer to refund the 14¢. A mistake had been made on his bill, and he wanted the account corrected. Poulson carried the crusade step by step to the head office. Eventually, Utah Power and Light reopened its accounts for that month, issued a correct bill, then reconciled its bookkeeping.

He chafed under the endless church appeals for donations and contributions in addition to the tithe, and finally settled the matter by informing the ward bishop that he would give a lump sum each year to be applied where most needed. "And in the meanwhile, I expect to be left alone."

This satisfied the bishop, but two members of the Building Fund Committee took it upon themselves to labor with Poulson regarding a donation for the new chapel. He explained his policy, then as they continued their sales pitch, he said, "Brethren, since my time is valuable, I make it a policy to deduct five dollars from my yearly contribution for every five minutes consumed to listening to appeals for donations. You have now squandered fifteen dollars of the church's money." The two hastily bade good-bye.

Budro took the plunge as a junior. The baptism of fire in Psych 11 was everything he'd dreaded, and more, particularly since he got in Poulson's doghouse through a column he was writing for the college newspaper. One item announced the Budro Theme Writing Company—papers prepared for any course, with grade A guaranteed, $15; Poulson's courses, $100. Budro fondly considered this a humorous spoof, but Poulson was sensitive about his reputation, and next day in class he announced that a certain columnist for the *Y News* couldn't *get* an A from him. Grades had never meant much to Budro, but now he really dug in for that A. His term paper was good enough to be accepted for publication by a national magazine—but it didn't get an A from Poulson. When he received a C for the course, Budro logged another first by confronting the teacher with the charge of grading on personal dislike, not scholarship. This impeachment of his integrity was the very worst affront to offer Poulson, and the clash was monumental.

Despite the experience, Budro scrapped his planned curriculum, and for next quarter signed up for every course under Poulson he could get—not because of psychology, but because of M. Wilford Poulson. The man was irascible, yes; he was a martinet and a tyrant, yes; but he had something tremendous to offer, which was worth the price.

If Poulson was surprised to see Budro's shining face back for more, he gave no sign of it. But, though the feud continued, there now was a difference. Budro's return was the greatest compliment he could have paid a teacher whom he detested; in turn, the professor gave the feisty student a certain respect.

"All you have to do to get along with me," Poulson announced the first day of every class, "is to do as I say." He meant it, right down to the last *ibid*. Papers had to be in specified form, with spacing, indentation, italicization, punctuation, and footnotes exactly as specified. What it amounted to was the accepted form of a scientific paper; but, with Poulson, if the form was wrong, too bad.

One student turned in a theme and also submitted a copy to the annual Talmage Essay contest. Poulson singled it out as a horrible example, and was cutting it to ribbons when George H. Brimhall, president emeritus of the Y, entered to congratulate the author for having won first prize. When Brimhall left, Poulson calmly demolished the remainder of the paper.

Among his peer group on the faculty, Poulson would likewise have won no popularity contests. When a fellow teacher working for an advanced degree suggested that Poulson extend professional courtesy by giving him credit for a course without attending classes, for merely reading the text and passing a snap exam, Poulson not only denounced the man to his face but indignantly related the outrage to all his classes. While he didn't mention names, the identity of the faculty member soon was an open secret when he enrolled for the required course.

"I don't teach psychology," Poulson said in every class, "I teach young ladies and gentlemen." This actually was the subject of all his courses, the eternal verities that added up to a philosophy of life based upon absolute integrity and the search for the kingdom of heaven within each individual. He was fond of quoting another Mormon teacher, William H. Chamberlain, who said that personality—basic character—was the highest quality of life, and the enhancing of it the greatest aim. "If you would know what is real and eternal, look into your own hearts and know your own selves."

Poulson made a fetish of the scientific method—an open mind; insistence upon primary sources; willingness to accept data wherever they might lead; caution in forming conclusions; an attitude of skepticism; a habit of challenging assertion, hearsay, superlatives, and sweeping statements; and the law of parsimony, acceptance of the simplest hypothesis which fit the facts.

One day a bill collector walked in during class and confronted Poulson with an overdue account. The two men engaged in a wrangle. After the collector slammed out, Poulson said to the class, "Write down what you have just witnessed." It was, of course, prearranged. A comparison of the widely divergent reports of an impressive event fresh on their minds made class members skeptical even of eyewitness testimony.

The average person, Poulson declared, rarely used his brain for thinking. Even college students didn't average five minutes a day in genuine thought. What passed for reasoning in solving a problem was the selection of facts to fit a preconceived answer. As he forced students to think, Budro discovered the stimulation of mental exercise, which was just as invigorating as breaking into a sweat with a physical workout.

Poulson's withering contempt of bombast, ostentation, pomposity, and pretense caused him to put his worst foot forward. But, like him or hate him, he was real; in a phony world of compromise and expediency, he was genuine.

"You'll notice he rode only the men," a former student said. "But any pretty girl who sat on the front row and crossed her legs was a cinch for an A."

It was true that Poulson had an old-fashioned gallantry with future mothers of Zion. Yet a former campus beauty said, "I could charm the other profs—but Poulson made me work. Being the daughter of an apostle smoothed the way with the others; but with Poulson it was two strikes against me." Then with a dazzling smile she said, "The world expanded for me in Psych 11."

Budro came to have a perverse pride in being in Poulson's doghouse; it meant he was worthy of special attention. The professor never picked on weaklings; he was considerate with students having personality handicaps, speech problems, emotional disturbances, or physical disabilities. He was endlessly patient and helpful with an Indian girl whose background left her with severe academic deficiencies. Largely because of his personal tutoring, she graduated.

A course in theology was required each quarter at BYU. Budro found Poulson's Theology of Religion the landmark class of his college career. The text was William James' *Varieties of Religious Experience;* and for the first time Budro found the spiritual concept beautifully presented by both the author and the teacher, two great minds in harmony.

Returned missionaries were shocked when he presented primary source material which proved they hadn't known all they thought they did about the gospel they'd preached in the vineyard. Poulson, who'd been on two missions himself, was caustic about selection of half-truth, mythology, and unrelated proof-texts. He added his thunder to Job's:

Hear now my reasoning, and hearken to the pleadings of my lips. Will ye speak wickedly for God? and talk deceitfully for him?

How much more faith we all would show, he said, by quietly demonstrating the divinity of our religion as it enriched our lives and personalities.

Budro never forgot the day Poulson swept his hand over the

blackboard. "All of you can spend the remainder of your lives in research, and never be able to explain exactly why the dust sticks to my fingertips. Adhesion; yes—but what is adhesion? There is not enough time in your lives to find the final answer to anything, including religion. You must accept any doctrine on the basis of known evidence. You can't know all the answers. Be satisfied with just a few important ones, then quit worrying about it. Don't invite a lifetime of torment seeking the unanswerable."

This one precept was, to Budro, worth the price of admission.

One day Poulson asked, "To what school of psychology do I belong?" This brought the class up short. Budro was in the second year of taking every course of his he could get, yet so rigorously impartial had been the presentation that there had been no hint of Poulson's personal leanings.

Budro left the Y with respect for Poulson's principles, but a cordial dislike for him as a person. It was almost a decade later when a mutual interest in Mormon history brought him and Poulson in communication on a professional level. And then one morning—New Year's day, of all times—Poulson phoned from the bus station at Redwood City. Just passing through, he said hesitantly, and he'd like to say hello if Budro had a few minutes and he wasn't imposing. Budro brought him out to the house, and in the living room, with the student-teacher relationship gone, Budro became acquainted with a Poulson he'd never known—a delightful person with a dry wit and an endless fund of anecdote, his mind so stimulating that Budro hated to let him go to bed.

It had taken considerable urging to get him to stay overnight, repeated assurances that he was entirely welcome. Poulson couldn't abide obligation, and in leaving next morning presented a reproduction of William Clayton's 1848 booklet, *The Latter-day Saints' Emigrants Guide from Council Bluffs to the Valley of the Great Salt Lake.*

The visit became an annual event, though Budro didn't know why Poulson always happened to be in Redwood City on New Year's day. It took another five years or so before Poulson took Budro into his confidence. On a trip to Provo, Budro spent an evening at his home, and as they chatted he thought how lonely Poulson must be, this unpopular teacher with his abrasive public personality who remained aloof from social and community affairs.

He lived alone. His wife had died, his children grown up and moved away. A second marriage had failed.

Then presently Poulson swore Budro to secrecy, unlocked a door, and took him downstairs. The full basement contained bookcases reaching from floor to ceiling in closely spaced rows. The shelves were crammed with books, documents, papers, journals—most of the material rare, all of it pertaining to Mormon history. With ordinary rare books he had two perfect copies; with something extremely rare, he generally had three.

Here was the secret life of M. Wilford Poulson. This was why he'd ridden a bicycle and made full use of every gray suit. All of his surplus money and time had gone into the adventure of research and the pursuit of rare historical material.

Now the reason was clear for his visits on New Year's. During the holidays he was scouring California on a book hunt, and on that date stores were closed.

Lonely? He'd lived life to the brim. There was a fortune in this basement—he'd sold a spare copy of the first compilation of Joseph Smith's revelations, *The Book of Commandments,* for more than $2,000—but, aside from that, here were the trophies of one of the most exciting hunts in the world. The pursuit required patience, intuition, diplomacy, vast knowledge, the deductive ability of Sherlock Holmes, and the gambling nerve of Bet-A-Million Gates. He had ferreted out his treasures from attics and barns and bookstores all over the United States. He'd also made a trip to Europe. He'd written thousands of letters; he'd cultivated untold numbers of skeptical and suspicious individuals. He'd lost great gambles of time, effort, and travel expense; but, again, he'd hit many jackpots. Working in secret, he'd assembled what probably was the finest private collection of early Mormon source material in existence.

The gem of his collection was the complete duplication of every book in the library to which Joseph Smith had had access during the prophet's formative years. There had been unending controversy regarding the environmental influences on Joseph. How much of his translations and revelations was original to him, and how much might he have known from the world about him? To a large degree, the answer lay in the library that Joseph frequented. M. Wilford Poulson was the first man to reconstruct it. While on a trip he came upon a portion of that library, together with a list of the remainder.

He made the discovery at a time when his schedule left less than an hour to examine and catalogue the books. Some had lost covers and title pages; from these, he jotted down chapter titles.

Ten years later, he had recreated the library, except for one volume. All he had for the missing book was a chapter heading. He'd advertised for it year after year, ransacked bookstores, trunks, attics, and basements. And then one day while browsing in his own collection he opened a book he'd purchased years previously merely because it had been published during the period under study, and found himself looking upon that elusive chapter heading. The library was complete.

Another research feat was breaking the code of James Strang's diary. Strang was an ambitious Saint who had attempted to take control of the church at Nauvoo after Joseph Smith's death. Failing this, he led a group of disciples to Beaver Island, Michigan, where he ruled the cult until assassinated in 1856. Strang's diary had tantalized historians ever since his death. Much of it was obviously written for posterity in high-sounding platitudes. But there were passages in a private code, evidently Strang's secret thoughts. Nobody had been able to break the code, until Poulson did so. This revealed the double life of Strang, intensely ambitious but frustrated until he deliberately became a fake prophet strictly for what was in it for Strang—the pomp and trappings of authority, the wealth from tithes, the adulation of the flock, and the choice of pretty girls as plural wives.[1]

Although Poulson had become the world's greatest authority on the origins of Mormonism, this was only preparatory to his ultimate goal. He considered his library as research material for the writing of a definitive history of the subject.

Why the elaborate caution? Why the secrecy? For one thing, Poulson followed Brigham Young's maxim, "Mind Your Own Business." There was another and deeper reason: the recent excommunication of Fawn Brodie, despite her being a niece of David O. McKay of the First Presidency, was an example of what could happen to anyone who tampered with the idealized concept of the

---

1. Working independently, another Mormon scholar, Dale Morgan, also broke Strang's code at this time. Fawn M. Brodie was doing research for her biography of Joseph Smith, *No Man Knows My History*. She learned of the Strang code from Poulson, and applied Strang's attitudes to Joseph. This concept couldn't be documented, and resulted in her expulsion from the church.

prophet as officially portrayed. Joseph Smith had been canonized; he was revered as a saint without fault or blemish. Even his own personal account of vital incidents in his life had been censored and improved by apologists.[2]

The church had its official story, and didn't want any tampering with it. At this time Salt Lake assumed that it owned the facts of history, and that any attempt to "sensationalize" them was an unfriendly act. Research on Mormon origins was frowned upon. Not only pioneer journals, but files of early church newspapers were locked away in the official archives, unavailable to scholars and historians. Incredibly enough, even the public sermons of the church authorities during the pioneer period, delivered from the rostrum and published in the twenty-six volumes of the *Journal of Discourses,* were suppressed. In fact, people had been called on the carpet and even cut off for persistently trying to gain access to them, and asking too many questions about their content.[3]

Meanwhile, Poulson's position at the university had become insecure. Perhaps it was inevitable that he should come under attack. Word had leaked out about his research. His compulsion to prick pretension, deflate pomposity, and challenge cherished half-truth and mythology had ruffled important feathers. His insistence upon maintaining an open mind and establishing facts from primary sources—even in religious matters—had caused zealous students to rush to Salt Lake with complaints. Among the faculty, his role as the caustic critic had alienated a number of his peers. His effectiveness as a teacher, it was charged, had declined. With growth of the school the Psychology Department had expanded;

2. Compare, for example, Joseph's account of the circumstances surrounding the visitation by the angel Moroni, as written and published by himself in the *Times and Seasons,* at Nauvoo, and subsequently incorporated into early editions of *The Pearl of Great Price,* with the modern revised version.

3. The Salt Lake City Public Library cooperated by refusing access to the *Journal of Discourses.* Subsequently, the Fundamentalists began reprinting them for *samizdat* circulation, whereupon the church republished them and put them on sale at Deseret Book Store—and the roof didn't fall in. However, at the time Poulson was doing his major research, internal censorship was stringent. People were afraid to be seen carrying *No Man Knows My History* from the Salt Lake Library, and brought their own dust jackets to conceal it. In the town of Heber, the local library circulated it, together with Hugh Nibley's refutation of it (*No, Ma'am, That's Not History*), as a unit, poison and antidote. A curious instance of suppression concerns the journal of Nibley's grandfather. After Nibley had deposited the journal with the church archives, he subsequently was refused permission to see it again.

now that students could get courses from other teachers, fewer and fewer enrolled for the baptism of fire under Poulson. Had he outlived his usefulness to the university?

When a friend on the faculty tipped him off that a hearing was scheduled to decide whether or not the employment of M. Wilford Poulson should be terminated, he thought he knew what had triggered it. The dilettante son of a general authority of the church had found his path smooth at the Y, until Poulson lowered the boom for lack of preparation, and flunked him. The arrogant young man never before had received such treatment, and, confronting Poulson, gave notice that he'd nail the professor's hide to the wall.

While the hearing was in progress, Poulson waited for the verdict in his office, humiliated that he should be on trial without being informed of it, without knowing the charges, without being able to prepare a defense or face his accusers. He had been a member of the faculty more than thirty-five years, professor of psychology and head of the department for a quarter century. He had received national recognition in his field.[4]

How important in his trial was his habit of challenging the mythology of Mormonism? He had tweaked important noses with an article on the background of the Word of Wisdom, which demolished the fond belief that nobody realized the harmful effects of coffee, tobacco, and strong drink until Joseph Smith received the information by revelation. He was known to have helped Fawn Brodie with her research. When the Catholic writer, Thomas F. O'Dey, was doing research for his book, *The Mormons*,[5] Poulson clashed with him at a meeting for making incorrect statements received during his carefully guided tour of materials in Salt Lake. Poulson was subsequently helpful in separating fact from half-truth for the Gentile. Yet how did this set with the Salt Lake sources of O'Dey's incorrect information?

4. He was a life member of the American Psychological Association; past vice president of the Library Department of the National Education Association; past president of the Utah Library Association, and also of the Utah Academy of Science, Arts and Letters; and during World War II he was a government psychologist at the Salt Lake and Provo induction centers.

In church activity he had taught Sunday school, the elders quorum and the high priests quorum; had been a member of the elders quorum presidency, a member of the Stake Aaronic Priesthood Committee, and superintendent of the stake religion classes.

5. Chicago: University of Chicago Press, 1957.

Poulson would have to depend upon his friends in the faculty to defend him. But who were they? The barbs of his abrasive honesty had pricked almost everyone.

He had been waiting almost two hours when his door opened. The friend who'd alerted him to the trial entered, beaming. One by one, faculty members had arisen to defend the accused. "There are so many temptations for all of us to be just a little phony," one said. "We need an utterly honest man." The meeting adjourned with a vote of confidence for M. Wilford Poulson.

He went out, got on his bicycle, and took a long ride. He was deeply injured by the fact that he'd been put on trial. He'd given his service to the BYU at considerable sacrifice, turning down several better offers from other universities. His heavy schedule of duties here left no time for writing the book that was to be his life's work. And he wasn't getting any younger.

Well, he now owed the BYU no further loyalty.

The following New Year's day he elatedly told Budro that an eastern university had made him a handsome offer. He would receive a healthy increase in salary, and a position of greater prestige. He would be required to teach just one course, which would leave time to write his book. It was good to know that he was appreciated elsewhere. This was exactly what he wanted.

Budro was surprised by his visit the following New Year's. He'd decided to reject the eastern offer. "The church has supported me during my adult life," he said. "I'll stay at BYU as long as I can be of service."

On his last visit to Redwood City, Poulson carried a stout yellow cane. Legend had it that it once had belonged to Brigham Young, though Poulson was quick to point out that he hadn't corroborated this from primary sources. Something was wrong with his foot, which, he said with his habit of ruthless veracity, was incurable and would get worse.

He was finished at BYU. He hadn't wanted to retire. "But there's no use chewing your pills," he said. "Swallow them."

The reason for secrecy concerning his collection was past. The years had brought a change in the attitude toward research on Mormon subjects. He even was being encouraged to write his book.

At the bus station next morning Budro asked if he had the

book underway yet. Poulson explained that he was on the track of an obscure journal on this trip, "And if I get it and a few other items, I'll be almost ready to begin."

Watching the white-haired man limp toward the bus with the help of the cane, Budro remembered that day in class long ago when Professor Poulson wiped his hand along the blackboard and said that a lifetime was too short to find why the chalk clung to his fingertips, or the final answer to anything else. In the twilight of life he was still seeking material, the final answer before he began his book. He'd forgotten his own maxim. On the night some twenty years previously when he'd taken Budro into the basement, he already had material for a half-dozen books. But he couldn't begin until he had absolutely everything, which meant he never would write page one.

This didn't exactly mean that he'd left his fight in the gymnasium. The quest in itself was a notable lifetime career. In assembling his library he had performed a tremendous service for his people, his church, and the community of scholars and historians.

In a paper written during Mormonism's Centennial year, he said:

It is regrettable that the latest edition of the *Encyclopaedia Britannica* must record that "no impartial and critical history of the Mormons yet exists." There is a great need for a conscious collection of material dealing with the background of Mormonism.[6]

Twenty-eight years later, in filling out a biographical questionnaire, he wrote that he had made a special project

of studying the social context of the rise of Mormonism and gathering relevant interview, picture, pamphlet and book material. The total job is both big and important so have tried to get many others interested and willing to spend the time and money before too much mythology obscures & before too much crucial material gets hidden away or lost altogether.

He had done that total job, big and important as it was. With what time remained, he worked with a secretary and tape recorder, to preserve his concept of the historical background for the BYU

6. "Library Resources for the Scientific Study of Mormonism," *Proceedings, Utah Academy of Science,* July 15, 1930.

archives. He had assembled the material for the use of someone who followed to write, someday, the definitive history of the rise of Mormonism.

Considering his reputation as the irascible tyrant, he surprisingly listed in the questionnaire that his prime hobby was "Being a friend and making new friends"—rating this above his monumental research achievements and the collection of his library.

In turn, he was best remembered, by the generations of students who attended his classes over a period of more than a half century, as the martinet who sacrificed popularity and good will in his dedicated passion to instill the eternal verities of life into young ladies and gentlemen, whether they liked it or not.

16

The Wasatch Front

AFTER LEAVING THE Y, Budro followed a girl to California. There to his vast surprise he found that, by and large, Gentiles were remarkably like Mormons—mostly good people with human foibles and conceits, and, occasionally, with a rotten apple in the barrel. Here he was no longer a member of the dominant ethnic group, but belonged to a tiny minority.

The really remarkable thing was discovering that the Wasatch Front wasn't confined to the central valleys of Utah. It was not a matter of geography, but of the Peculiar People. The Redwood City Ward was exactly like his Fourth Ward at Provo, the members of it as interchangeable as Ford parts. A Saint could move from Provo to Redwood City, arrive on Monday, be visited by the

ward bishop, assigned a job, and the following Sunday be a functioning part of the intricate mechanism. The Wasatch Front was
as near as the local meetinghouse, anywhere he might be. Here
could be found his own kind; and, Budro realized, like it or lump
it, he was one of the Peculiar People.

Although the San Francisco Bay area was the location of the
oldest Mormon settlement of the West (Sam Brannan brought a
shipload of Saints through the Golden Gate a full year before
Brigham Young's pioneer party arrived at the Salt Lake valley),
two factors had blighted the growth in this acre of the Lord's vineyard. One was that Brannan was a rascal, who shattered the faith
and the solidarity of his colony; the other was that the people were
recalled to Zion at the time of the Utah War of 1857, and, what
with the turmoil of carpetbag government in Deseret, and the long
struggle with the United States over polygamy, they never returned.

As late as 1927, when George W. Rose arrived at Redwood
City on June 20, he was, so far as he knew, the only Mormon in
this county seat of 6,000 population. The town was distinguished
by the slogan, "Climate Best by Government Test," and by the fact
that it had no redwood trees—years previously loggers had clean-
cut the area and moved on.

George Rose was a thirty-eight-year-old millwright and machin-
ist who had arrived to help set up the Pacific Portland Cement plant
to utilize the limitless shell beds underlying San Francisco Bay.
Della Rose came down from Washington with the four children to
join her husband in time for school that fall. Zion was growing.

That winter two LDS missionaries knocked on the Rose door
and were startled to be welcomed by a fellow Saint. They brought
news that there was a branch of the mission at Palo Alto, 5 miles
away, which held services in a lodge hall over the post office. There,
Rose met J. D. Clark, a carpenter who also lived in Redwood City,
and had been there for two years. This made Clark the first Mormon resident of record since pioneer days.

By 1929 a total of thirty-four Mormons were living in Redwood
City, so a local butcher, Frank Mortenson, organized a local Sunday school as a twig of the Palo Alto Branch. The stock market
crashed that fall, and as the chill of depression settled over the
land, people left to seek work, until by the next spring the town's
LDS population had dwindled to the Rose and Clark families. Then

Sunday school attendance took an abrupt drop when the Clark kids all got whooping cough. For the next five years Redwood City Saints attended services at Palo Alto.

In the fall of 1935 a design engineer named W. Yates Farnsworth moved to Redwood City. He was forty-eight, and during the depression had done everything that came handy, including housework, until he latched on at the Schlage Lock Company. He became superintendent of the Redwood City Branch, organized that December. It held services at Forester's Hall on Middlefield Road, in an upstairs room above a saloon. There was always a party at the place Saturday night, so George Rose would get there early next morning to sweep up butts, tote out empties, mop up puke, open windows, and set up chairs.

Farnsworth's wife, Theda, led the choir with such zeal that practically everyone belonged. In fact, at times when the choir sang the entire adult congregation took places at the front, leaving only children for the audience.

As ward teachers, Rose and Farnsworth called each month at Budro's home. The branch boundaries covered an area of 700 square miles, from the bay over the mountainous spine of the peninsula to the Pacific. For more than twenty years they never missed a month of this duty, though at the time the branch was organized it took three hard days of driving more than 125 miles over switchback mountain roads to cover the route.

Farnsworth had two hobbies, composing songs and receiving letters from important people. He wrote both words and music, and published the songs himself. Whenever he had a new composition, he'd bring it on his monthly visit to Budro, and play piano accompaniment while he and Rose sang. His songs were sung at Schlage socials, and were popular at the Balconades, a dance hall at San Jose featuring old-time melodies. In 1945 he composed the "Victory March" to celebrate the end of World War II. He sent complimentary copies to the president and forty governors, and proudly showed Budro letters of thanks from the White House and fifteen state capitols. However, a copy sent to the editor of a magazine came back with a rejection slip.

With membership grown to 260, Redwood City Branch became a ward on October 5, 1941, Farnsworth bishop and Rose first counselor. The following July Rose arrived at Forester's Hall on a

Sunday morning to find the hall gutted by fire; the Independence day shindig had been hotter than usual. Nothing to do but hold church services downstairs, in the barroom.

Farnsworth utilized the bar as both sacrament table and pulpit, but, "I do not feel at ease," he admitted, "with a beer sign over my head like a halo."

Rose was more philosophical. "We should consider ourselves fortunate," he pointed out. "Here we have Lucky Strike; there, Lucky Lager; and, if we wish to rest, there is Chesterfield."

The fire provided the incentive for purchasing a meeting place. Liberty Hall, farther down Middlefield Road, was a former beer joint, on the market for $6,000—an appalling price for depression-scarred people—but when Annie May Riggs, a widow and oldest member of the ward, donated $400 toward the purchase, the deal was made.

"Best investment we ever made," George Rose said. "Maybe Liberty Hall wasn't much, but it was *ours.* We gained strength and membership."

Everyone pitched in to rehabilitate and remodel the new meetinghouse. Women tackled the floor with scrapers, knives, and scrubbing brushes, getting off the gum, grime, and ingrained dirt of years. Men installed tile, built a circular staircase to make a classroom of the overhead projection booth, strung wires for curtains to partition the chapel into several classrooms. The back room held the bar, which was handy as a serving table for ward dinners until stake officials paid a visit; then it had to go.

Budro was overseas, fighting the war with his typewriter, when, in September 1944, Farnsworth was released as bishop. In pioneer days, a man became bishop for life. Modern policy, however, was based on the new-broom concept; tenure for a bishop might be five years or so, but almost never ten.

James P. Johnson, the new bishop, was a foreman at the National Motor Bearing plant. He chose Raymond Varney as first counselor, but for a while he had no second, because of difficulty in persuading Louis H. Osterloh to accept the call. Osterloh, a ticket agent for Southern Pacific Railroad, didn't feel worthy. A gregarious man, he liked to go out with the boys on occasion, and have a beer. One night Johnson labored with him until 1 A.M. Finally Osterloh said with a sigh, "Well, all right, if you think I can cut it."

After Budro returned from overseas, the great Mormon boom in California got into high gear. New wards and stakes proliferated in the bay area; the boundaries of Redwood City Ward shrank until the ward teaching route of Farnsworth and Rose became a snap, including only the city itself and the neighboring town of San Carlos.

When the stake was divided in 1946, Bishop James Johnson was released to become stake clerk of the newly created Palo Alto Stake. Lou Osterloh was a happy man. "I'm glad to be getting out of this," he told Johnson. "And I'll tell you something, Jim—from now on, no more church jobs for me."

Louis H. Osterloh was sustained the next bishop of Redwood City Ward, an office he was to hold for eight years.

On July 24, 1947, the day Utah celebrated its centennial, the Redwood City *Tribune* carried an item about the local ward, whose membership was 422 souls. As a welfare project, it had a quota of canning 40 cases of pears, 25 cases of peaches, and 100 cases of string beans. The ward also raised the beans, having planted a quarter acre locally and the same amount near Mountain View on property owned by George Rose, who had left the cement company for the well-drilling business. Members plowed the soil and planted the beans, laid pipe for irrigation, drove 1,600 stakes, and were picking and canning at the time the newspaper item appeared. Everyone helped. Irene Albretsen had a new baby, which she put in a cardboard box and pulled down the rows as she picked.

Other welfare projects of the period were fruit picking, prune drying, the raising of rabbits and chickens. But Tony Terranova never forgot the sanctimonious sisters and the acre of tomatoes. This was a project of the Elders' Quorum, Terranova and Andy Jones in charge. The two ladies generously allowed use of their land for the worthy cause until, after the acre was planted, they made the horrifying discovery that the nice young men were *Mormons*. The sisters rushed to their minister in dismay. Had they sinned? "My daughters, you have given your sacred word that they could use the land," the spiritual leader advised. "But—you haven't promised *water*, have you?" So all summer long Tony Terranova buzzed back and forth in his pickup, hauling water in a 50-gallon barrel, while Andy Jones and his crew irrigated the acre of tomatoes with buckets.

242

During this period the ward built two homes for needy members, donating all labor, and obtaining bargain rates for materials from sympathetic Gentile dealers. There was a party spirit with such activities. Weenie roasts made fun out of picking string beans. At the steamy kitchen of Liberty Hall women sang as they canned the acre of tomatoes in kitchen pressure cookers.

In 1948 the wards of Palo Alto Stake built a welfare cannery at Redwood City. Corrugated sheet metal for walls and roof came free as the government dismantled Camp Shoemaker, across the bay. Total cash outlay for building and machinery was only $20,000. The structure also housed the bishop's storehouse, which issued supplies for the needy. As Liberty Hall became more crowded, the choir practiced at the cannery, and the Relief Society ladies used it for meetings and quilting bees.

Two more stakes joined in the cannery operation, their wards taking turns using the facility for their welfare quotas. On an unforgettable Saturday night Redwood City Ward was finishing the canning of tomatoes, and all except seven people had gone home when a truckload arrived, having been delayed by a flat tire. The load was dead ripe, and, since there could be no canning on the Sabbath, would be spoiled by Monday. It took the entire crew of seven to operate the machinery, so they all peeled until they had enough for a cooker full, then moved over to the equipment, packed the cans, put them through the steam belt, sealed them and filled the cooker, then went back to peeling again. Slow work, but no tomatoes spoiled. It was daylight when they left the cannery, with just time enough to go home, clean up, and get to church. Of course the cannery worksheet showed they'd signed out at midnight, for it was unthinkable to work Sunday on a church project.

When David B. Haight became stake president, he suggested that a new chapel for Redwood City Ward was necessary. Liberty Hall forthwith went on the block, and was sold for $15,000. Once more the ward went into rented quarters, at Arroyo Hall, above a San Carlos plumbing shop. Rent, $75 a month.

After the ward purchased a building site on lower Edgewood Road, in a choice residential district, the Mormon Menace made headlines. Neighbors secured 250 names on a petition of protest. After several hearings—and national publicity—Redwood City Mormons were denied a building permit. So Salt Lake took over the lot, and the ward went farther out Edgewood Road into the boondocks for another site, three quarters of an acre, price $9,000. Again a building permit was denied, the lot being too small for off-street parking. After the ward spent another $14,000 for parking space, the County Health Department got in the act, refusing to allow septic tanks. The only sewer line belonged to the city of San Carlos, which refused permission for use.

At this point Bishop Osterloh touched the hearts of the San Carlos city fathers with a letter outlining the ward's plight, and finally the Redwood City *Tribune* headlined on June 21, 1951, "LATTER-DAY SAINT CHURCH GETS PERMIT TO BUILD."

For a year and a half after the permit was granted, the site remained untouched, while the ward wrestled with plans, specifications, estimates, and bids, everything requiring approval from Salt Lake. Key problem was money. The same congregation which just eight years previously had had serious misgivings about the $6,000 plunge for Liberty Hall had undertaken a $240,000 project. That was a lot of money for a congregation of plain people, and it took five hard years to finish the job.

Before beginning construction, the ward had to own the land free and clear. Salt Lake would pay half the building costs, but the ward would have to have a cash fund of 30 percent of its share before beginning. Labor, all of it donated, would count toward the ward's share.

Claude Stevens went around to every family in the ward, active and inactive, seeking pledges of a month's income to the building fund. This was a stiff levy for most members, particularly the devout, who already were dollared to death with tithes, welfare assessments, and literally dozens of other contributions. (The LDS Church is an expensive organization for the active member, so much so that the Internal Revenue Service finds the contributions hard to believe.)

After the first round, Stevens again visited every family for pledges. Some of the faithful gave another month's income, some two months, some three; and a few contributed five months' income toward the new chapel. (Yes, it was a chapel, now, no longer a meetinghouse.)

Finally, with money on hand or pledged, the congregation hauled a piano on to the site in a pickup truck on February 21,

1953, stuck an American flag in the soil, and officially broke ground.

Oral Nelson contributed the excavation work and grading. When he arrived with his tractor, somebody said, "While we're at it, why don't we add a classroom in the basement, and a good-sized rumpus room for the Boy Scouts down there?" Bishop Osterloh nodded approval, and Oral Nelson scooped it out, nothing said about it.

Jim Johnson and Orion Packer were the builders. It was the first big construction job for the former bishop and his partner, and they often sought practical advice from J. D. Clark, with his long experience as a carpenter. Johnson and Packer hadn't bid the job in; it was a call. Instead of the usual commission, they received modest wages—the only money expended for labor by ward members.

Saturday was the big building day, men doing the heavy work, women cleaning up. The Relief Society donated the food and cooked lunch. A problem with volunteer labor was that someone giving his time free felt independent. And nobody could be fired. As tempers occasionally flared, soft-spoken Jim Johnson had a sure cure. When somebody blew his stack, Johnson quietly led him away. A worker crossing into the corner where they had retired might find them kneeling in prayer.

Johnson never forgot the day when Elder LeGrand Richards arrived from Salt Lake to inspect work in progress. In the basement, the apostle looked about curiously at the classroom and Boy Scout room. "Hmmm—let me see those blueprints again."

"Er—these two rooms aren't *on* the blueprints."

"What's that?"

"We were afraid Salt Lake wouldn't give us permission."

"Well, you'd better *get* permission, right away."

Salt Lake did approve what already existed.

In the three years of hard work it took to build the ward house, certain days stood out, and the high point in Jim Johnson's memory was the Saturday they framed the roof. They'd made the girders on the ground, stacked them in huge piles. It was expected that several weeks would be required to get them into place. But E. H. Bean arrived with rigging equipment and hoisted them up deftly, until when Osterloh arrived to help that afternoon, the job was finished and the men sitting in a circle on the floor of the future chapel room eating watermelon.

E. H. Bean submitted a bill for $400, marked "PAID IN FULL."

When the roof was ready to go on, Peninsula Roof and Tile underbid two LDS contractors. Then after receiving payment the company returned its $800 profit for the job.

Gentiles were good people, also.

With a roof overhead, Primary, Mutual, Relief Society and other activities moved under it, even though a diagonal subfloor was underfoot.

Because the entire building was stucco outside and plaster within, an enormous burden fell on the only two journeymen in the ward capable of doing this work, George Grubb and Cub Ross. They were on the job every afternoon after work until dark, as well as Saturdays. Soon after the chapel was finished, George Grubb went to the hospital with an attack of arthritis. Cub Ross had developed a bad shoulder from overwork, and had to give up the trade.

Subsequently, when Cub Ross decided that he'd like to go through the temple with his wife, Vida, to be married for time and eternity and have their children sealed to them in the hereafter, he was dubious. "I don't know if I can qualify," he admitted to Budro. The bishop, however, was certain that he was worthy of a recommend.

Original plans called for a bishop's office. During construction there was a change of plans to provide for two of them. Divide and prosper—such is the church's method of growth. By splitting the congregation into two wards, a new bishopric and some 250 other positions were created. That's the number of officers (all unpaid) required to staff a ward completely. Seventy-five of them were of sufficient importance to receive the status symbol of a key to the building. At least another seventy-five felt hurt at not rating a key.

With division of the wards came new bishoprics. William R. Callister, a department manager for Del Monte Corp., became Budro's bishop, with Claude Stevens taking office at San Carlos Ward.

Division of a ward is like a divorce. Old friends no longer see each other. Two congregations use the same meetinghouse—even three, as subsequently happened—but meetings are so deftly dovetailed that one group never encounters another. In this case, the usual wrenching separation of the tightly knit group was somewhat eased because both congregations continued working together on the building.

At a stake conference following his call to office, Bishop Callister was appalled when someone clouted the hat of the visiting authority from Salt Lake, LeGrand Richards. Callister joined the vain search, incredulous that a fellow Saint would cop the headgear of one of the Lord's anointed at a time of worship. A few days later as he prepared for work on a sunny morning, Callister reached for his hat and noticed that it seemed particularly shiny. He looked inside to find the ZCMI label and the initials "L.R." on the sweatband. Certainly it was the most embarrassed bishop in the entire church who sat down to write a letter to a member of the Twelve.

Callister never did find out who stole his own hat.

"We're in!" a circular announced January 26, 1955.

Yes, although the chapel pews have not been installed and there is yet a great deal to do, we are in our chapel and the recreation hall is serving as a temporary improvement over Arroyo Hall.

Now began the big push for completion. In addition to Saturdays, the volunteer labor force worked every evening when the meetinghouse wasn't in use—but with two wards scheduling events, just *when* was there an opportunity for work? In addition to the regular schedules of MIA, choir practice, Primary, Relief Society, and meetings-meetings-meetings, both wards held a series of dinners, bazaars, dinners, festivals, dinners, rummage sales, stage shows, and dinners to make fun out of the incessant pressure for funds.

The faithful acquired a curiously waxen look. They'd been drained of the last drop of financial blood, yet, somehow. . . . It was cash on the barrelhead as work went on—no notes, no loans, no mortgages. Kitchen equipment arrived, couldn't be paid for, went back. With a total membership of 362 families in the two wards, only about one third of them carried the burden.

A huge truck and semi arrived with the knocked-down chapel pews, and Budro helped a crew assemble them and screw them into place. With services now held in the chapel, the finish floor could

247

be laid in the recreation hall and the stage completed. But the roadshow was coming up, both wards using the stage for rehearsals. Every time hammers and saws got going, someone would rush out of a meeting: "Hold it! We're having prayer!" Finally Jim Johnson said in his quiet way, "I am giving you notice. If you want this place finished, we've got to be able to work."

But if anyone supposes that church activity ceased merely to allow the meetinghouse to be built, he is indeed naïve.

The date for dedication was set. Activity reached a frenzy. There were a thousand touch-up jobs. Women washed windows, shined floors, cleaned up after the men. Everything must be spic-and-span-new, as if the place hadn't been in use night and day for two years. Budro kept his tools and overalls in his car during the final weeks, dropping around to help every spare hour; yet he, it must be remembered, really didn't qualify as an active member. In fact, despite his gray hair his progress had been so retarded that he held the priesthood office of deacon, generally bestowed on boys at the age of twelve.

During this final building push, Budro met W. Aird McDonald, first president of San Francisco Stake, at a luncheon. When Mc-Donald was introduced as the area's oldest stake president, Budro replied, "I'm the oldest deacon."

Dedication meant the meetinghouse was not only finished, but paid for—"We don't dedicate a debt to the Lord." In getting over the final hump, there were many generous gestures. Just one: Jim Johnson and Orion Packer, who drew wages for a forty-hour week and worked eighty, went to Salt Lake to present their case for a modest builders' commission of $4,000. When this was granted, they turned it to the ward building fund, which, matched by the church, made an $8,000 credit.

However, the firm of Packer and Johnson got more than treasures in heaven for their dedication. The chapel project was a springboard in the construction business, which made both men wealthy.

According to persistent legend, on the day of dedication heavenly hosts joined in as the combined choirs and congregations of the two wards sang the Hosannah Anthem. Certainly this group of dedicated people, and particularly the "Middlefield Roaders" who had worked together almost thirty years, felt an overwhelming sense of ecstasy and spiritual exaltation at the culmination of the ceremony.

Now that it was finished, there was criticism: The women wanted to know why there was no outside door to the kitchen, why it had restaurant-type equipment which housewives couldn't handle. The drama directors were unhappy with the stage. Restrooms had been carved out of the wings, leaving no backstage space for scenery and props. The professional stage lighting was a nightmare of jacks and dimmers which needed a stage electrician to handle.

But the big and basic mistake was that the chapel was located on the west side of the building, its entire wall of window glass, reaching from floor to ceiling, exposed to the unblinking glare of the afternoon sun. It would have been so simple, at the beginning, to have reversed the plan, putting the chapel on the east. . . .

It must be understood that criticism was strictly within the group; any outside suggestion that the Lord's house wasn't perfect would have been met with the fury of tigers.

A ward, however, is not a thing of brick and stucco, walls, roof, foundation, pews, pulpit. It is a living entity—the body of the congregation, the Peculiar People. Peculiar in what way? In reverence for authority. A woman takes her sample ballot to the bishop, for him to mark by inspiration. A pregnant wife who has measles refuses to have an abortion when her bishop assures her the Lord will see to it that her baby is perfectly normal. When it proves not to be, her marriage breaks up and her faith is devastated.

They are a record-keeping people. The Lord notes the fall of a sparrow, and the church keeps a record of almost everything else. If it isn't a matter of record, it didn't happen. Budro's father-in-law lived in a small Idaho town where the records went into the attic instead of to Salt Lake. When the meetinghouse burned down, he and others discovered they weren't members of the church, for no record existed. For the record he was again baptized, confirmed, ordained to the priesthood offices of deacon, teacher, priest, elder, and high priest.

A people to whom matters of record are so important can come to value observance of the letter of the gospel above the spirit of it. Obeying the Word of Wisdom looms so large in modern practice that at BYU students listed the breaking of it the most serious sin of all; murder was relegated to number seven on the list. Observing it, by the same token, was the greatest virtue. One faithful member so implicitly believed in the Lord's law of health that he expected to live 500 years, he told Budro. He planned to retire at 65, and spend 435 golden years on Social Security.

Salt Lake never loses a piece of paper, but it can be curiously wary about releasing information. When Budro needed a birth certificate for a passport (being the child of a plural wife, his birth was not a matter of public record), he applied to the Church Historian's Office for a copy of his baptismal record. It arrived with the mind-boggling stipulation that if the information was not used within two years for the purpose stated, the document was null and void.

In 1967 the Middlefield Roaders gathered from the four corners for a ward reunion, forty years from the time George Rose arrived at Redwood City to find that the only other Mormon family in town was J. D. Clark's. Clark had gone to his reward, but his wife, LaRue, attended. Theda and Yates Farnsworth arrived from their retirement home in Washington for the shindig, and three others of the seven bishops who had led the ward, James P. Johnson, William Brew, and Don Reid.

It was a night of memories for George Rose. It seemed only yesterday when the identical twins, Caroline and Marilyn Hill, were confirmed members. Yates Farnsworth laid hands on a pretty head and confirmed Caroline; but as the girl resumed her seat, her mother whispered to Farnsworth that *that* one was Marilyn. So back came a twin, and Farnsworth confirmed Marilyn. Then as the girl sped to her seat the mother whispered that *that* one was Caroline. Shaken, Farnsworth again put hands on a head, and was in the midst of confirmation when the mother interrupted—wrong twin again. So, with the mother standing by, the confirmations at last were correctly performed. However, one of the Hill twins—which one, George Rose never knew—had the distinction of being two and a half times a Mormon.

George Rose had his problems with the food storage program, and in this he was not alone. For more than a century the church had been urging its members to have a year's supply of food, two if possible; and, during pioneer days, the brethren urged a seven-year supply. The problem was twofold, keeping it and using it.

Ward members joked wryly about finding weevils in the kitchen cupboard, and, upon climbing into the attic discovering the year's supply of wheat literally crawling. Joe Budro purchased his year's supply from a family that was moving; but he discovered the canned goods were mush, cereals wormy. The evaporated milk was stringy, so he fed it to the cat. The only thing his family could use was the package of toothpicks. On hearing the story, a ward member asked seriously, "Is your cat all right?"

Men of the Elders' Quorum manufactured an ingenious storage rack to simplify the problem of using year-old food while keeping the stored supply fresh. It consisted of a rack with shelves built on an incline, so as you took the oldest can from the lower end all the others on the sloping shelf made a half turn in moving into place. Then you could put a fresh can at the top of the shelf. After Budro wrote an item about the device for the *Church News* the quorum received requests for plans from all over the nation and one came from Australia. Obviously, there was a problem. It took a really devout housewife to put a fresh can of corn at the rear of the rack, then serve her husband and children corn a year or more old taken from the front; the taste just wasn't there, nor the food value.

Then came the boom in dehydrated food. Budro, who'd slowly grown hollow while living on powdered rations for two years overseas in World War II, had had more than enough to last a lifetime. But many Mormons found this the answer. For $575 one company, SamAndy, offered a "basic unit" only 24 × 18 × 53 inches in girth, which would supply 1,500 calories a day for one person for a year. The unit contained powdered apples, carrots, potatoes, vegetable stew, margarine, and even powdered cheese, powdered peanut butter, and powdered hamburger. You could just stick the unit in a closet, hallway, garage, or attic, and forget it. As for eating the stuff, SamAndy took the bull by the horns in an enlightening brochure.[1]

There are two basic approaches to food storage programs. One is to rotate the food carefully and methodically at all times, staying well within the known limits of flavor and palatability. . . . However, because this involves so much record keeping, so much storage space, and is so time consuming, there are not any (very few?) who have ever done this

1. *The Family Food Reserve Story,* SamAndy, Inc., 1969.

for a complete year's supply or well enough to prevent a great deal of spoilage and waste.

The alternative is to select the most stable foods, package them properly, store them in the best locations available and replace them when they reach the end of their storage life.

Certainly this attitude was frank and refreshing. Powdered food wasn't supposed to be eaten, just stored for its "shelf life," then thrown away.[2] Considering food storage as a religious practice, along with the Word of Wisdom, tithing, fasting for two meals each month, or qualifying for a temple recommend, it really didn't matter if your basic unit sat in a hot attic twenty years or more; you had obeyed counsel regarding food storage.

In the 1970s the nation and the world caught up with the Mormon catastrophe concept. Suddenly everything was a "crisis"— ecology, pollution, environment, oil, gas, water, energy. Not to be outdone, SamAndy offered the Saints a survival newsletter for $100 a year; a coal-burning kitchen range with reservoir and warming oven, $489; a hand-operated washing machine with crank wringer, $119.95; a 640-gallon fuel storage tank, $349; a wood-tub dough-maker, $24.95; and, for when things got really tough, a do-it-yourself childbirth kit, $19.95 plus postage. Jack Wilson of the ward, however, kept even ahead of SamAndy. He not only had water tanks stored under the house, but a huge bag of fresh, clean air to suck on when the Day of Judgment arrived.

The ward had a champion in Bruce Voyce, who at nine won the annual Little People's Coloring Contest locally, then came second in the national competition. He received a set of the *Junior Encyclopaedia Britannica* and a $100 savings bond, though he had little use for the books because he'd won the same set the previous year. Bruce wouldn't talk about his coloring secrets, nor would his eleven-year-old sister, Terri, who'd won a trip to Disneyland. "When we're too old to compete," Terri said, "we'll pass on our secrets to some worthy child."

The ceaseless activity of the Mormon group gave rise in 1915 to the official "Home Evening," one night a week for Mom, Dad,

2. Dr. Clayton Huber, professor of food science and nutrition at BYU, studied the shelf life of dehydrated foods while working on the NASA Sky Lab program. He found that they may lose considerable nutritional value if stored more than one year. See *BYU Today*, February 1978.

and the kids to stay home and get acquainted. But the pressure of activity encroached on that handy evening until the concept was forgotten, then revived and forgotten several more times until it rose to prominence again in the 1960s. To have only six nights a week imposes a hardship on those scheduling activities, and at times they display considerable ingenuity in observing it, such as having a Family Home Evening picnic for the ward at Hudardt Park, or a Family Home Evening Christmas party; or when some 2,000 Saints gathered at the Oakland Interstake Center for Family Home Evening with Billy Casper, the golfer.

Casper sponsored a church-wide golf tournament. To qualify, an entrant had to sign an affidavit that he never played golf on Sunday. Casper, of course, on the pro tour, made his living playing golf on Sunday. It's okay to do it for money, but sinful to do it for fun.

A stranger might wonder how the active member has time for everything. Actually, he doesn't, but he learns a little trick. He never misses a meeting or an event, but he doesn't stay long. After putting in an appearance, shaking hands around—getting *credit*—he slips away.

This explains the mystery of the one hundred Mormons who vanished during a cruise of San Francisco Bay. It was the maiden voyage of the *Harbor Princess,* chartered by the Specialaires, a stake social group, for a three-hour night cruise of the bay. The crew noticed something strange from the beginning. With 235 passengers, the bar was closed, and the snack counter didn't sell coffee. After that, the crew would believe anything.

As the *Harbor Princess* cruised in the night, there was dancing, there was rubbernecking at the city lights gleaming across the water, at the two great bridges, at Alcatraz. Despite the fact they drank nothing but pop, the Mormons were having a great time.

And then the crew noted an eerie circumstance. While the ship was churning through the middle of the bay, the Mormons began shaking hands and saying good-bye. "Our babysitter has to be home early." . . . "We must attend another meeting." . . . "Have to do my ward teaching." . . . "It's been grand." . . .

The crew rubbed their eyes as the passengers began disappearing. There was no place to *go.* No other boat approached. Nobody was seen swimming, nor walking on the water. But the crowd dwindled away, as it always did at a Mormon shindig. Only 135 remained aboard when the *Harbor Princess* docked. The other hundred had left early.

When Budro sent the story to the *Church News,* the editor asked what *happened.* Budro replied that there was no reason at all for a tall story.

Dedication of the Oakland Temple in 1964 put an end to that remarkable activity known as the temple excursion. George Rose remembered temple excursions by chartered bus to Salt Lake, Mesa, or St. George, two days going, a day at the temple, two days returning. After the Los Angeles Temple was dedicated, some unsung genius figured that by embarking from Redwood City at 9 o'clock Friday night, the bus would reach Los Angeles in time for four sessions at the temple Saturday, then leave at 4 P.M. and arrive home before midnight, thus avoiding Sunday travel.

The one thing left out of this schedule was sleep. Also, it didn't take into account that the buses would be at least twenty years old, fume-filled, prone to breakdown, and with square wheels.

Aside from theological considerations, Budro felt much as he had during World War II when his company was alerted for overseas. With the big show on, he didn't want to sit home and miss the main event.[3]

Could he qualify? He braved an interview with Bishop John Weaver to find out.

"Do you obey the Word of Wisdom, Joe?"

"No," Budro said, "I'm ten pounds overweight."

"Hmm." The bishop might have been violating the counsel for moderation by about the same degree. At any rate, he issued the recommend.

When Budro arrived with his wife at the chapel Friday evening he noticed that the other seventy-four people all carried pillows. Old-time excursionists such as George Rose had a special model of horseshoe shape that fit around the neck to hold the head steady through every wrench and lurch of the journey. Then as the bus arrived in a cloud of blue smoke, there was a mad scramble to get

---

3. Temple ceremonies include marriage for time and eternity, sealing of children to parents in the hereafter, and baptism for the dead. Accounts of the rites have been published many times. A modern example is William J. Whalen's *The Latter-day Saints in the Modern Day World* (New York: John Day Company, 1964).

aboard. Politely bringing up the rear, Budro didn't realize his mistake until he found all seats taken except the end bench—an expanse of slick plastic, nothing to brace against or cling to. He slid back and forth like a shuttlecock as the smelly rattletrap lurched through the night.

Presently the entrapped passengers began screaming in unison. Budro joined with groans until he realized the inmates actually were singing. He thought of the dauntless pioneers crossing the plains, singing "Come, Come, Ye Saints." The singing didn't last long. Presently everyone subsided into a drugged stupor as the exhaust fumes seeped through the heating system.

Dawn was breaking as the bus pulled up at a café on the outskirts of Los Angeles. Out of it, bent, limping, and groaning, crept seventy-four brave souls and one craven. Right then, Budro would have traded his chances for the celestial glory for a single cup of coffee; but he didn't have the guts to order it.

It was not yet 6 o'clock when the bus parked at the temple. The first session didn't begin until 7:45. Budro stretched out on that rear seat. Ahh! "All out!" the driver bawled, and seventy-five miserable wretches crept from the torture chamber to huddle in the thin chill at the temple entrance like roosters in the rain for two hours.

At last the doors opened. Processing began. "We will form two lines," an attendant said, "one here for living endowments, and another over there for the dead."

Budro's wife murmured, "Where's the line for the half-dead?"

That afternoon at four, reeling with fatigue, Budro inched onto the rear bench and began sliding back and forth on the return trip. Of course the bus broke down on schedule. Of course it didn't get back until 4 A.M. But seventy-four pilgrims were up and at church a few hours later, bright-eyed and bushy-tailed. "Wasn't it wonderful!" "What a marvelous experience!" "We won't want to miss the excursion next month!" Budro, eyeballs full of sand and rust in every joint, was baffled until he realized a simple fact: Sacrifice is part of the religious experience. The greater the suffering, the more glorious the reward. These people *loved* temple excursions, not despite travail but because of it.

With completion of the Oakland Temple, just across the bay, things seemed almost too easy. Old-timers such as George Rose looked back at the excursions to Salt Lake, Mesa, St. George, and Los Angeles as memories of a golden past. He missed the fellowship that comes of suffering together.

While the Saints prided themselves on avoidance of ritual, lack of vestments, no collection plates, a society of brotherhood and equality, they actually had an elite corps—holders of a current temple recommend. While it might be assumed that to qualify once would be sufficient to establish spiritual worth, such is not the case. The recommend must be renewed annually, and an essential requirement is payment of tithes. Special clothing is worn in the temple, and there is a rather elaborate ritual which, in pioneer times, occupied eight hours.[4]

As with any other status symbol, some people will go to almost any length to have a current recommend. Budro wasn't impressed by the spiritual qualities of a missionary whose girl greeted him so affectionately on his return home that she became pregnant. Then he jilted her, because now she couldn't qualify for temple marriage.

In an earlier day, missionaries were mature men. Many left families as they went out without purse or scrip to labor in the Lord's vineyard. Modern policy is to call young men of nineteen or twenty, who are supported by checks from the family at home. These youngsters are full of zeal and untroubled by lack of background. They memorize the lessons of the missionary manual, which is an excellent sales pitch for the gospel, arranged to lead the investigator into a series of minor concessions until he is ready for baptism.

The regimen of these young men is incredible; they are studying, preaching, or praying from 5:45 in the morning until 10 at night. If that isn't enough to quell the exuberance of youth, the sword hangs over their head—to be sent home in disgrace. This can be a shattering experience to the boy and his family. When a missionary was sent home in Budro's area, the family moved out of the ward and out of California.

The Saints are reminded time and again, "Every member a missionary." Stake missionaries—mature men and women—till the vineyard locally of an evening. Untold numbers await the golden opportunity to pop the Golden Questions to unwary associates on the job, the golf course, or over the back fence. The Golden Ques-

4. The modern ceremony has been shortened.

tions are, "What do you know about the Mormons?" and "Do you wish to know more?" To evince interest can mean that missionaries will knock at your door.

Roy and Georgia Markow had their private missionary projects. A salesman of surgical supplies, Roy Markow convinced motel owners in the area to put the Book of Mormon alongside the Gideon Bible in 2,000 of their rooms.

His wife, Georgia, ran a one-woman boiler room, making converts by telephone, cold turkey. She made a business of soliciting magazine subscriptions by phone, and just how she managed to switch the pitch from *Reader's Digest* or *Playboy* to the gospel, was something she herself didn't understand. "It's always when I feel discouraged and about ready to chuck it all," she said. "And then I have a wonderful gospel discussion on the phone. With Roy it's the same way. When he's had a bad week and feels discouraged, he places the Book of Mormon in another motel."

Nothing so typified her spirit as the story of the irate plumber and the leaky faucet. As the plumber worked, Georgia Markow belabored him with the gospel. "Lady, I'm here to fix your tap," the plumber said, "not listen to your religion."

"I see. And how much is your time worth?"

"Three dollars an hour." (Ah, those bygone days before plumbers had Cadillacs, private planes, and country estates.)

She checked her purse, gave him $15, then launched into five solid hours of the gospel.

At a stake conference the morning session was devoted to missionary work, every member exhorted to till the vineyard. Meanwhile, Jehovah's Witnesses were doing a bit of tilling, putting their tracts in the parked cars at the stake center. This caused the stake president to wax wroth that afternoon at the outrage. This reminded Budro of the story about the Mormon who went to heaven. St. Peter showed him a small group standing apart from millions of others. "These are the Mormons," Peter said, indicating the small group. Then he pointed at the vast assemblage. "And here are the others."

"What others?" the Mormon asked.

George Rose had gone to his reward by 1977, which marked fifty years since he arrived at Redwood City to find one other Mormon family in town. Now three wards used the meetinghouse.

Of the nine bishops who had led the Redwood City Ward, only three were Middlefield Roaders, while the last four had arrived after the new chapel was built.

The handful of Middlefield Roaders still around were stunned by a decision to tear the chapel down and build another. Why? Because the edifice that had seemed the culmination of dreams just twenty years ago was now considered not elegant and ostentatious enough for the modern image of the wealthy church. Other chapels in the area were newer, larger, more imposing "silent missionaries." Redwood City's was an embarrassment.

Oh, it wasn't stated in just that *way*. There was rationalization of the type which justifies buying a new car—the old clunker was almost three years old, the rearview mirror was loose, there was a rattle somewhere, it needed a new fan belt, and from now on there'd be repairs. Get rid of it.

The building was, it seemed, too small; but if they added two classrooms they'd have to bring the entire structure up to the city building code (it originally conformed to the county code); the stage lighting was a complicated nightmare; so was the restaurant-type kitchen equipment; and they'd have to do something about that glass wall facing the afternoon sun, which made the chapel an oven in summertime.

A grand plan for remodeling would cost $500,000. Why not spend another $200,000 and have a completely new building, which people wouldn't be ashamed of?

The new building wouldn't be constructed by the ward members. Unions. So they'd contract the job to a professional builder, shove the money over the transom, and let him have at it. That's how things were done these days.

Oh, yes, there'd be a meeting, where a decision would be made —rather, as everyone knew, a *fait accompli* would be "sustained." Even so, and realizing its complete futility, Budro attended, and from the floor presented the Middlefield Roader case to the three sundowner bishops on the rostrum who were obediently pushing for demolition and elegance.

Plans for the proposed $500,000 remodeling job, Budro said, were so fantastic in design that it could only be concluded that they were concocted for the purpose of causing the congregations to sustain the decision to demolish the building.

Regarding problems with the present building, the remedies were simple:

Tear out the complex stage-lighting system and replace it with a couple of wall switches.

Tear out the restaurant equipment in the kitchen and replace it with household appliances.

As to the glass wall of the chapel, just why, he asked, hadn't deciduous shade trees and shrubs been planted twenty years ago to provide summer shade and winter sun? Why couldn't it be done now?

As to additional classrooms, if they were made in a separate building, no remodeling would be required of the existing structure, no elaborate reconstruction to conform to the new code. The separate building, connected by a breezeway, might cost $100,000, or even half that if the people did it themselves, as they had the present meetinghouse. Why couldn't they do it the same way now? There were unions twenty years ago. Nobody bothered a congregation making a place of worship with their own hands.

Ask the old-timers; ask the Middlefield Roaders about the fellowshiping and spirituality of the ward during the construction period. Would there be a legend of heavenly hosts joining the singing at the dedication of a building which no member had touched?

Budro then reminded the congregation of basic pioneer values —thrift, frugality, avoidance of debt, lack of ostentation. Brigham Young exhorted his people to make do or do without. Brigham came from New England, where a man reaching the age of twenty-one received a stout pair of boots and an overcoat, which were supposed to do him the remainder of his life. Brigham liked to tell how his grandmother used her wedding dress for Sunday best until the day she died.

What had happened to the Saints? When had they come to value ostentation to the point where they would demolish a perfectly good building, of good design, approved by Salt Lake, only twenty years old and in good condition, just because it wasn't as impressive as newer chapels in the area? Since when did we put on such airs?

He sat down knowing that he'd just tilted at another windmill. Decisions came from above. There was no appeal. At the time plans for the Oakland Temple arrived in the bay area, Budro had been appalled. So were some local Mormon architects, though they dutifully kept silent. Only Budro had been brash enough to write to Salt Lake. He advised Hugh B. Brown of the First Presidency that he believed the design was an architectural disaster, and that, particularly in view of the great rivalry between the San Francisco and Los Angeles areas, the Oakland plans were particularly unfortunate compared with the good design of the Los Angeles Temple.

In reply, President Brown said that he felt exactly the same way, and that nothing could be done about it.

Budro felt somewhat like his father, and his grandfather before that. Each had clung to old values during a time of transition. The church had changed direction. He felt like a fish in the old channel, swimming around with a few Middlefield Roaders in a diminishing pool.

Bibliography

Abbreviations

BYU   Wilkinson and Skousen, *Brigham Young University, A School of Destiny*

CHC   Roberts, *A Comprehensive History of the Church*

CR   *Conference Reports*

D&C   *Doctrine and Covenants*

HP   *The Most Holy Principle*

JD   *Journal of Discourses*

MFP   Clark, *Messages of the First Presidency*

SI   Smoot investigation

UHQ   *Utah Historical Quarterly*

Newspapers Cited

Church News, Salt Lake City
Deseret News, Salt Lake City
The Evening and the Morning Star,
     Independence, Missouri
Los Angeles *Times*
New York *Globe*
New York *Herald*
New York *Journal*
New York *Sun*
New York *Times*
New York *Tribune*
New York *World*
Norfolk *Pilot*
Ogden *Standard*

Philadelphia *Ledger*
Provo *Herald*
St. Louis *Globe Democrat*
Salt Lake *Herald,* and *Herald-*
     Republican
Salt Lake *Times*
Salt Lake *Tribune*
San Francisco *Chronicle*
San Francisco *Examiner*
San Jose *Mercury*
Springfield *Republican*
Times and Seasons, Nauvoo, Illinois
Washington *Post*

Documents and Letters

CLARK, JAMES R. *Messages of the First Presidency.* Vols. 1 to 5. Salt Lake: Bookcraft, 1965–1971.

Conference Reports. Discourses at general conferences held April and October at Salt Lake City. Pamphlets, 1880, 1897–1930. Published by the church.

Congressional Record.

POULSON, M. WILFORD. *Library Resources for the Scientific Study of Mormonism.* Proceedings, Utah Academy of Science. July 15, 1930.

SAM ANDY, INC. *The Family Food Reserve Story.* Pamphlet, 1969.

SMITH, JOHN HENRY. "Letters." University of Utah, Special Collections.

BIBLIOGRAPHY

SNOW, ERASTUS. "Letters." University of Utah, Special Collections.
TAYLOR, JOHN. *"Letters,"* 1839–1887. University of Utah, Special Collections.
UTAH COMMISSION. *Annual Reports,* 1887–1896.
WELLS, GOVERNOR HEBER M. *Executive Communication,* March 14, 1901.
WEST, GOVERNOR CALEB W. *Annual Report to the Secretary of the Interior,* October 27, 1888.

Periodicals Cited

Brigham Young University Today
Business Week
Dialogue: A Journal of Mormon Thought
Improvement Era
Juvenile Instructor
Ladies' Home Journal

Literary Digest
National Geographic
Newsweek
The Outlook
Playboy
The Star of Truth
Truth

Articles

"A Biographical Sketch of the Life of Mary Evelyn Clark Allred." *The Star of Truth,* November 1954.
ARRINGTON, LEONARD J. "The Settlement of the Brigham Young Estate." *Pacific Historical Review,* February 1952.
BARRY, RICHARD. "The *Mormon* Method in Business." *Pearson's,* November 1910.
BEECHAM, BILL, AND BRISCOE, DAVID. "Mormon Money & How It's Made." *Utah Holiday,* March 22, 1976.
BITTON, R. DAVIS. "The B. H. Roberts Case of 1898–1900." *Utah Historical Quarterly,* January 1957.
BRUDNOY, DAVID. "Of Sinners and Saints: Theodore Schroeder, Brigham Roberts, and Reed Smoot." *Journal of Church and State,* Spring 1972.
CLARK, JAMES R. "The Kingdom of God, the Council of Fifty, and the State of Deseret." *Utah Historical Quarterly,* April 1958.
DE VOTO, BERNARD. "The Centennial of Mormonism: A Study in Utopia and Dictatorship." *American Mercury,* January 1930. Revised version in *Forays and Rebuttals.* Boston: Little, Brown, 1936.
HARROW, JOAN RAY. "Joseph L. Rawlins, Father of Utah Statehood." *Utah Historical Quarterly,* Winter 1976.
JEPPSON, JOSEPH H. "Merging Business and Religion." *Dialogue: A Journal of Mormon Thought,* Autumn 1966.
LA MAR, HOWARD R. "Statehood for Utah: A Different Path." *Utah Historical Quarterly,* Fall 1971.
LEWIS, ALFRED HENRY. "The Great Mormon Conspiracy." *Collier's,* March 26, 1904.
———. "The Viper on the Hearth"; "The Trail of the Viper"; "The Viper's Trail of Gold." *Cosmopolitan,* March, April, May 1911.

Bibliography

MORGAN, NEIL. "Utah: How Much Money Hath the Mormon Church?" *Esquire*, August 1962.

QUINN, D. MICHAEL. "The Flag of the Kingdom of God." *BYU Studies*, Autumn 1973.

SMITH, GARY M. "Sacred Cows of the News Media: ... The Story They Wouldn't Touch." Logan *Herald Journal*, February 27, 1976.

TAYLOR, SAMUEL W. *"Time and the Dream Mine." Esquire*, May 1941.

Books, Manuscripts, Graduate Studies

ALLEN, JAMES A., AND LEONARD, GLEN M. *The Story of the Latter-day Saints*. Salt Lake: Deseret, 1976.

ALLRED, B. HARVEY. *A Leaf in Review*. Caldwell: Caxton, 1933.

ALTER, J. CECIL. *Early Utah Journalism*. Salt Lake: Utah State Historical Society, 1938.

Anonymous. *The Most Holy Principle*. 4 vols. Salt Lake: Gems Publishing Co., 1970, 1971, 1975.

ARRINGTON, LEONARD J. *Great Basin Kingdom: An Economic History of the Latter-day Saints*. Cambridge: Harvard University Press, 1958.

ASHTON, WENDEL J. *Voice of the West: Biography of a Pioneer Newspaper*. New York: Duell, Sloan & Pearce, 1950.

BENNETT, JOHN C. *The History of the Saints; or, An Exposé of Joe Smith and Mormonism*. Boston: Leland & Whiting, 1842.

BENNION, HEBER. *Gospel Problems*. Salt Lake: The Author, 1920. Published anonymously. Reprinted under author's name, with additional material, Dugway: Pioneer Press, 1976.

BISHOP, LYNN L. AND STEVEN L. *The Keys of the Priesthood Illustrated*. Draper: Review and Preview Publishers, 1971.

BRODIE, FAWN M. *No Man Knows My History: The Life of Joseph Smith, the Mormon Prophet*. New York: Alfred A. Knopf, 1945.

BROOKS, JUANITA. *The Mountain Meadows Massacre*. Palo Alto: Stanford University Press, 1950.

CALL, LAMONI. *2000 Changes in the Book of Mormon*. Bountiful: The Author, 1898.

CANNON, FRANK J. AND O'HIGGINS, HARVEY J. *Under the Prophet in Utah*. Boston: C. M. Clark Publishing Co., 1911.

COLLIER, FRED C., AND BLACK, ROBERT R. *The Trials for the Membership of John W. Taylor and Matthias F. Cowley*. Pamphlet. Salt Lake: The Authors, 1976.

FIFE, AUSTIN AND ALTA. *Saints of Sage and Saddle: Folklore among the Mormons*. Bloomington: Indiana University Press, 1956.

GARDNER, HAMILTON. *Economic Activities of the Mormons*. Typescript, 1925. Copy at Utah State Historical Society.

GREGORY, MARVA HODSON. *The Life and Educational Contribution of Eugene Lusk Roberts*. M.S. thesis, University of Utah, 1952.

HANSEN, KLAUS J. *Quest for Empire: The Political Kingdom of God and the*

BIBLIOGRAPHY

Council of Fifty in Mormon History. East Lansing: Michigan State University Press, 1967.

HICKMAN, BILL. *Brigham's Destroying Angel: Being the Life, Confession, and Startling Disclosures of the Notorious Bill Hickman, the Danite Chief of Utah*. Ed. J. H. Beadle. New York: 1872; 2nd ed., Salt Lake: Shephard Publishing Co., 1904.

HOWE, EBER D. *Mormonism Unvailed: Or, A Faithful Account of that Singular Imposition and Delusion from Its Rise to the Present Time*. Painesville, Ohio: The Author, 1834.

IVINS, STANLEY S. *The Moses Thatcher Case*. Salt Lake: Modern Microfilm Co., n.d.; circa 1965.

JENSON, ANDREW. *Church Chronology. A Record of Important Events Pertaining to the History of the Church of Jesus Christ of Latter-day Saints*. 2nd ed. Salt Lake: Deseret News, 1914.

Journal of Discourses. 26 vols. Liverpool: Published by various presidents of the British Mission, 1854–86.

KNIGHT, JESSE WILLIAM. *The Jesse Knight Family*. Salt Lake: Deseret News Press, 1940.

KRAUT, OGDEN. *Complaint against Ogden Kraut*. Dugway: Pioneer Press, 1972.

LARSON, GUSTIVE O. *The "Americanization" of Utah for Statehood*. San Marino: Huntington Library, 1971.

LDS Church Standard Works: The Bible, King James Version; The Book of Mormon; *Doctrine and Covenants; The Pearl of Great Price*. Salt Lake: Deseret, many editions.

LUNDWALL, N. B. *Temples of the Most High*. Salt Lake: Bookcraft, 16th printing, 1968.

MALMQUIST, O. N. *The First 100 Years: A History of the Salt Lake Tribune, 1871–1971*. Salt Lake: Utah State Historical Society, 1971.

MERRILL, MILTON R. *Reed Smoot: Apostle in Politics*. Ph.D. dissertation, Columbia University, 1950.

―――. "Reed Smoot, Apostle-Senator." *Utah Historical Quarterly*, October 1960.

MUSSER, J. W. AND BROADBENT, J. L. *Supplement to the New and Everlasting Covenant of Marriage*. Salt Lake: The Authors, circa 1935.

NIBLEY, HUGH. *No, Ma'am, That's Not History: A Brief Review of Mrs. Brodie's Reluctant Vindication of a Prophet She Seeks to Expose*. Salt Lake: Bookcraft, 1946.

O'DEY, THOMAS F. *The Mormons*. Chicago: University of Chicago Press, 1957.

PARDOE, T. EARL. *The Sons of Brigham*. Provo: Brigham Young University Alumni Association, 1969.

PETERSEN, MARK E. *The Great Prologue*. Salt Lake: Deseret Book Co., 1975.

PIERCE, NORMAN C. *The Dream Mine Story*. Salt Lake: The Author, 1972.

―――. *The 3½ Years*. Salt Lake: The Author, 1963.

QUINN, DENNIS MICHAEL. *The Mormon Hierarchy, 1832–1932: An American Elite*. Ph.D. dissertation, Yale, 1976.

REASONER, CALVIN. *Church and State: The Issue of Civil and Religious Liberty in Utah*. Pamphlet. Salt Lake, 1896.

ROBERTS, B. H. *A Comprehensive History of the Church of Jesus Christ of Latter-day Saints; Century I*. 6 vols. Salt Lake: Deseret News, 1930.

————. *The Life of John Taylor, Third President of the Church of Jesus Christ of Latter-day Saints*. Salt Lake: George Q. Cannon & Sons Co., 1892. Reissued with additional material, Salt Lake: Bookcraft, 1963.

————. *Recent Discussion of Mormon Affairs; Answer to the Ministerial Association Review*. Pamphlet. Salt Lake, 1907.

————, ed. *History of the Church* (known as the "Documentary History"). 7 vols. Salt Lake: Deseret News, various editions.

ROBERTS, EUGENE L., AND CLUFF, MRS. ELDON REED. *Benjamn Cluff, Jr.; Scholar, Educational Administrator, and Explorer*. Typescript. Provo: 1947. Brigham Young University, Special Collections.

SMITH, JOSEPH FIELDING. *Life of Joseph F. Smith, Sixth President of the Church of Jesus Christ of Latter-day Saints*. Salt Lake: Deseret Book Co., 1938.

Smoot investigation. Short title of *Proceedings before the Committee on Privileges and Elections of the United States Senate in the Matter of the Protests against the Right of Hon. Reed Smoot, a Senator from the State of Utah, to Hold His Seat*. 4 vols. Washington: Government Printing Office, 1904, 1905, 1906.

Songs of Zion. Salt Lake: Deseret Sunday School Union, various editions.

STEGNER, WALLACE. *Mormon Country*. New York: Duell, Sloan & Pearce, 1942.

STOUT, WAYNE. *History of Utah*. Vols. 1 and 2. Salt Lake: The Author, 1967, 1968.

TANNER, JERALD AND SANDRA. *3,913 Changes in the Book of Mormon*. Salt Lake: Modern Microfilm Co., 1965.

————. *Changes in the Pearl of Great Price*. Salt Lake: Modern Microfilm Co., 1968.

————. *Mormonism—Shadow or Reality*. Salt Lake: Modern Microfilm Co., 1964. Enlarged ed., 1972.

TAYLOR, JOHN. "Revelations." Typescript, University of Utah, Special Collections.

TAYLOR, SAMUEL W. *The Kingdom or Nothing: The Life of John Taylor, Militant Mormon*. New York: Macmillan Publishing Co., 1976.

————. *Nightfall at Nauvoo*. New York: Macmillan Publishing Co., 1971.

————. Interviews and correspondence over a period of thirteen years concerning the family of his father, John W. Taylor. Copies at Brigham Young University, University of Utah and Utah State University.

TSCHIFFELY, A. F. "Buenos Aires to Washington by Horse." *National Geographic*, February 1929.

————. *Tschiffely's Ride*. New York: Grosset and Dunlap, 1933.

BIBLIOGRAPHY

TURNER, WALLACE. *The Mormon Establishment*. Boston: Houghton Mifflin, 1966.

Utah: A Guide to the State. American Guide Series. New York: Hastings House, 1941.

A Vineyard by the Bay. Various authors. San Mateo: San Mateo Stake of Zion, 1968.

WERNER, M. R. *Brigham Young*. New York: Harcourt, Brace & Co., 1925.

WHALEN, WILLIAM J. *The Latter-day Saints in the Modern Day World*. New York: The John Day Co., 1964.

WHITNEY, ORSON F. *History of Utah*. 4 vols. Salt Lake: George Q. Cannon & Sons, 1892, 1893, 1904.

WILKINSON, ERNEST L., AND SKOUSEN, W. CLEON. *Brigham Young University: A School of Destiny*. Provo: Brigham Young University Press, 1976.

WOODRUFF, WILFORD. *Journal*.

YOUNG, KIMBALL. *Isn't One Wife Enough?* New York: Henry Holt and Co., 1954.

Index

INDEX